CW00822832

BILLY THE KID'S
OLD TIMEY ODDITIES
AND THE ORM OF LOCH NESS

writers
ERIC POWELL
and KYLE HOTZ

artist
KYLE HOTZ

colorist
DAN BROWN

letterer
NATE PIEKOS of BLAMBOT®

cover and chapter break art
KYLE HOTZ
with DAN BROWN

DARK HORSE BOOKS

editors
Scott Allie & Daniel Chabon

assistant editor
Shantel LaRocque

designers
Lia Ribacchi & Amy Arendts

president & publisher
Mike Richardson

Special thanks to Tracy Marsh.

Neil Hankerson *Executive Vice President* • Tom Weddle *Chief Financial Officer* • Randy
Stradley *Vice President of Publishing* • Michael Martens *Vice President of Book Trade Sales*
Anita Nelson *Vice President of Business Affairs* • Scott Allie *Editor in Chief* • Matt Parkinson
Vice President of Marketing • David Scroggy *Vice President of Product Development* • Dale
LaFountain *Vice President of Information Technology* • Darlene Vogel *Senior Director of Print,
Design, and Production* • Ken Lizzi *General Counsel* • Davey Estrada *Editorial Director* • Chris
Warner *Senior Books Editor* • Diana Schutz *Executive Editor* • Cary Grazzini *Director of Print
and Development* • Lia Ribacchi *Art Director* • Cara Niece *Director of Scheduling* • Tim Wiesch
Director of International Licensing • Mark Bernardi *Director of Digital Publishing*

This volume collects issues #1–#4 of the Dark Horse Comics miniseries
Billy the Kid's Old Timey Oddities and the Orm of Loch Ness.

Published by
Dark Horse Books
A division of
Dark Horse Comics, Inc.
10956 SE Main Street
Milwaukie, OR 97222

DarkHorse.com

To find a comics shop in your area,
call the Comic Shop Locator Service toll-free at (888) 266-4226.

First edition: July 2013
ISBN 978-1-61655-106-3

1 3 5 7 9 10 8 6 4 2

Printed in China

CHAPTER ONE

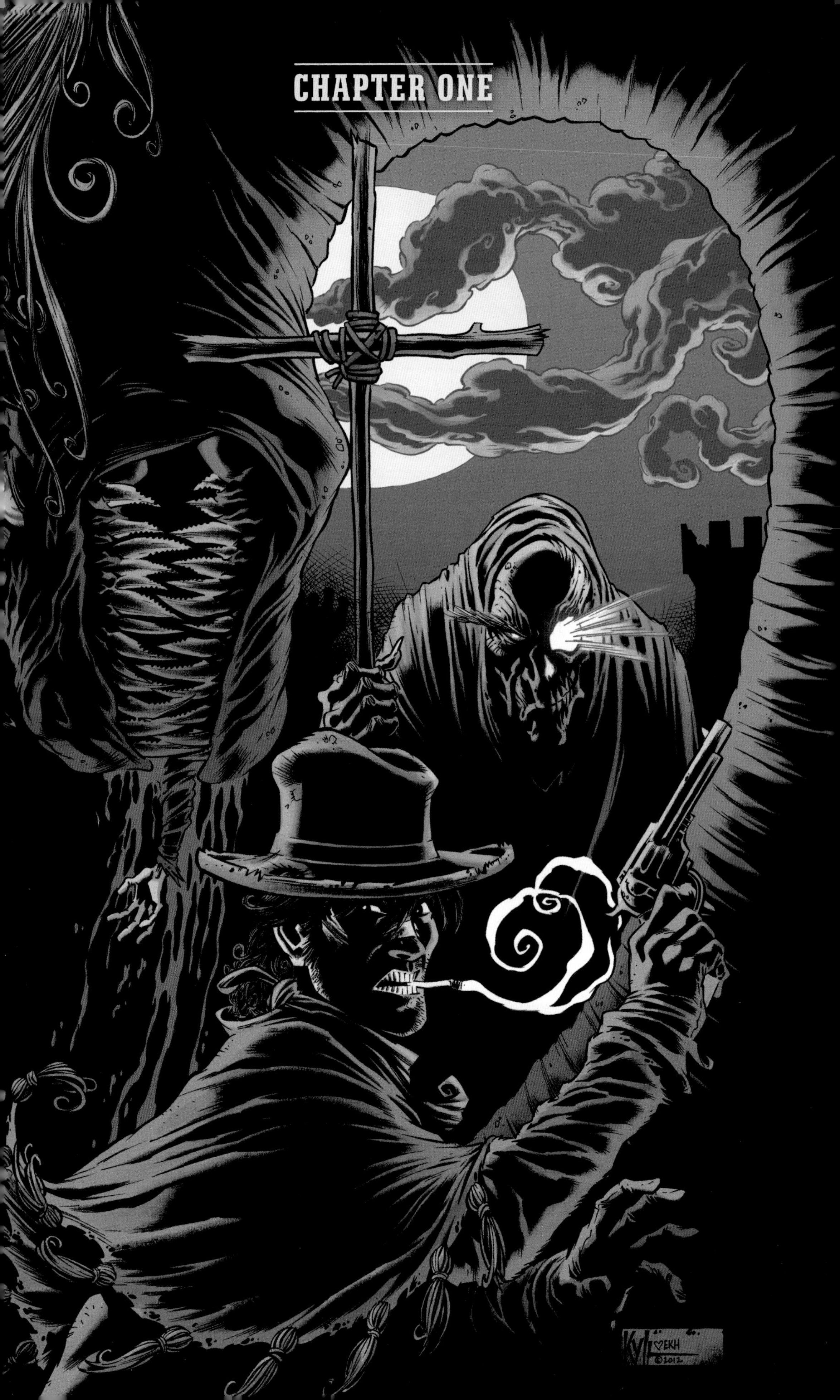

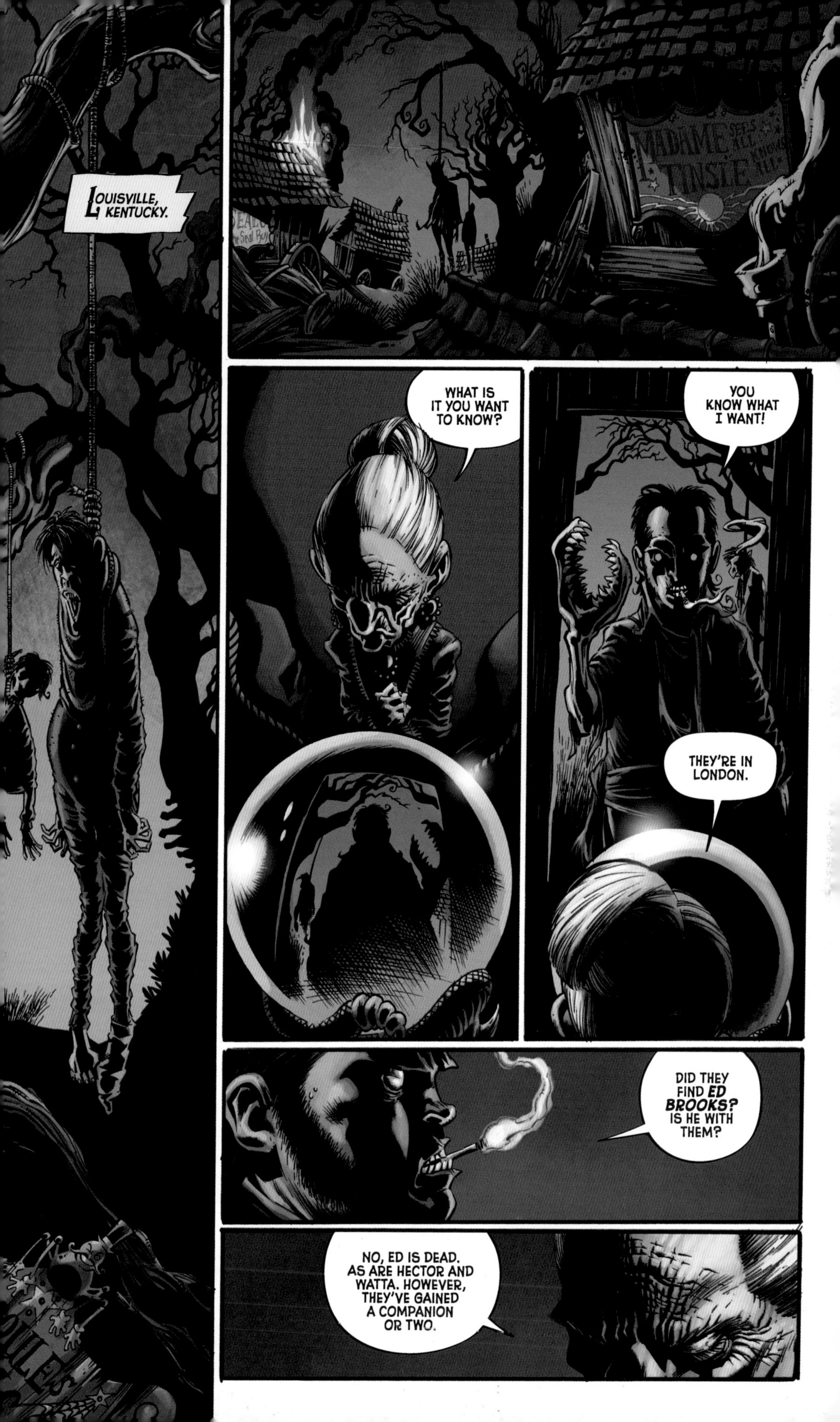
LOUISVILLE, KENTUCKY.
MADAME TINSLE
SEES ALL KNOWS ALL
WHAT IS IT YOU WANT TO KNOW?
YOU KNOW WHAT I WANT!
THEY'RE IN LONDON.
DID THEY FIND **ED BROOKS?** IS HE WITH THEM?
NO, ED IS DEAD. AS ARE HECTOR AND WATTA. HOWEVER, THEY'VE GAINED A COMPANION OR TWO.

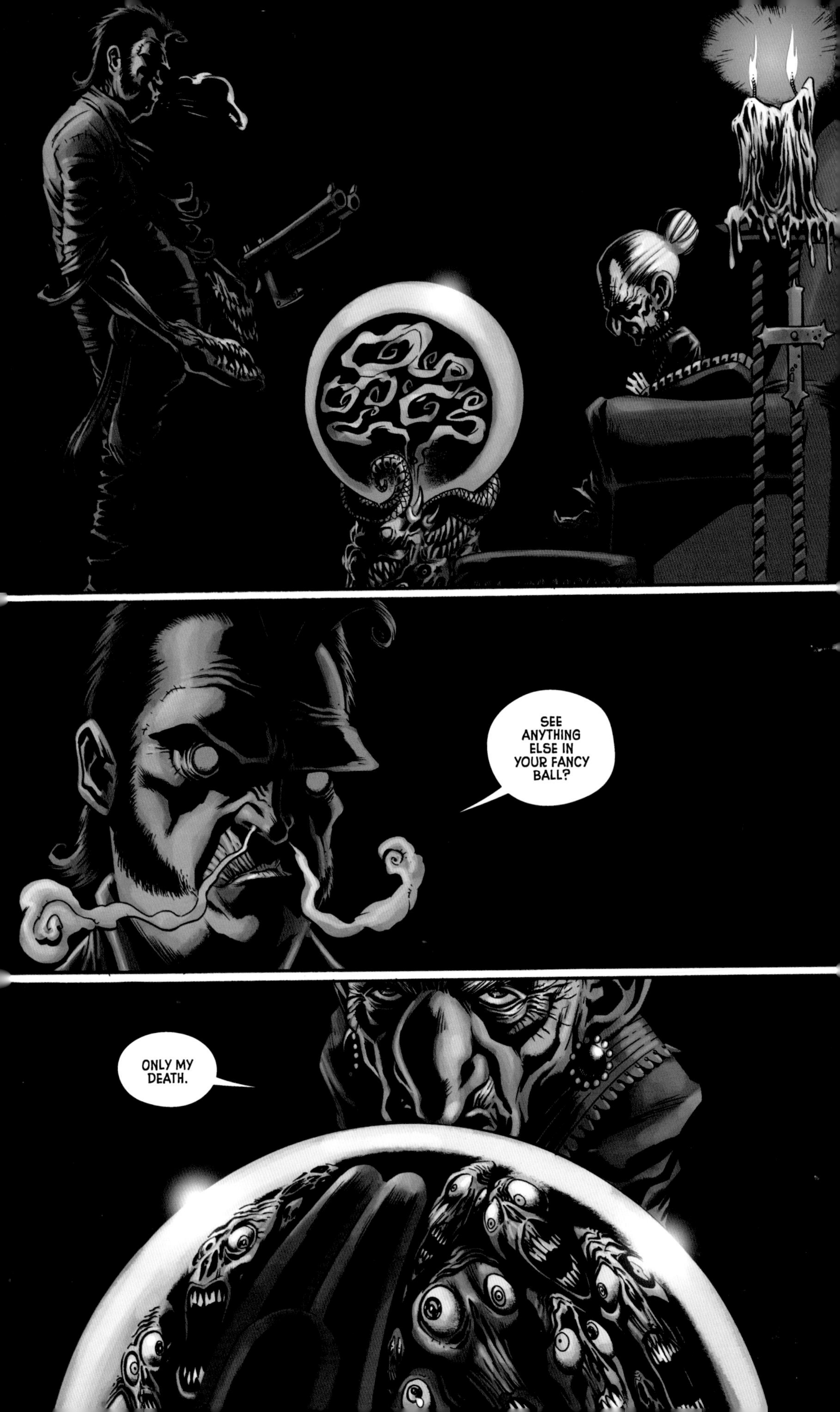
SEE ANYTHING ELSE IN YOUR FANCY BALL?
ONLY MY DEATH.

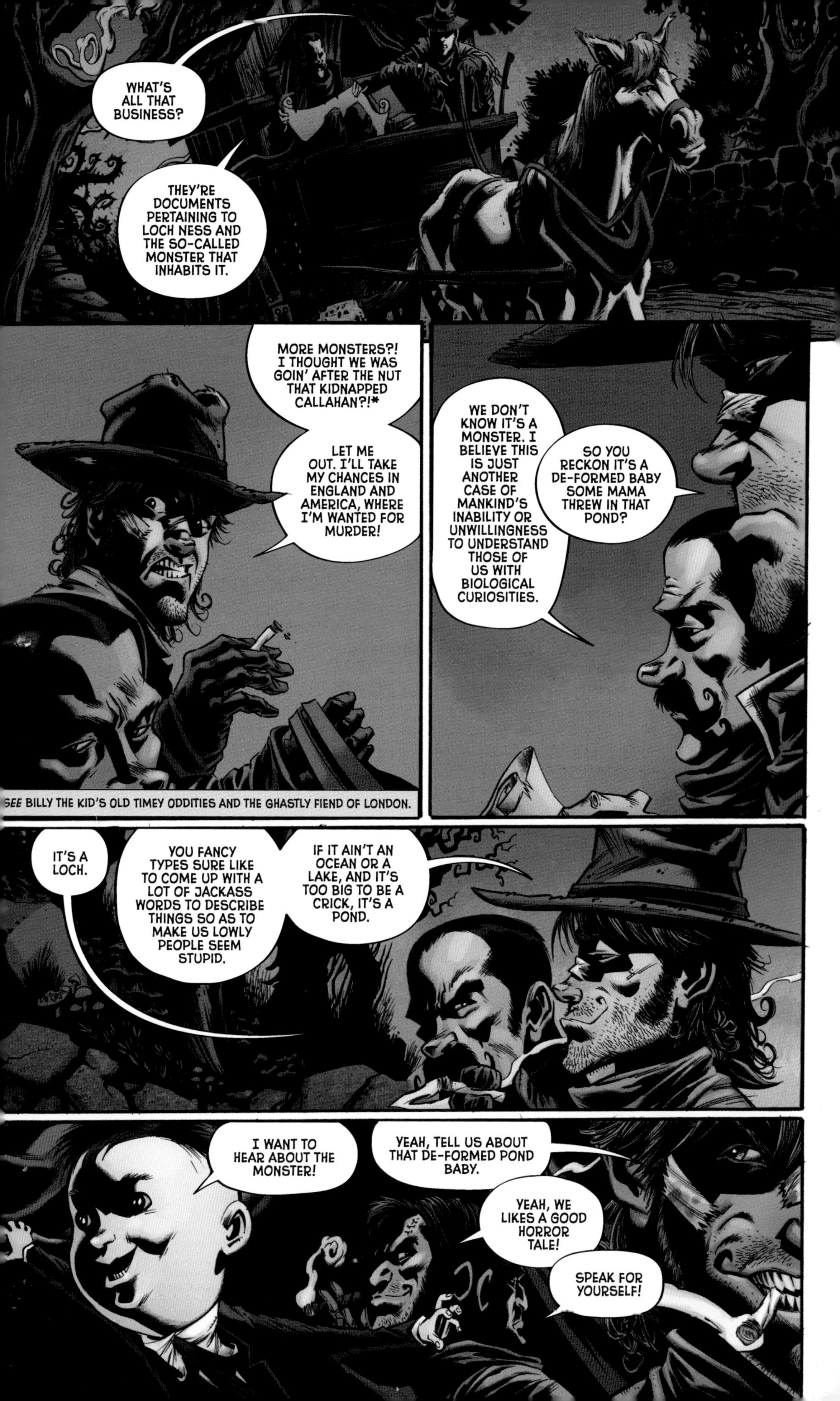
WHAT'S ALL THAT BUSINESS?
THEY'RE DOCUMENTS PERTAINING TO LOCH NESS AND THE SO-CALLED MONSTER THAT INHABITS IT.
MORE MONSTERS?! I THOUGHT WE WAS GOIN' AFTER THE NUT THAT KIDNAPPED CALLAHAN?!*
LET ME OUT. I'LL TAKE MY CHANCES IN ENGLAND AND AMERICA, WHERE I'M WANTED FOR MURDER!
*SEE BILLY THE KID'S OLD TIMEY ODDITIES AND THE GHASTLY FIEND OF LONDON.
WE DON'T KNOW IT'S A MONSTER. I BELIEVE THIS IS JUST ANOTHER CASE OF MANKIND'S INABILITY OR UNWILLINGNESS TO UNDERSTAND THOSE OF US WITH BIOLOGICAL CURIOSITIES.
SO YOU RECKON IT'S A DE-FORMED BABY SOME MAMA THREW IN THAT POND?
IT'S A LOCH.
YOU FANCY TYPES SURE LIKE TO COME UP WITH A LOT OF JACKASS WORDS TO DESCRIBE THINGS SO AS TO MAKE US LOWLY PEOPLE SEEM STUPID.
IF IT AIN'T AN OCEAN OR A LAKE, AND IT'S TOO BIG TO BE A CRICK, IT'S A POND.
I WANT TO HEAR ABOUT THE MONSTER!
YEAH, TELL US ABOUT THAT DE-FORMED POND BABY.
YEAH, WE LIKES A GOOD HORROR TALE!
SPEAK FOR YOURSELF!

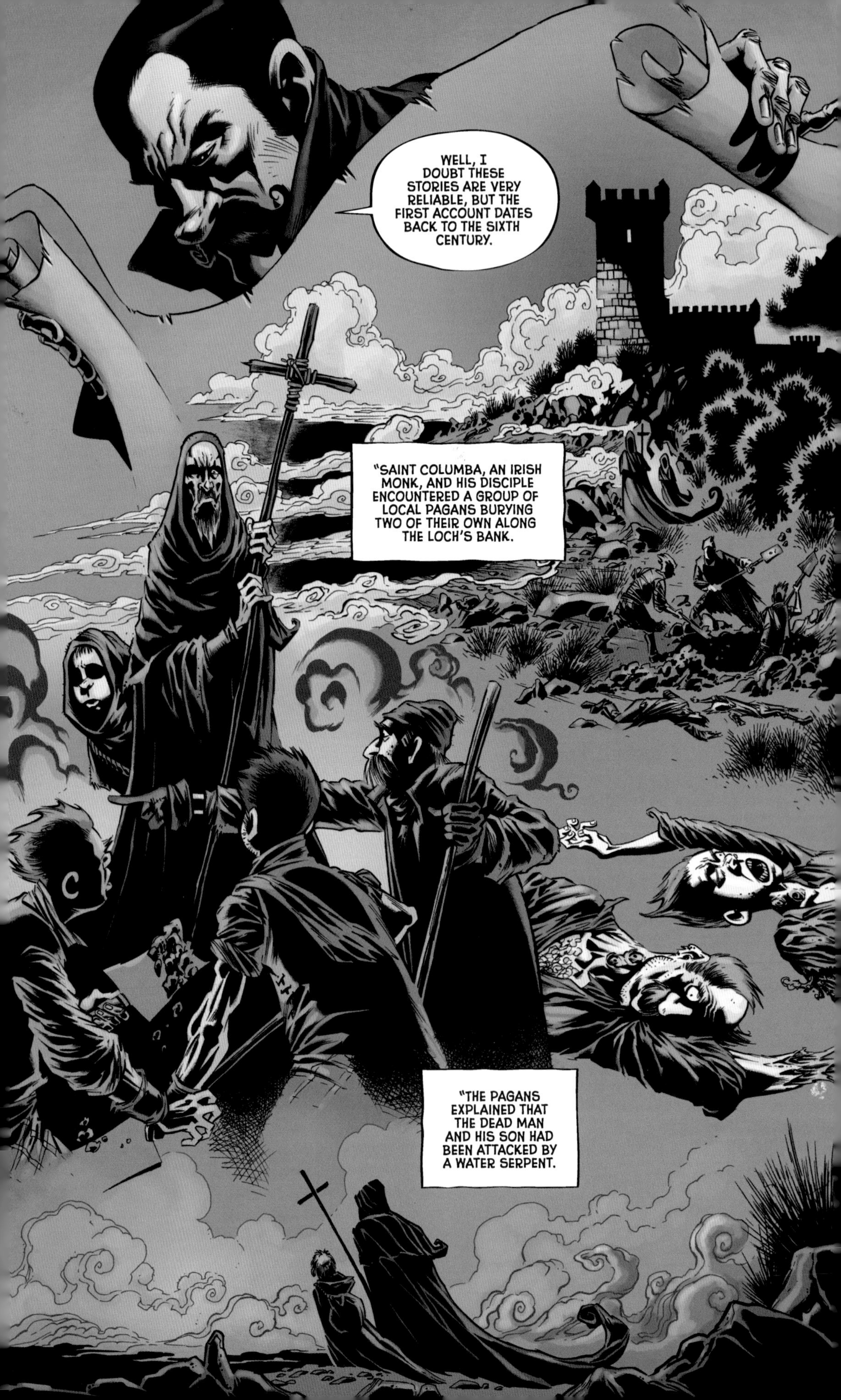
WELL, I DOUBT THESE STORIES ARE VERY RELIABLE, BUT THE FIRST ACCOUNT DATES BACK TO THE SIXTH CENTURY.
"SAINT COLUMBA, AN IRISH MONK, AND HIS DISCIPLE ENCOUNTERED A GROUP OF LOCAL PAGANS BURYING TWO OF THEIR OWN ALONG THE LOCH'S BANK.
"THE PAGANS EXPLAINED THAT THE DEAD MAN AND HIS SON HAD BEEN ATTACKED BY A WATER SERPENT.

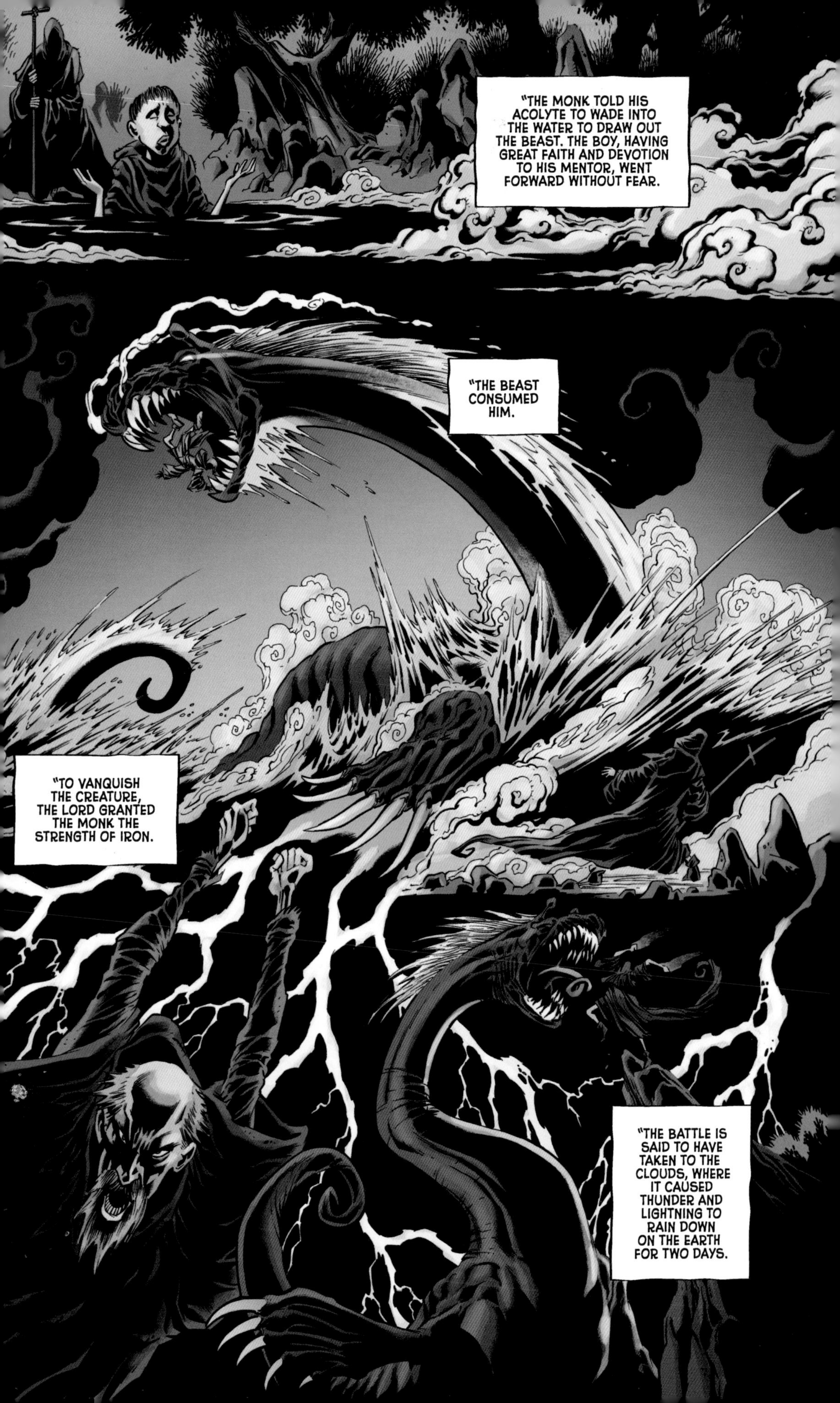
"THE MONK TOLD HIS ACOLYTE TO WADE INTO THE WATER TO DRAW OUT THE BEAST. THE BOY, HAVING GREAT FAITH AND DEVOTION TO HIS MENTOR, WENT FORWARD WITHOUT FEAR.
"THE BEAST CONSUMED HIM.
"TO VANQUISH THE CREATURE, THE LORD GRANTED THE MONK THE STRENGTH OF IRON.
"THE BATTLE IS SAID TO HAVE TAKEN TO THE CLOUDS, WHERE IT CAUSED THUNDER AND LIGHTNING TO RAIN DOWN ON THE EARTH FOR TWO DAYS.

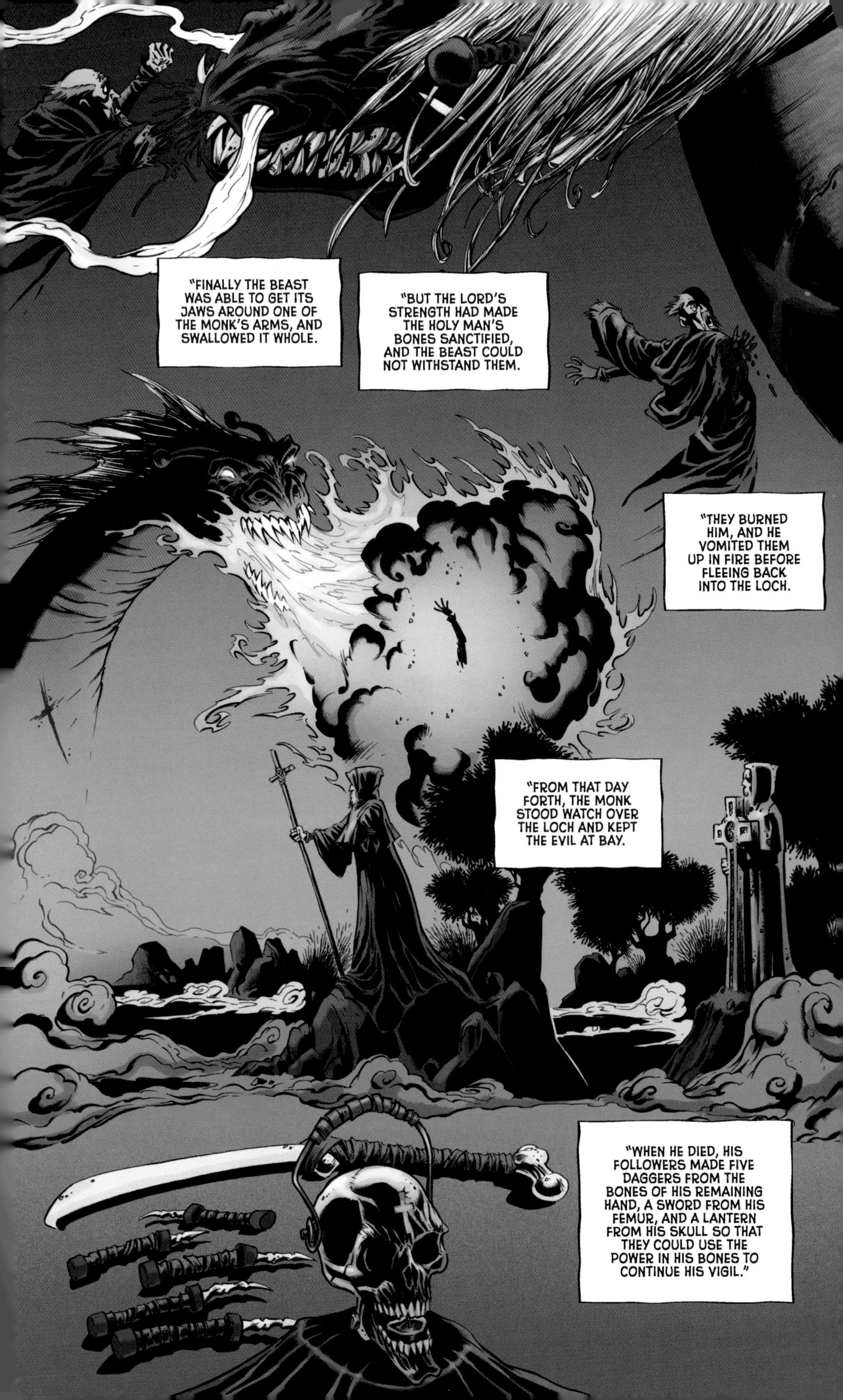
"FINALLY THE BEAST WAS ABLE TO GET ITS JAWS AROUND ONE OF THE MONK'S ARMS, AND SWALLOWED IT WHOLE.
"BUT THE LORD'S STRENGTH HAD MADE THE HOLY MAN'S BONES SANCTIFIED, AND THE BEAST COULD NOT WITHSTAND THEM.
"THEY BURNED HIM, AND HE VOMITED THEM UP IN FIRE BEFORE FLEEING BACK INTO THE LOCH.
"FROM THAT DAY FORTH, THE MONK STOOD WATCH OVER THE LOCH AND KEPT THE EVIL AT BAY.
"WHEN HE DIED, HIS FOLLOWERS MADE FIVE DAGGERS FROM THE BONES OF HIS REMAINING HAND, A SWORD FROM HIS FEMUR, AND A LANTERN FROM HIS SKULL SO THAT THEY COULD USE THE POWER IN HIS BONES TO CONTINUE HIS VIGIL."

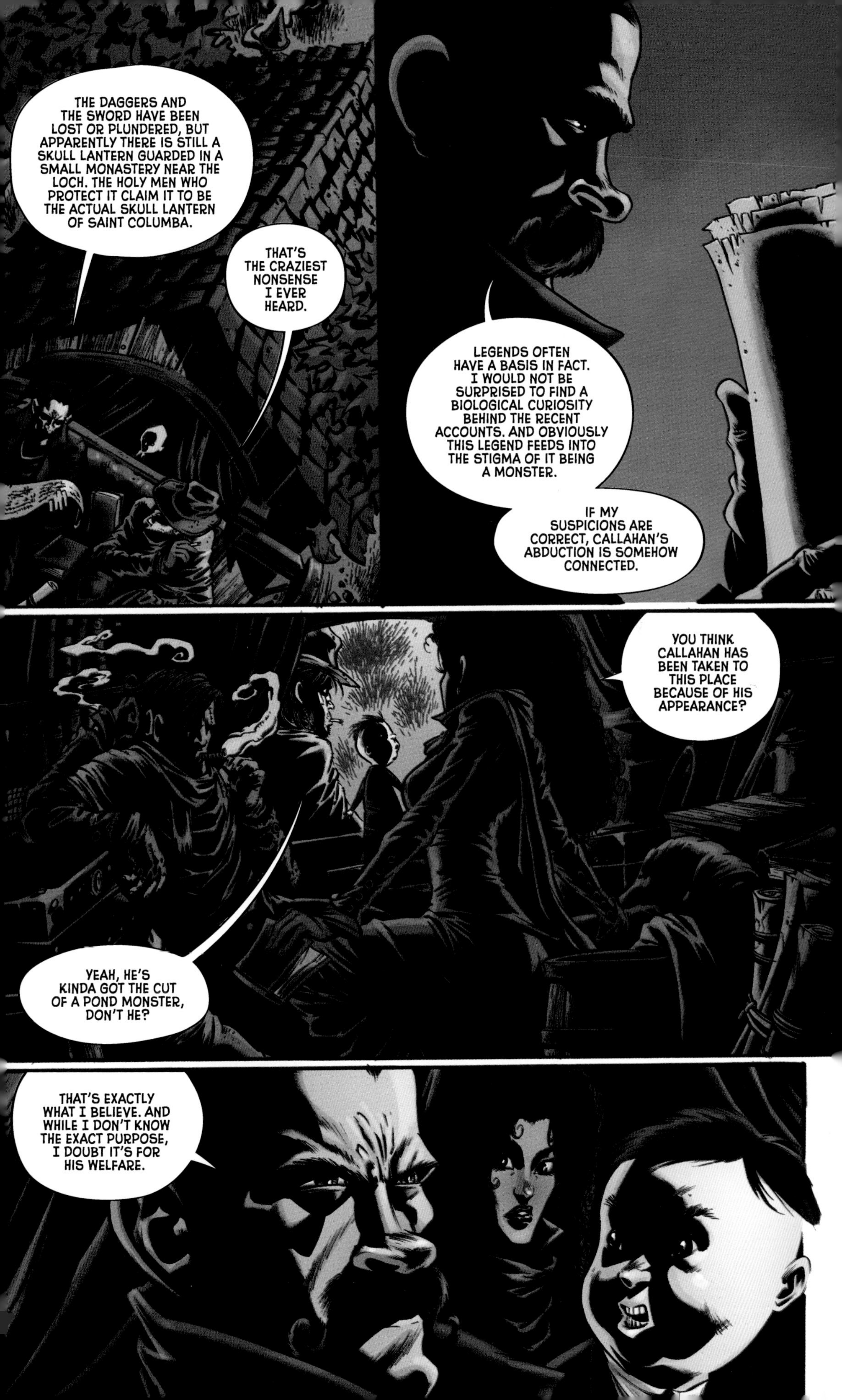
THE DAGGERS AND THE SWORD HAVE BEEN LOST OR PLUNDERED, BUT APPARENTLY THERE IS STILL A SKULL LANTERN GUARDED IN A SMALL MONASTERY NEAR THE LOCH. THE HOLY MEN WHO PROTECT IT CLAIM IT TO BE THE ACTUAL SKULL LANTERN OF SAINT COLUMBA.
THAT'S THE CRAZIEST NONSENSE I EVER HEARD.
LEGENDS OFTEN HAVE A BASIS IN FACT. I WOULD NOT BE SURPRISED TO FIND A BIOLOGICAL CURIOSITY BEHIND THE RECENT ACCOUNTS. AND OBVIOUSLY THIS LEGEND FEEDS INTO THE STIGMA OF IT BEING A MONSTER.
IF MY SUSPICIONS ARE CORRECT, CALLAHAN'S ABDUCTION IS SOMEHOW CONNECTED.
YOU THINK CALLAHAN HAS BEEN TAKEN TO THIS PLACE BECAUSE OF HIS APPEARANCE?
YEAH, HE'S KINDA GOT THE CUT OF A POND MONSTER, DON'T HE?
THAT'S EXACTLY WHAT I BELIEVE. AND WHILE I DON'T KNOW THE EXACT PURPOSE, I DOUBT IT'S FOR HIS WELFARE.

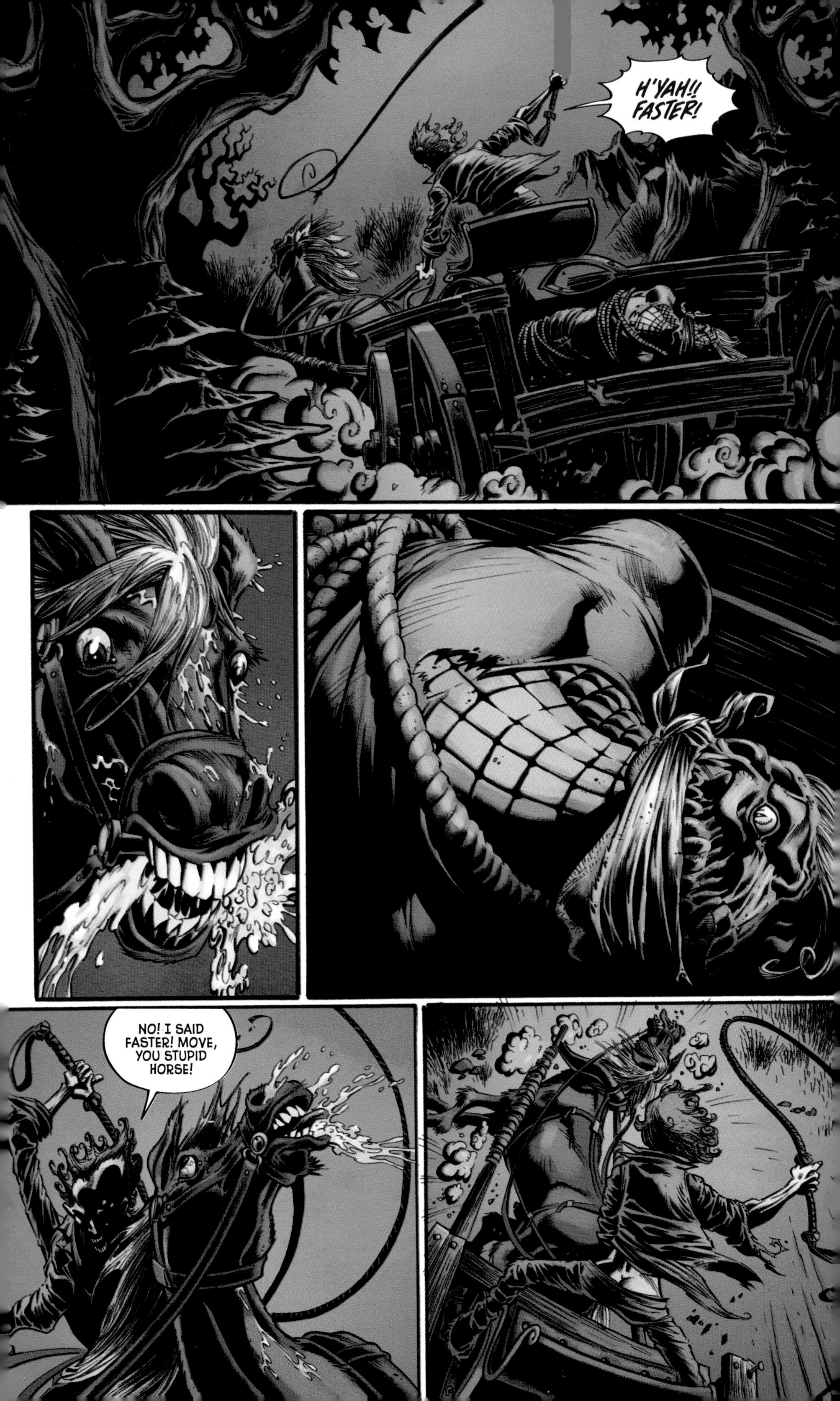
H'YAH!! FASTER!
NO! I SAID FASTER! MOVE, YOU STUPID HORSE!

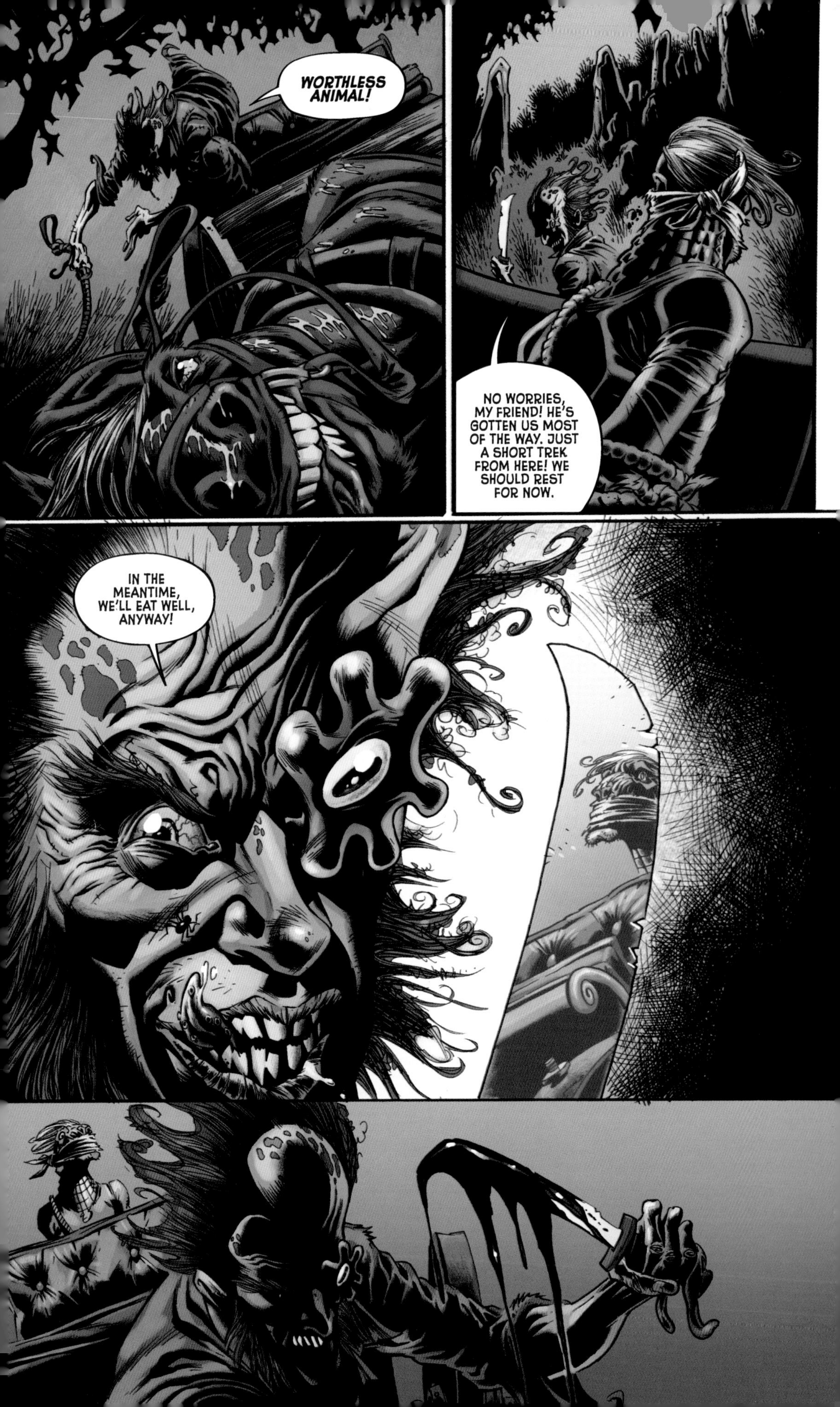
WORTHLESS ANIMAL!
NO WORRIES, MY FRIEND! HE'S GOTTEN US MOST OF THE WAY. JUST A SHORT TREK FROM HERE! WE SHOULD REST FOR NOW.
IN THE MEANTIME, WE'LL EAT WELL, ANYWAY!

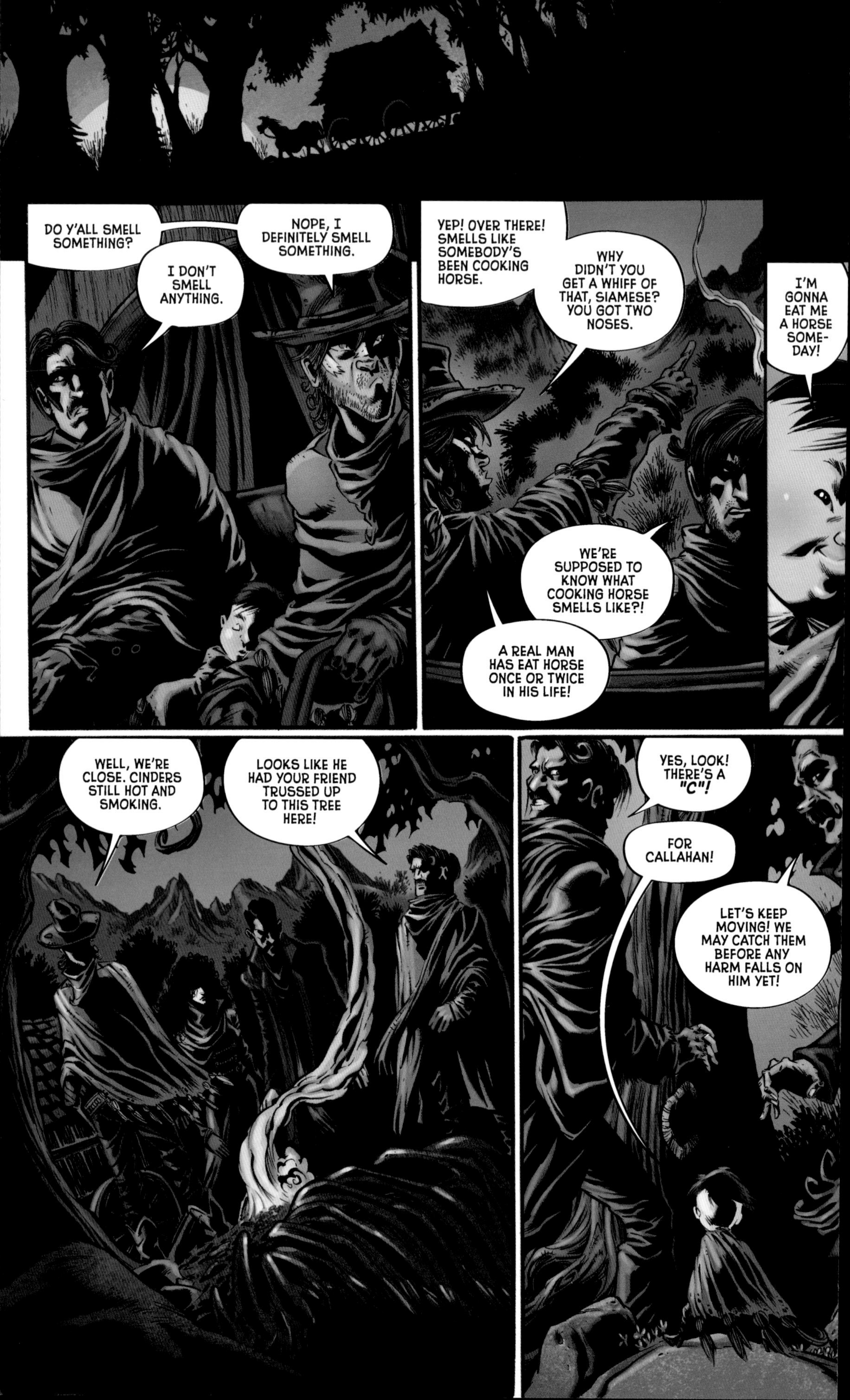
DO Y'ALL SMELL SOMETHING?
I DON'T SMELL ANYTHING.
NOPE, I DEFINITELY SMELL SOMETHING.
YEP! OVER THERE! SMELLS LIKE SOMEBODY'S BEEN COOKING HORSE.
WHY DIDN'T YOU GET A WHIFF OF THAT, SIAMESE? YOU GOT TWO NOSES.
WE'RE SUPPOSED TO KNOW WHAT COOKING HORSE SMELLS LIKE?!
A REAL MAN HAS EAT HORSE ONCE OR TWICE IN HIS LIFE!
I'M GONNA EAT ME A HORSE SOME-DAY!
WELL, WE'RE CLOSE. CINDERS STILL HOT AND SMOKING.
LOOKS LIKE HE HAD YOUR FRIEND TRUSSED UP TO THIS TREE HERE!
YES, LOOK! THERE'S A "C"!
FOR CALLAHAN!
LET'S KEEP MOVING! WE MAY CATCH THEM BEFORE ANY HARM FALLS ON HIM YET!

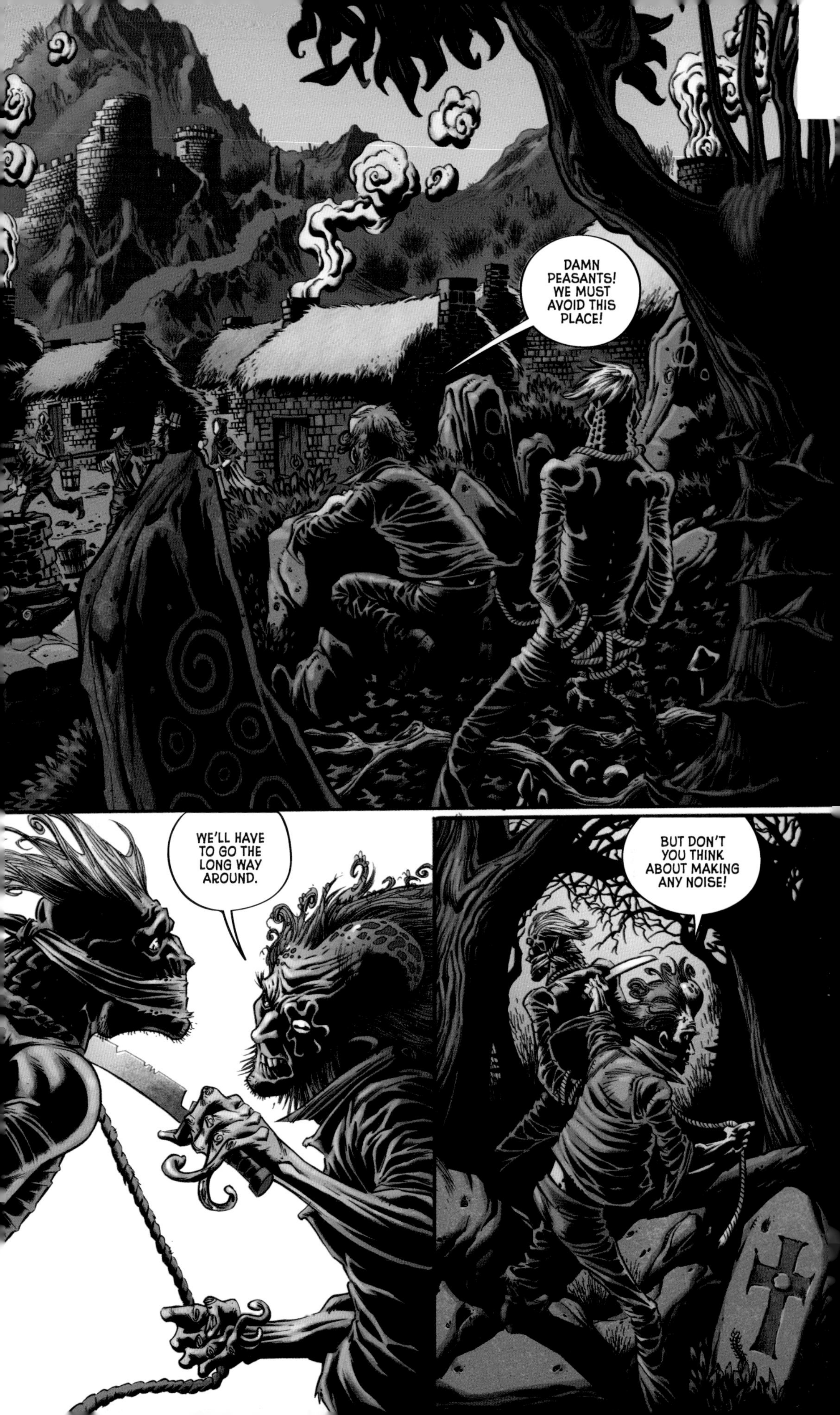
DAMN PEASANTS! WE MUST AVOID THIS PLACE!
WE'LL HAVE TO GO THE LONG WAY AROUND.
BUT DON'T YOU THINK ABOUT MAKING ANY NOISE!

LOOKS LIKE WE GOT A TOWN UP AHEAD.

SEEMS HOSPITABLE ENOUGH.

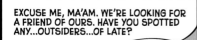

EXCUSE ME, MA'AM. WE'RE LOOKING FOR A FRIEND OF OURS. HAVE YOU SPOTTED ANY...OUTSIDERS...OF LATE?

NO, SIR. YOU ARE THE ONLY STRANGERS TO COME TO THIS VILLAGE IN YEARS.

ARE ALL THE LADIES IN THIS VILLAGE AS ATTRACTIVE AS YOU?

AND DO YOU HAVE A SISTER?

IT HAS TWO HEADS!

ABOMINATIONS FROM THE LOCH!

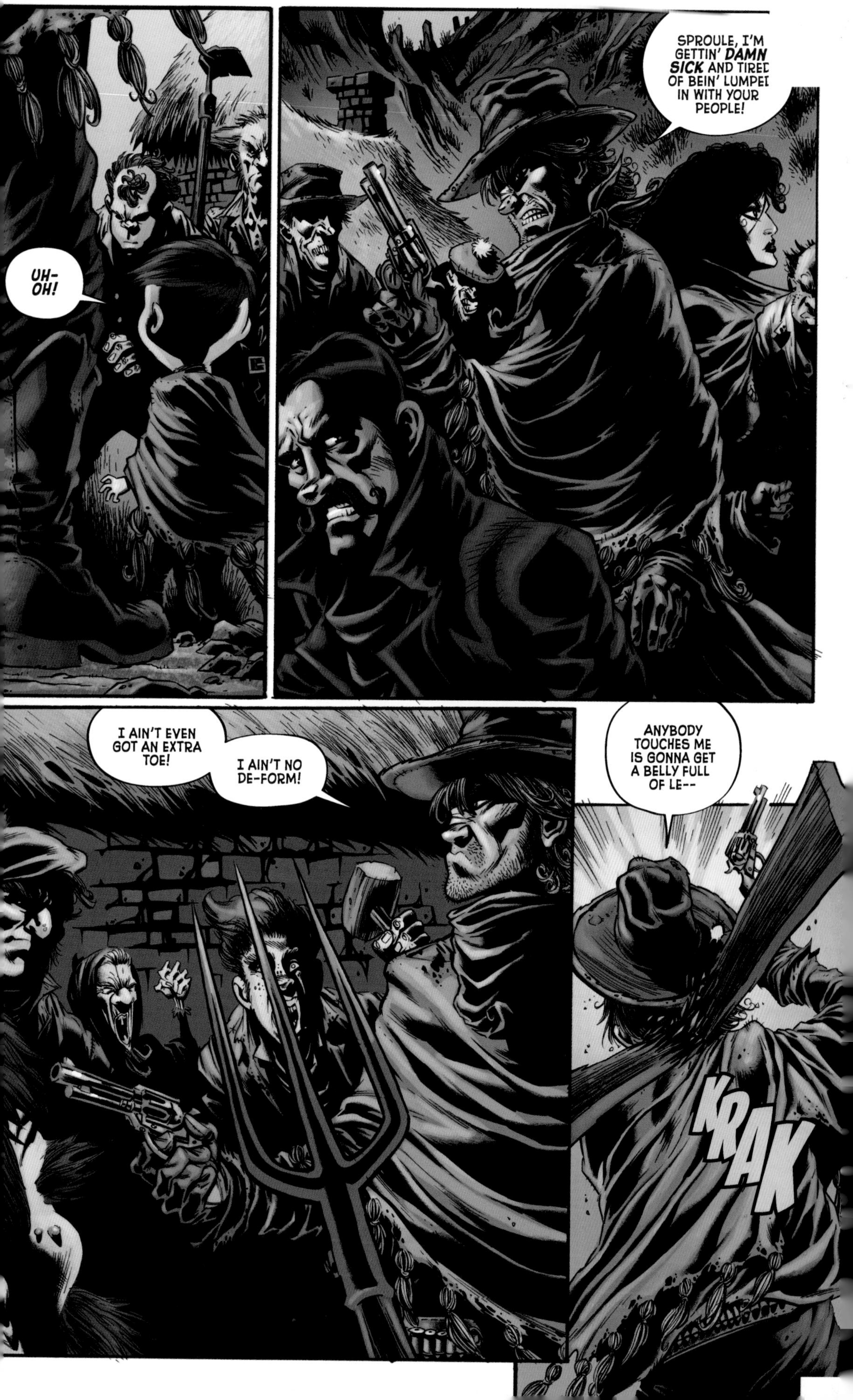
UH-OH!
SPROULE, I'M GETTIN' DAMN SICK AND TIRED OF BEIN' LUMPED IN WITH YOUR PEOPLE!
I AIN'T EVEN GOT AN EXTRA TOE!
I AIN'T NO DE-FORM!
ANYBODY TOUCHES ME IS GONNA GET A BELLY FULL OF LE--
KRAK

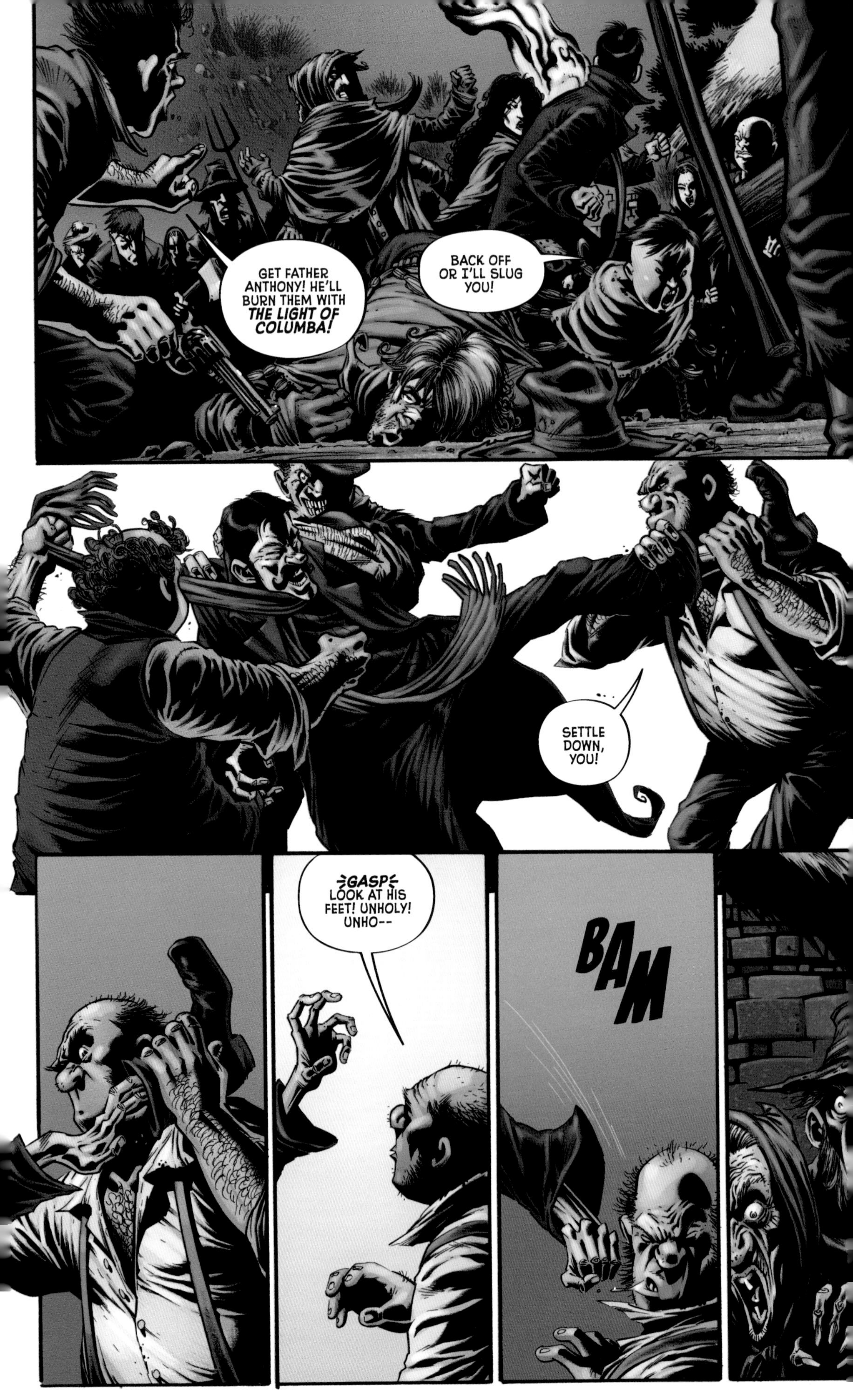
GET FATHER ANTHONY! HE'LL BURN THEM WITH *THE LIGHT OF COLUMBA!*
BACK OFF OR I'LL SLUG YOU!
SETTLE DOWN, YOU!
GASP LOOK AT HIS FEET! UNHOLY! UNHO--
BAM

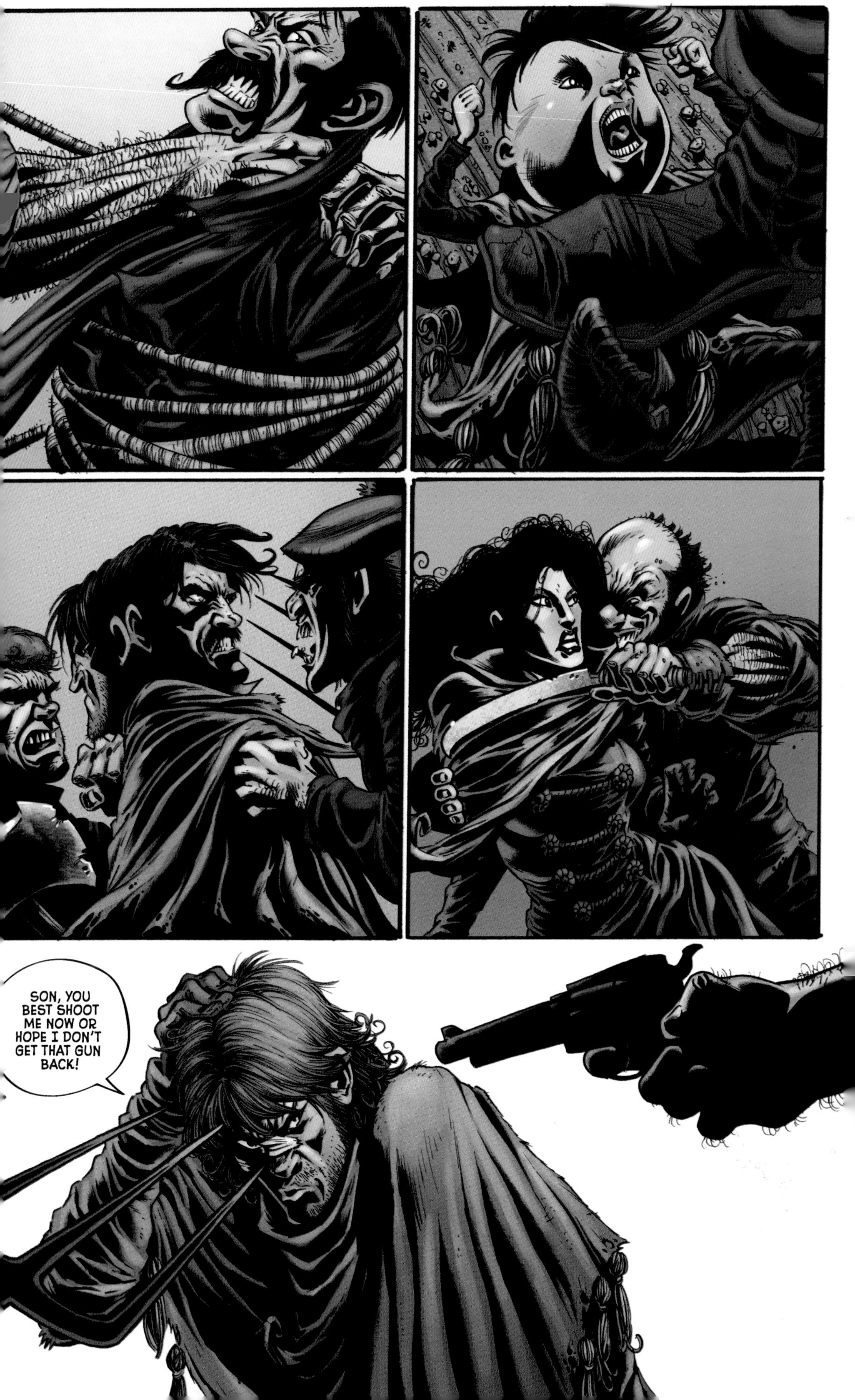
SON, YOU BEST SHOOT ME NOW OR HOPE I DON'T GET THAT GUN BACK!

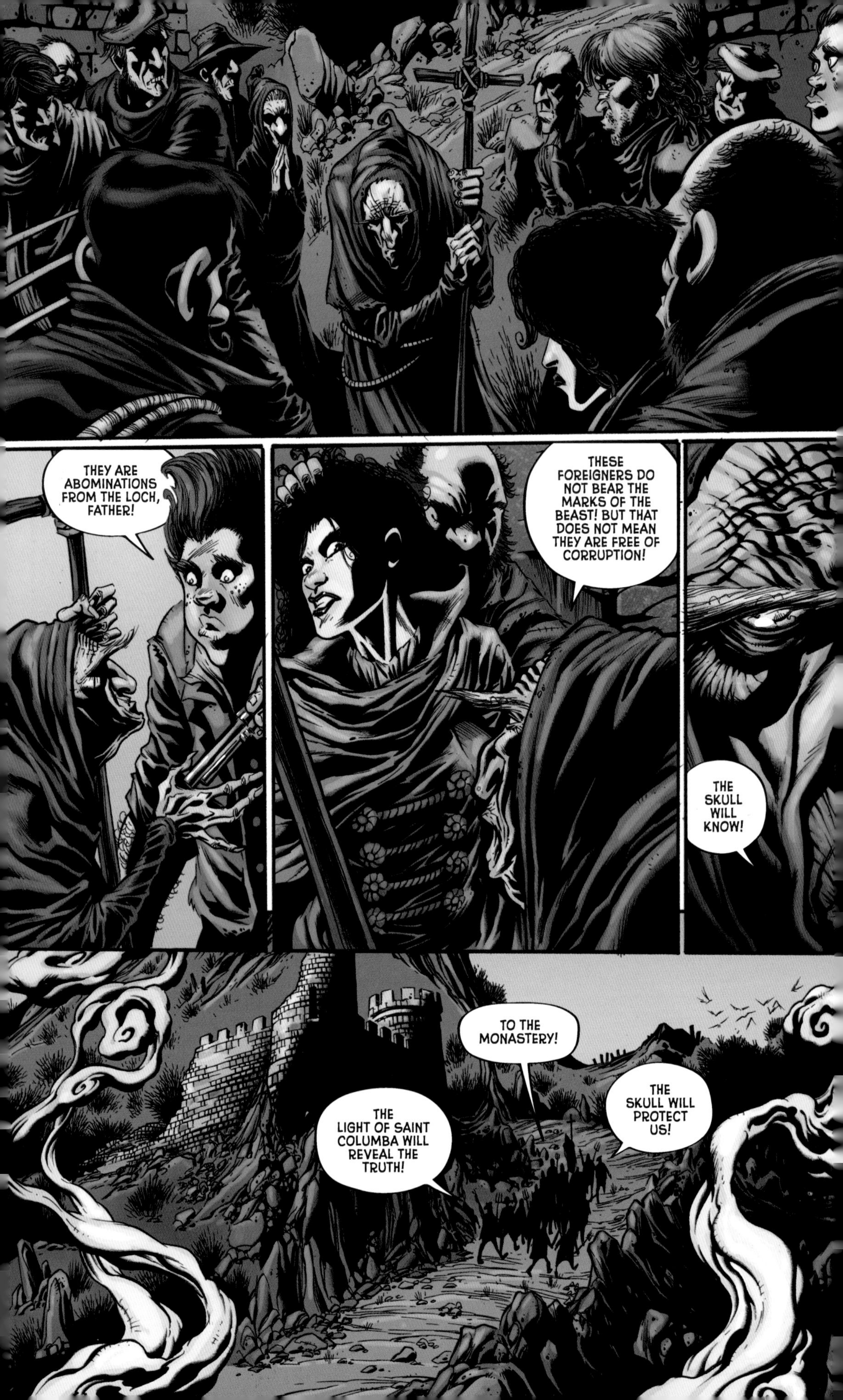
THEY ARE ABOMINATIONS FROM THE LOCH, FATHER!
THESE FOREIGNERS DO NOT BEAR THE MARKS OF THE BEAST! BUT THAT DOES NOT MEAN THEY ARE FREE OF CORRUPTION!
THE SKULL WILL KNOW!
TO THE MONASTERY!
THE LIGHT OF SAINT COLUMBA WILL REVEAL THE TRUTH!
THE SKULL WILL PROTECT US!

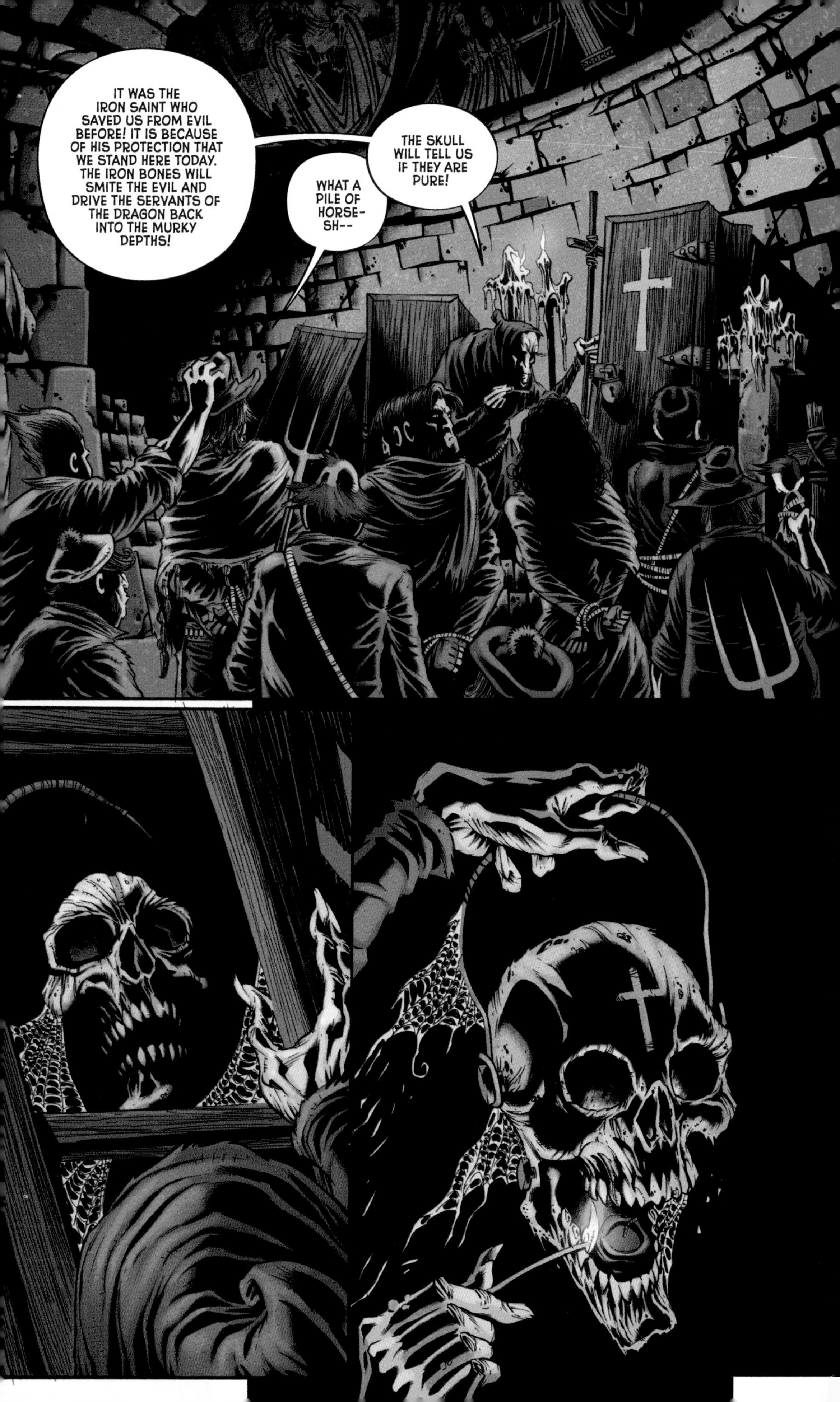
IT WAS THE IRON SAINT WHO SAVED US FROM EVIL BEFORE! IT IS BECAUSE OF HIS PROTECTION THAT WE STAND HERE TODAY. THE IRON BONES WILL SMITE THE EVIL AND DRIVE THE SERVANTS OF THE DRAGON BACK INTO THE MURKY DEPTHS!
THE SKULL WILL TELL US IF THEY ARE PURE!
WHAT A PILE OF HORSE-SH--

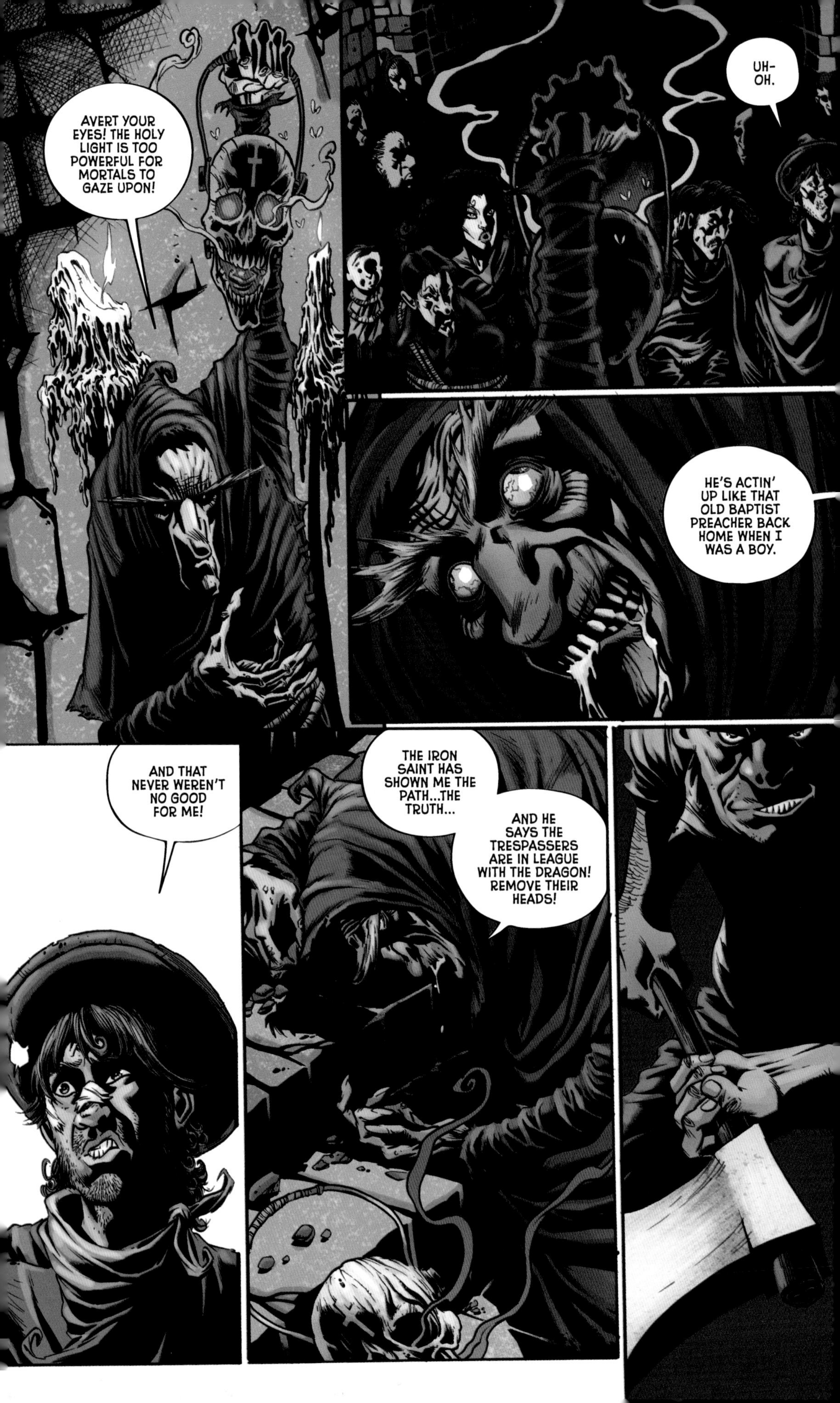
AVERT YOUR EYES! THE HOLY LIGHT IS TOO POWERFUL FOR MORTALS TO GAZE UPON!
UH-OH.
HE'S ACTIN' UP LIKE THAT OLD BAPTIST PREACHER BACK HOME WHEN I WAS A BOY.
AND THAT NEVER WEREN'T NO GOOD FOR ME!
THE IRON SAINT HAS SHOWN ME THE PATH...THE TRUTH...
AND HE SAYS THE TRESPASSERS ARE IN LEAGUE WITH THE DRAGON! REMOVE THEIR HEADS!

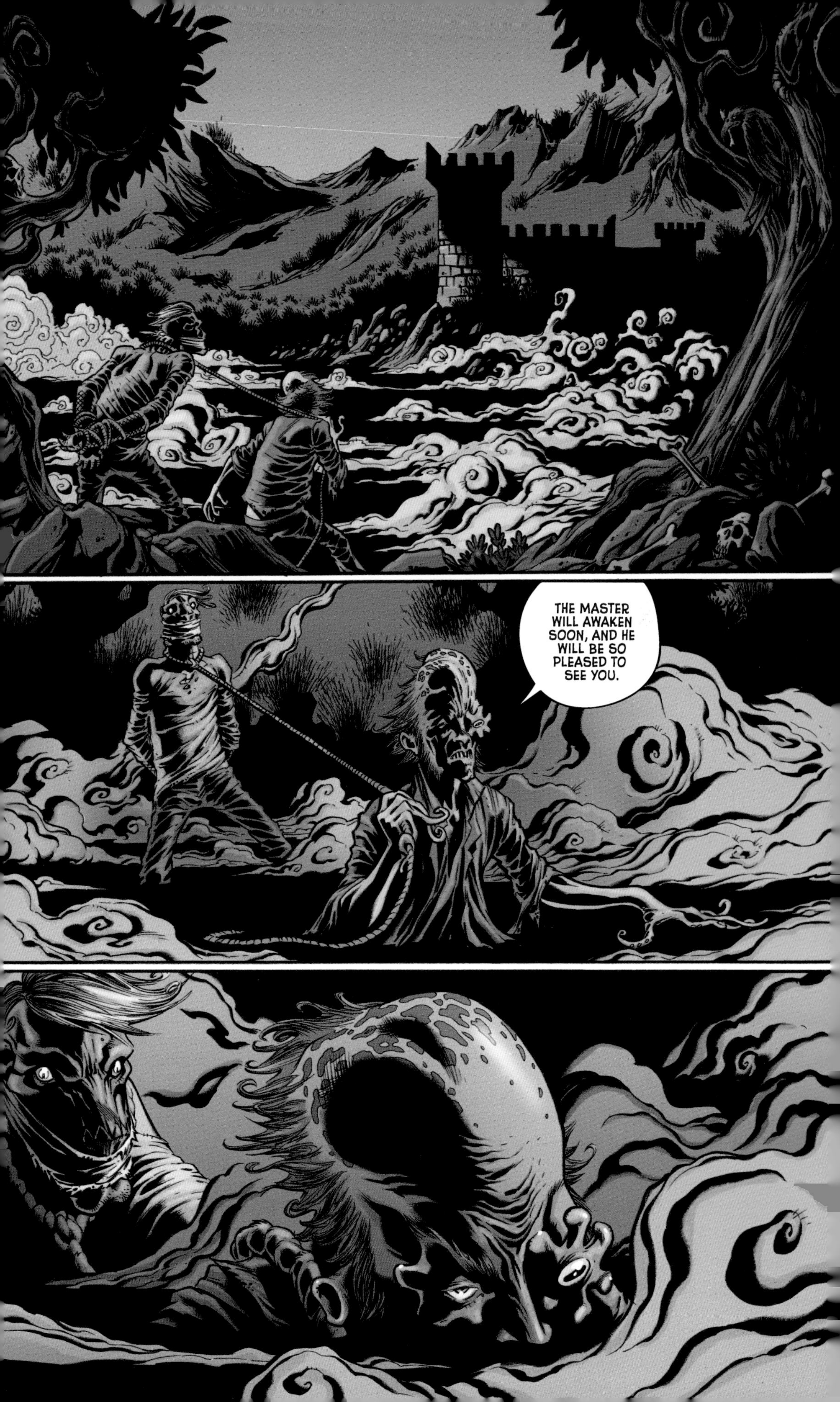
THE MASTER WILL AWAKEN SOON, AND HE WILL BE SO PLEASED TO SEE YOU.

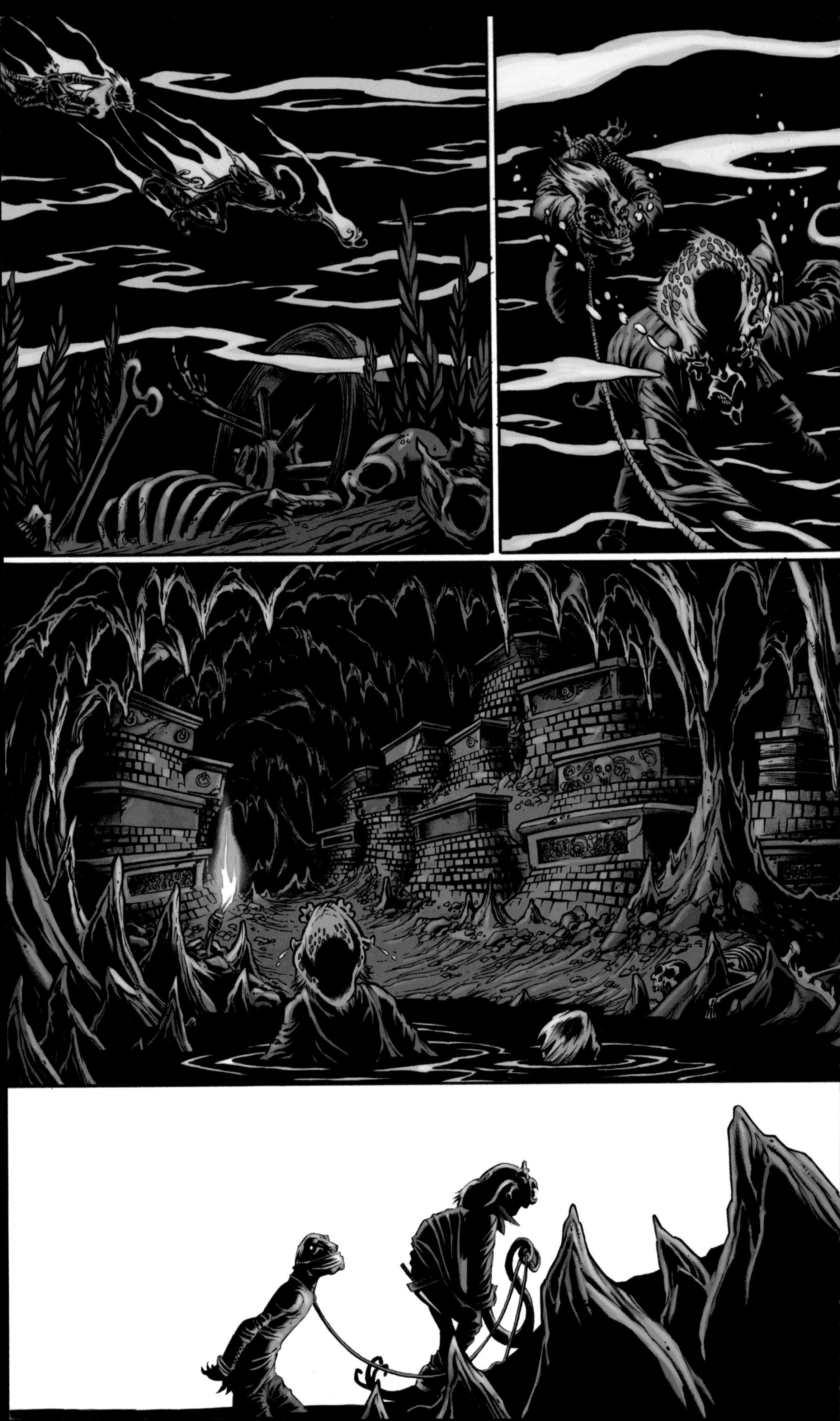

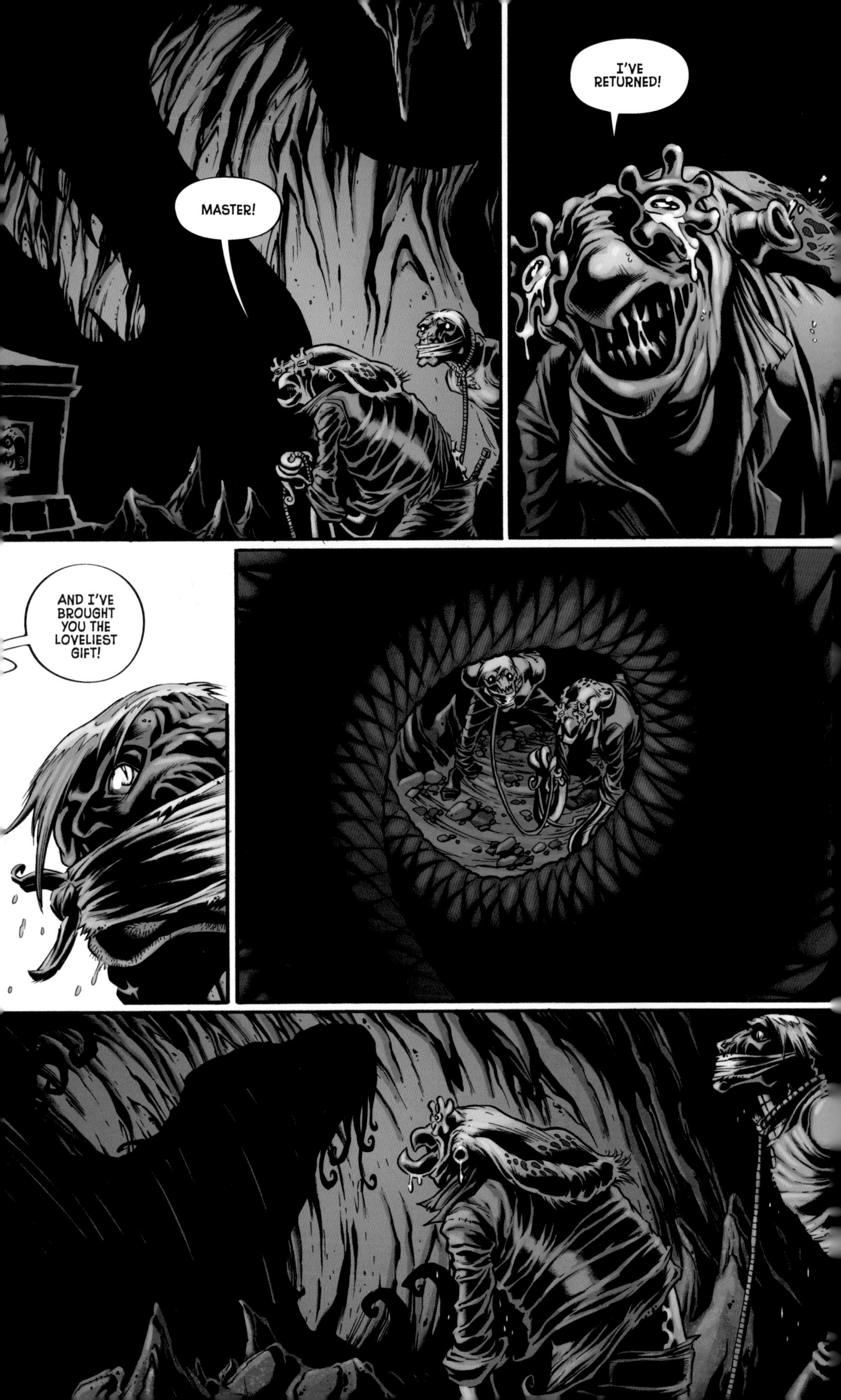
MASTER!
I'VE RETURNED!
AND I'VE BROUGHT YOU THE LOVELIEST GIFT!

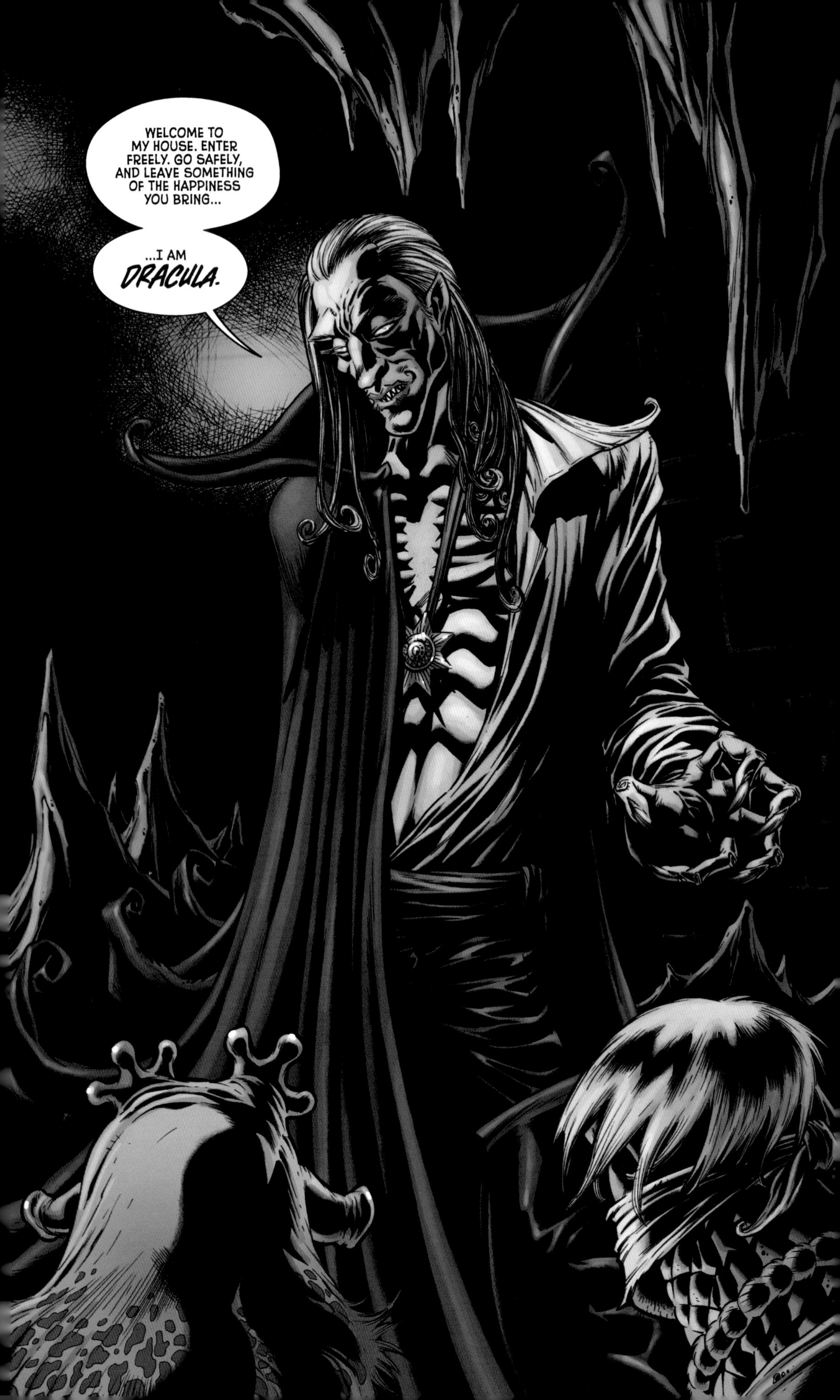
WELCOME TO MY HOUSE. ENTER FREELY. GO SAFELY, AND LEAVE SOMETHING OF THE HAPPINESS YOU BRING...
...I AM *DRACULA*.

CHAPTER TWO

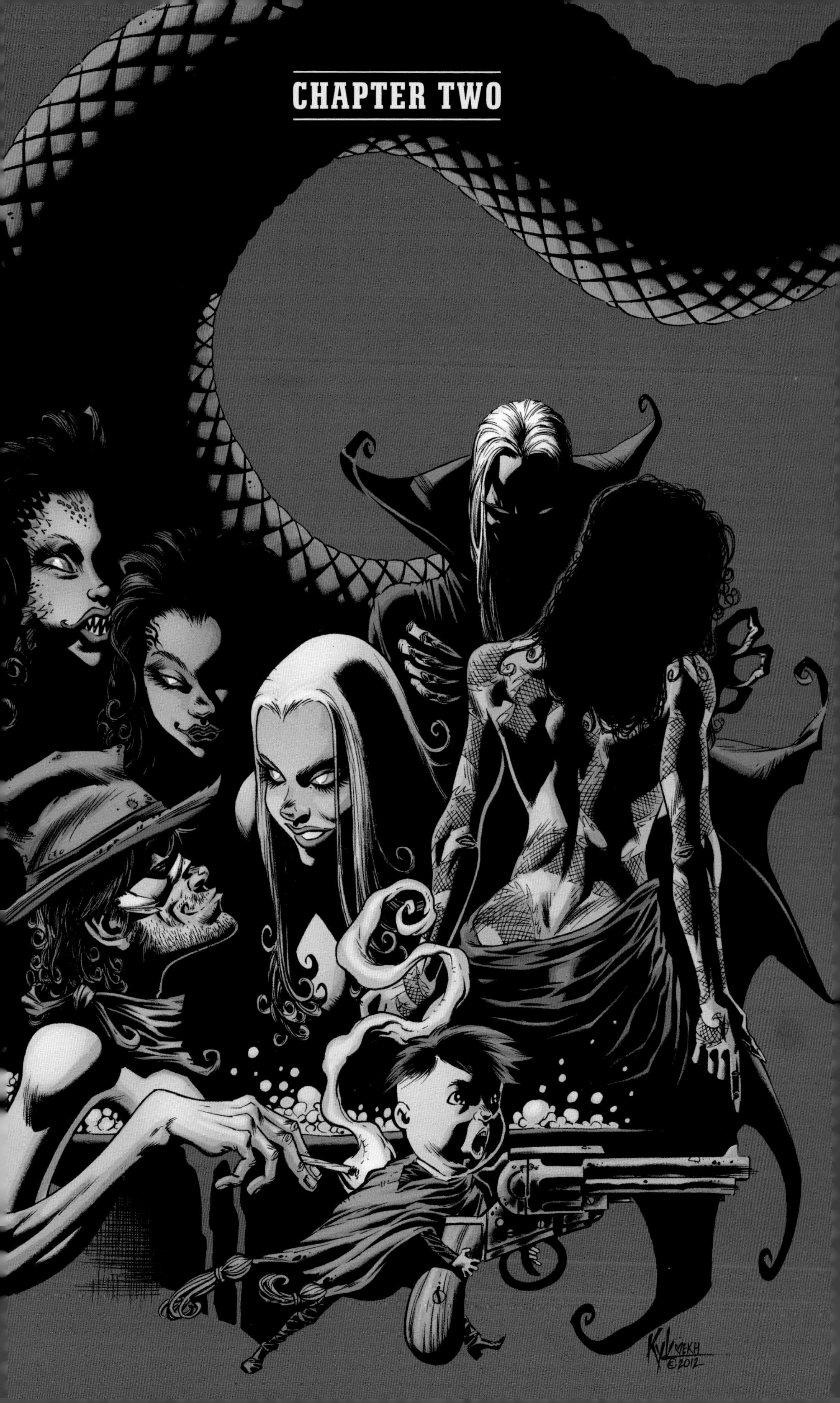

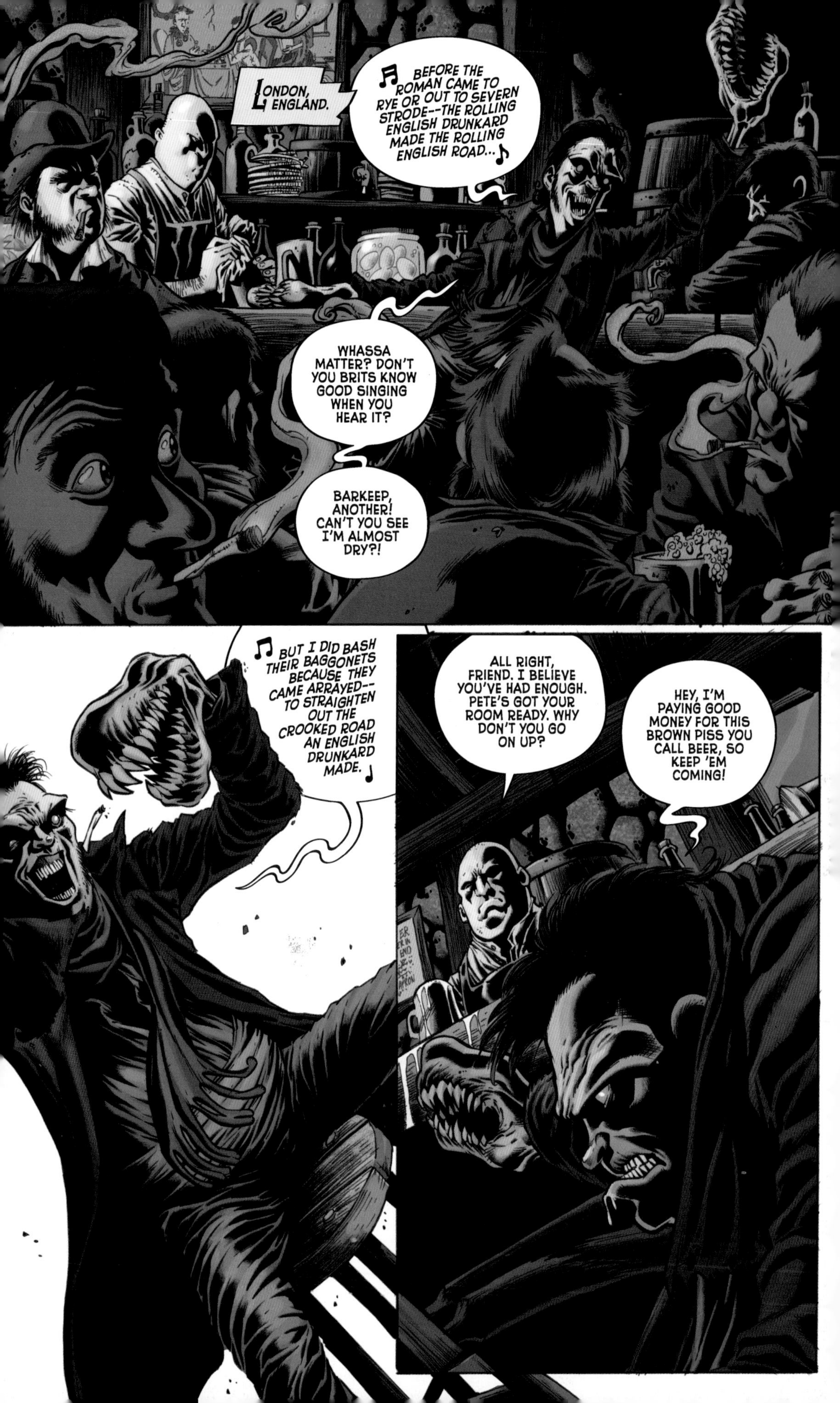
LONDON, ENGLAND.
BEFORE THE ROMAN CAME TO RYE OR OUT TO SEVERN STRODE--THE ROLLING ENGLISH DRUNKARD MADE THE ROLLING ENGLISH ROAD...
WHASSA MATTER? DON'T YOU BRITS KNOW GOOD SINGING WHEN YOU HEAR IT?
BARKEEP, ANOTHER! CAN'T YOU SEE I'M ALMOST DRY?!
BUT I DID BASH THEIR BAGGONETS BECAUSE THEY CAME ARRAYED-- TO STRAIGHTEN OUT THE CROOKED ROAD AN ENGLISH DRUNKARD MADE.
ALL RIGHT, FRIEND. I BELIEVE YOU'VE HAD ENOUGH. PETE'S GOT YOUR ROOM READY. WHY DON'T YOU GO ON UP?
HEY, I'M PAYING GOOD MONEY FOR THIS BROWN PISS YOU CALL BEER, SO KEEP 'EM COMING!

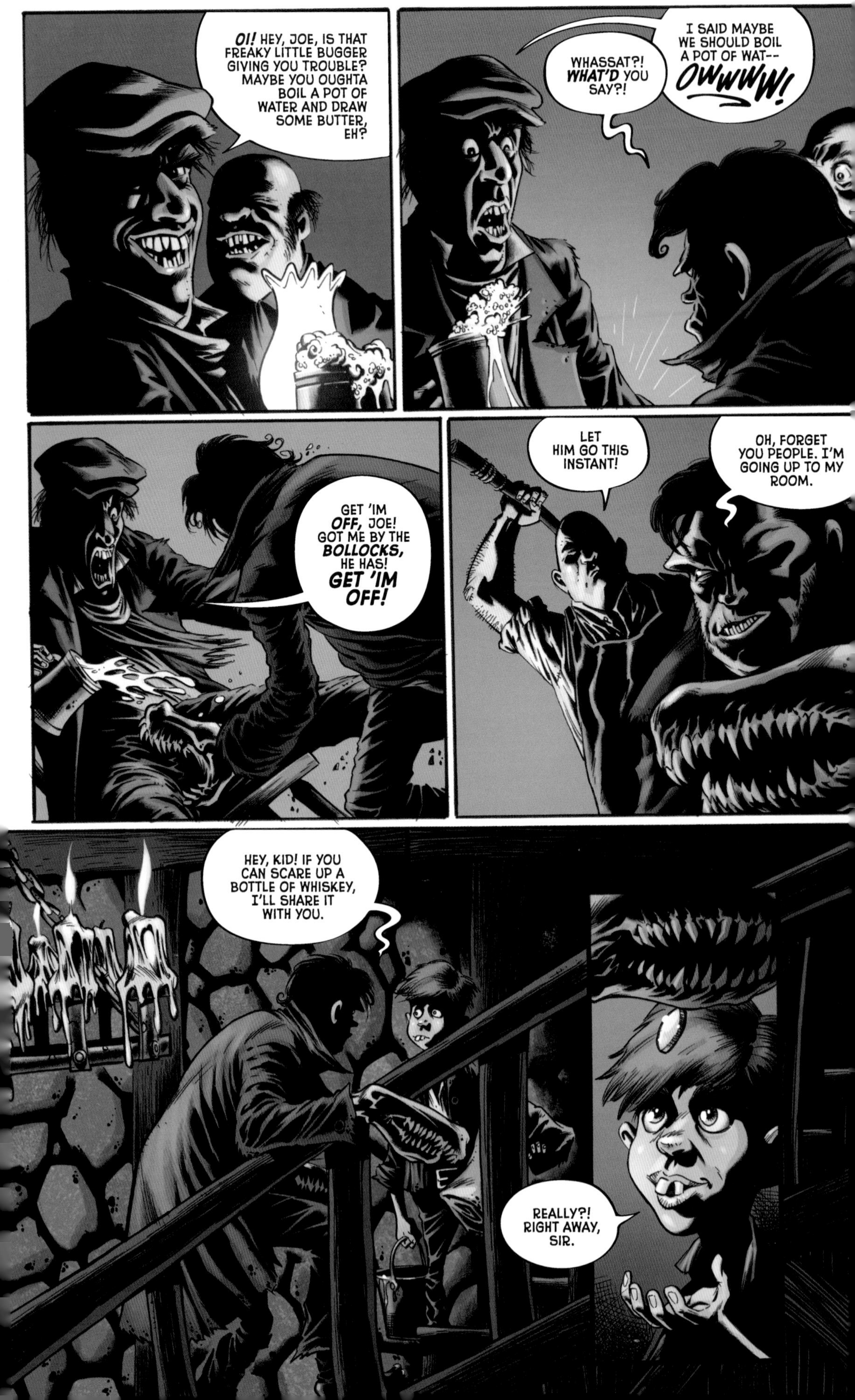
OI! HEY, JOE, IS THAT FREAKY LITTLE BUGGER GIVING YOU TROUBLE? MAYBE YOU OUGHTA BOIL A POT OF WATER AND DRAW SOME BUTTER, EH?
WHASSAT?! WHAT'D YOU SAY?!
I SAID MAYBE WE SHOULD BOIL A POT OF WAT-- OWWWW!
GET 'IM OFF, JOE! GOT ME BY THE BOLLOCKS, HE HAS! GET 'IM OFF!
LET HIM GO THIS INSTANT!
OH, FORGET YOU PEOPLE. I'M GOING UP TO MY ROOM.
HEY, KID! IF YOU CAN SCARE UP A BOTTLE OF WHISKEY, I'LL SHARE IT WITH YOU.
REALLY?! RIGHT AWAY, SIR.

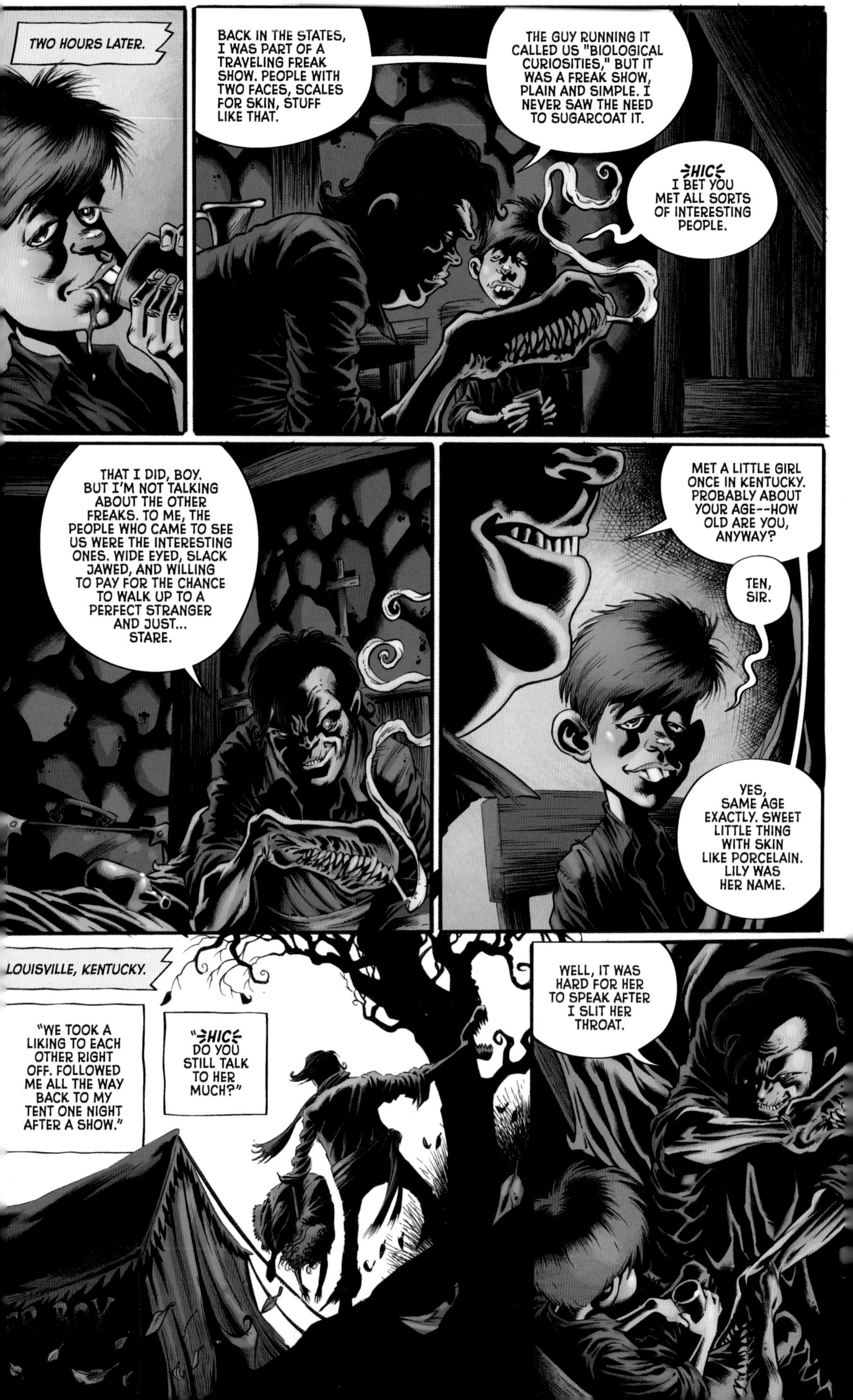
TWO HOURS LATER.
BACK IN THE STATES, I WAS PART OF A TRAVELING FREAK SHOW. PEOPLE WITH TWO FACES, SCALES FOR SKIN, STUFF LIKE THAT.
THE GUY RUNNING IT CALLED US "BIOLOGICAL CURIOSITIES," BUT IT WAS A FREAK SHOW, PLAIN AND SIMPLE. I NEVER SAW THE NEED TO SUGARCOAT IT.
HIC I BET YOU MET ALL SORTS OF INTERESTING PEOPLE.
THAT I DID, BOY. BUT I'M NOT TALKING ABOUT THE OTHER FREAKS. TO ME, THE PEOPLE WHO CAME TO SEE US WERE THE INTERESTING ONES. WIDE EYED, SLACK JAWED, AND WILLING TO PAY FOR THE CHANCE TO WALK UP TO A PERFECT STRANGER AND JUST... STARE.
MET A LITTLE GIRL ONCE IN KENTUCKY. PROBABLY ABOUT YOUR AGE--HOW OLD ARE YOU, ANYWAY?
TEN, SIR.
YES, SAME AGE EXACTLY. SWEET LITTLE THING WITH SKIN LIKE PORCELAIN. LILY WAS HER NAME.
LOUISVILLE, KENTUCKY.
"WE TOOK A LIKING TO EACH OTHER RIGHT OFF. FOLLOWED ME ALL THE WAY BACK TO MY TENT ONE NIGHT AFTER A SHOW."
"HIC DO YOU STILL TALK TO HER MUCH?"
WELL, IT WAS HARD FOR HER TO SPEAK AFTER I SLIT HER THROAT.

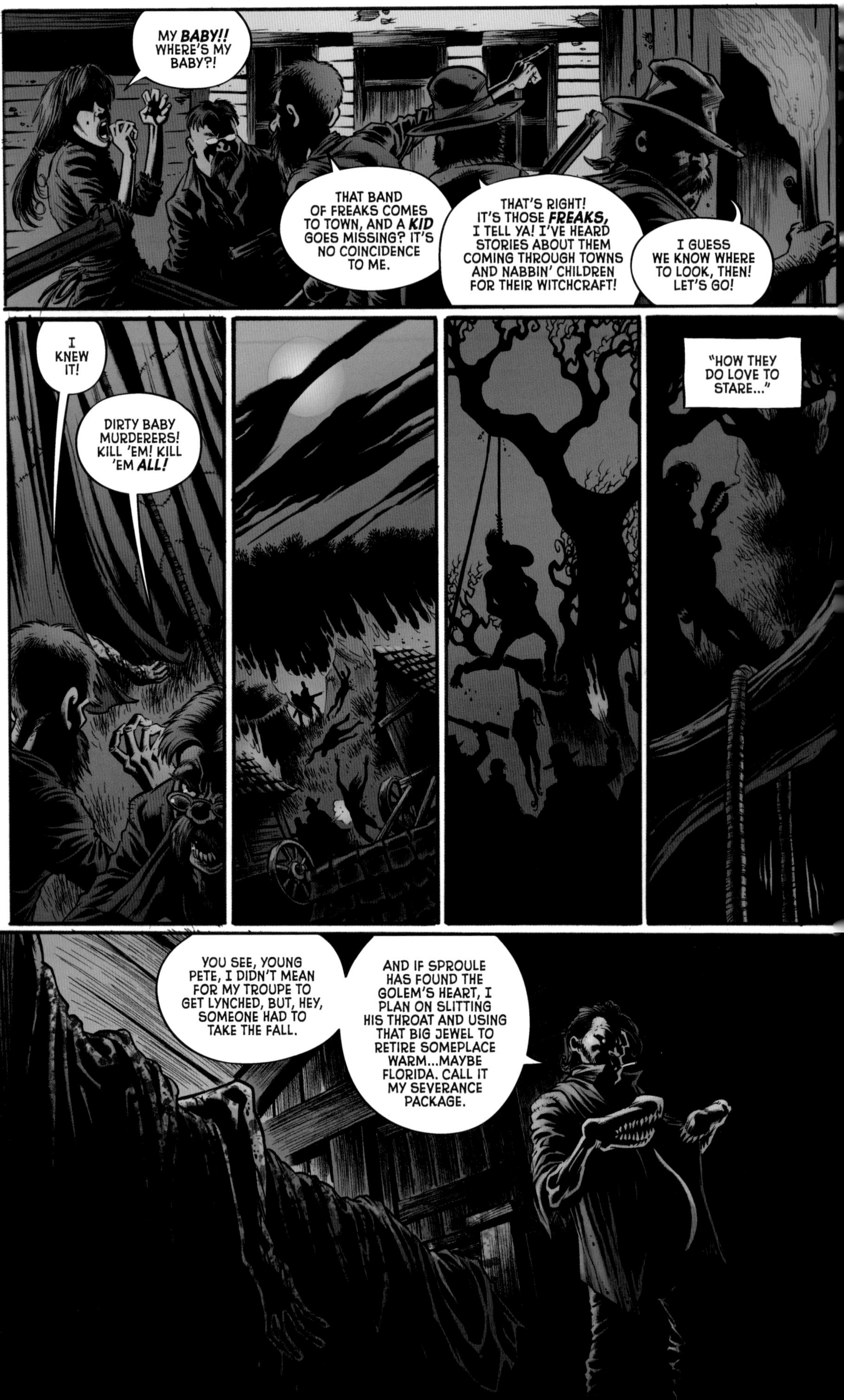

MY ***BABY!!*** WHERE'S MY BABY?!
THAT BAND OF FREAKS COMES TO TOWN, AND A ***KID*** GOES MISSING? IT'S NO COINCIDENCE TO ME.
THAT'S RIGHT! IT'S THOSE ***FREAKS,*** I TELL YA! I'VE HEARD STORIES ABOUT THEM COMING THROUGH TOWNS AND NABBIN' CHILDREN FOR THEIR WITCHCRAFT!
I GUESS WE KNOW WHERE TO LOOK, THEN! LET'S GO!
I KNEW IT!
DIRTY BABY MURDERERS! KILL 'EM! KILL 'EM ***ALL!***
"HOW THEY DO LOVE TO STARE..."
YOU SEE, YOUNG PETE, I DIDN'T MEAN FOR MY TROUPE TO GET LYNCHED, BUT, HEY, SOMEONE HAD TO TAKE THE FALL.
AND IF SPROULE HAS FOUND THE GOLEM'S HEART, I PLAN ON SLITTING HIS THROAT AND USING THAT BIG JEWEL TO RETIRE SOMEPLACE WARM...MAYBE FLORIDA. CALL IT MY SEVERANCE PACKAGE.

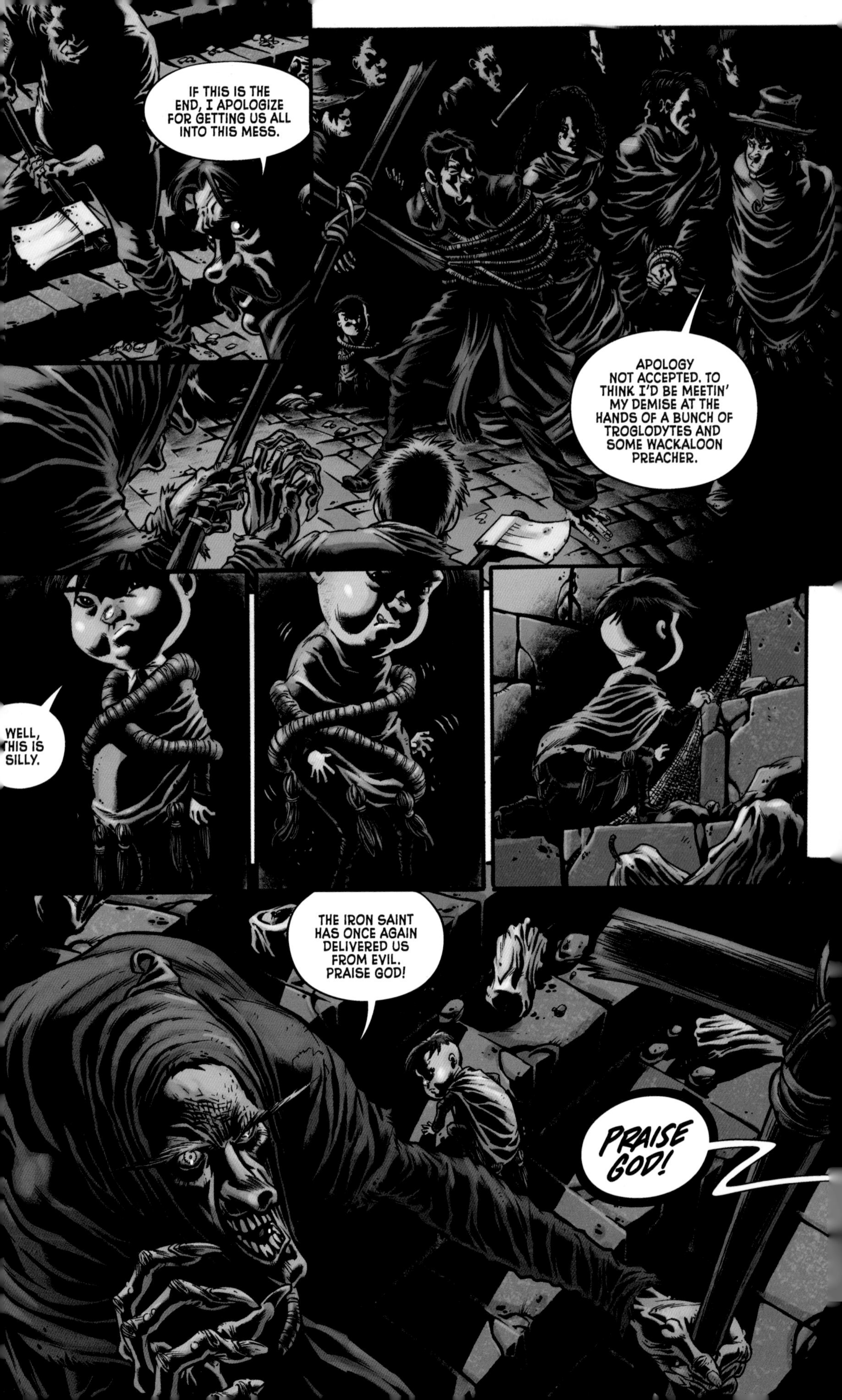
IF THIS IS THE END, I APOLOGIZE FOR GETTING US ALL INTO THIS MESS.
APOLOGY NOT ACCEPTED. TO THINK I'D BE MEETIN' MY DEMISE AT THE HANDS OF A BUNCH OF TROGLODYTES AND SOME WACKALOON PREACHER.
WELL, THIS IS SILLY.
THE IRON SAINT HAS ONCE AGAIN DELIVERED US FROM EVIL. PRAISE GOD!
PRAISE GOD!

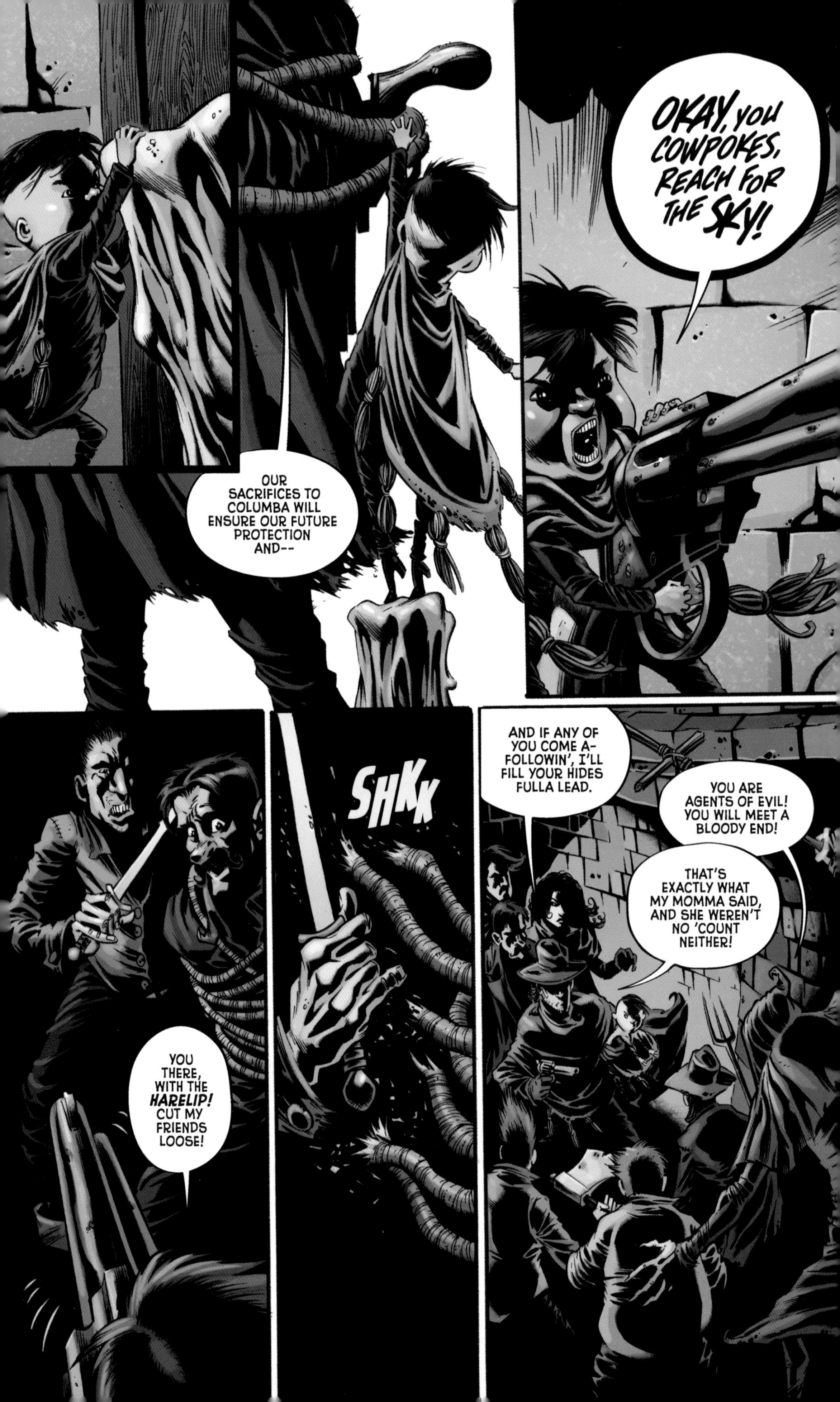

OUR SACRIFICES TO COLUMBA WILL ENSURE OUR FUTURE PROTECTION AND--
OKAY, YOU COWPOKES, REACH FOR THE SKY!
YOU THERE, WITH THE HARELIP! CUT MY FRIENDS LOOSE!
SHKK
AND IF ANY OF YOU COME A-FOLLOWIN', I'LL FILL YOUR HIDES FULLA LEAD.
YOU ARE AGENTS OF EVIL! YOU WILL MEET A BLOODY END!
THAT'S EXACTLY WHAT MY MOMMA SAID, AND SHE WEREN'T NO 'COUNT NEITHER!

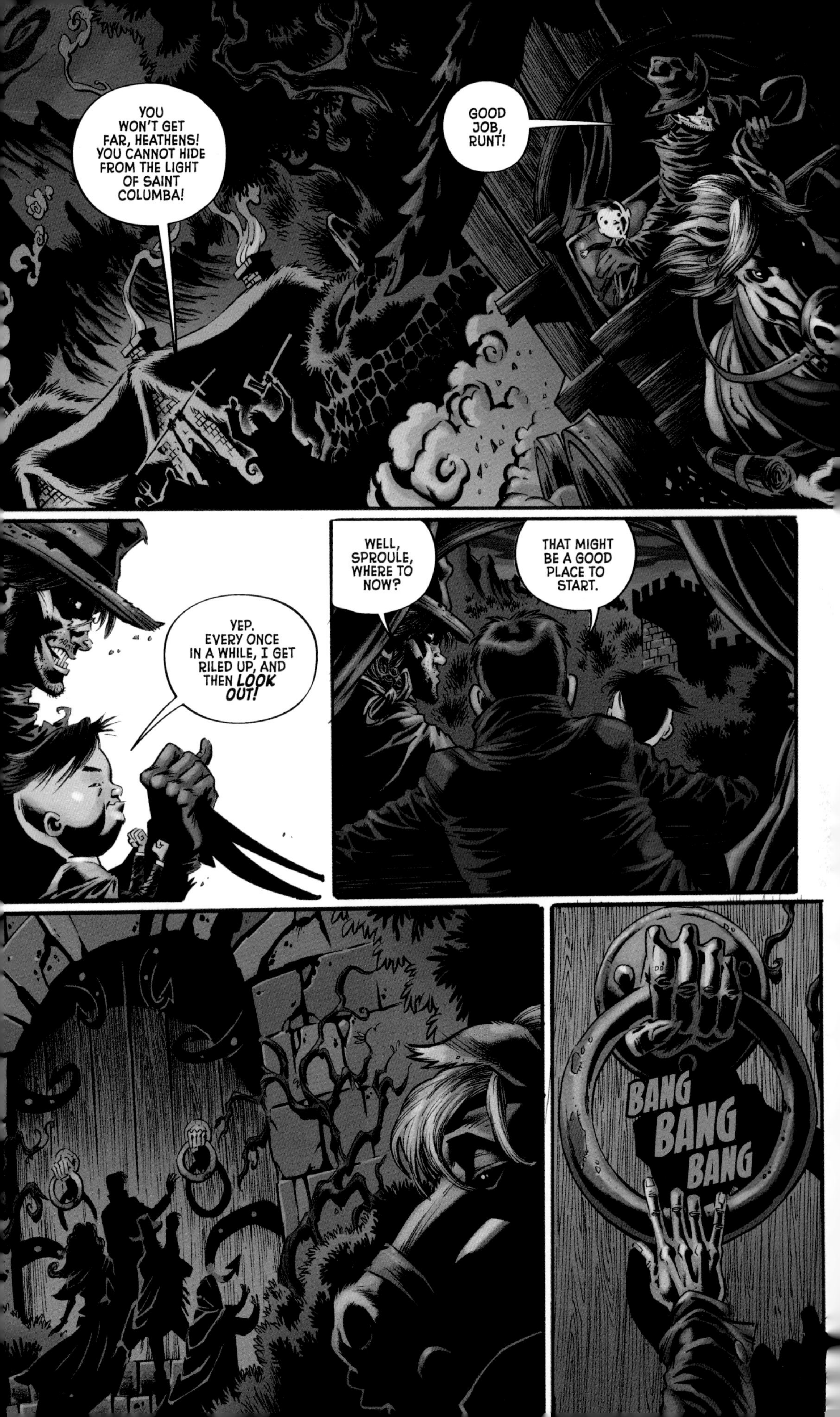
YOU WON'T GET FAR, HEATHENS! YOU CANNOT HIDE FROM THE LIGHT OF SAINT COLUMBA!
GOOD JOB, RUNT!
YEP. EVERY ONCE IN A WHILE, I GET RILED UP, AND THEN LOOK OUT!
WELL, SPROULE, WHERE TO NOW?
THAT MIGHT BE A GOOD PLACE TO START.
BANG BANG BANG

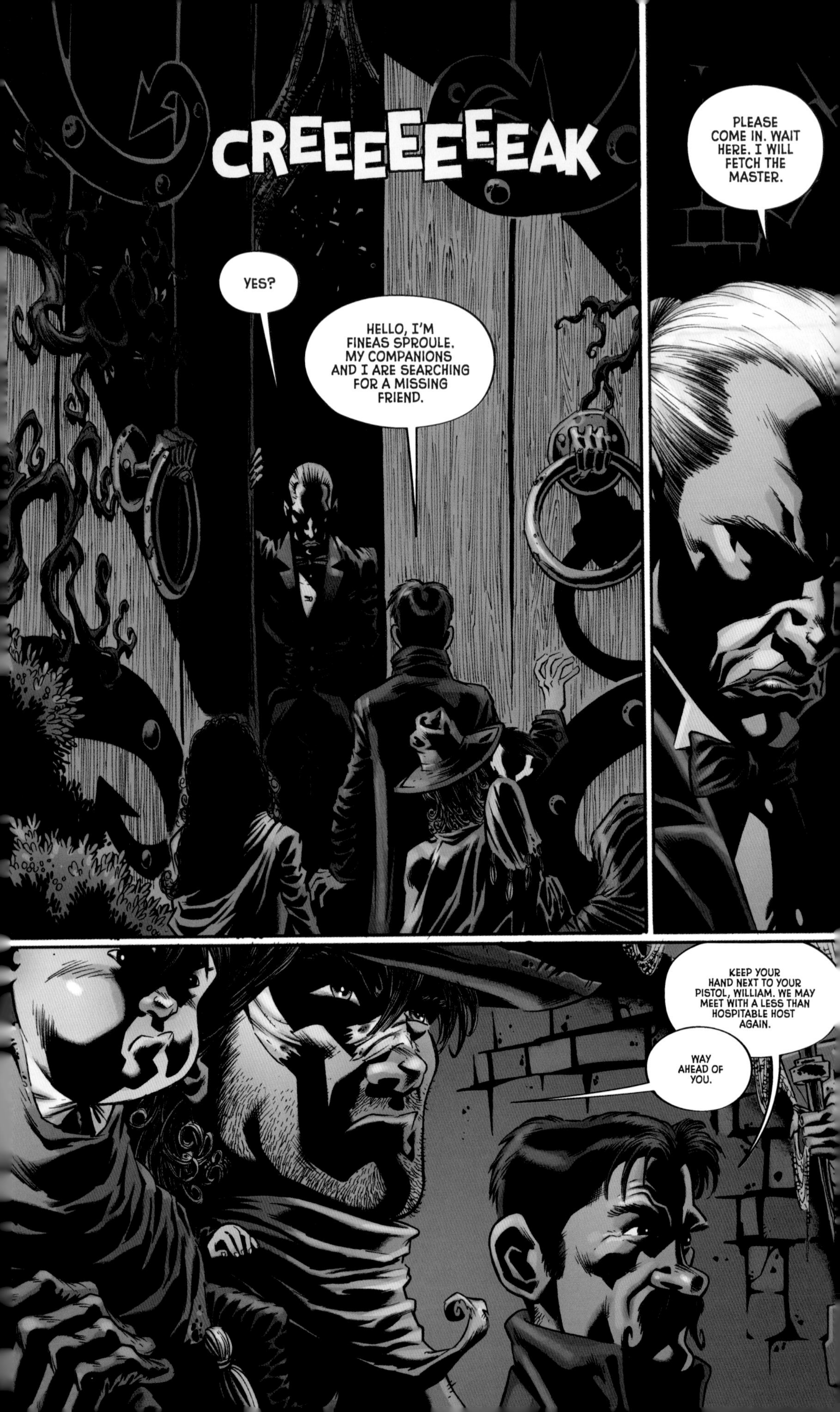
CREEEEEEEEAK
YES?
HELLO, I'M FINEAS SPROULE. MY COMPANIONS AND I ARE SEARCHING FOR A MISSING FRIEND.
PLEASE COME IN. WAIT HERE. I WILL FETCH THE MASTER.
KEEP YOUR HAND NEXT TO YOUR PISTOL, WILLIAM. WE MAY MEET WITH A LESS THAN HOSPITABLE HOST AGAIN.
WAY AHEAD OF YOU.

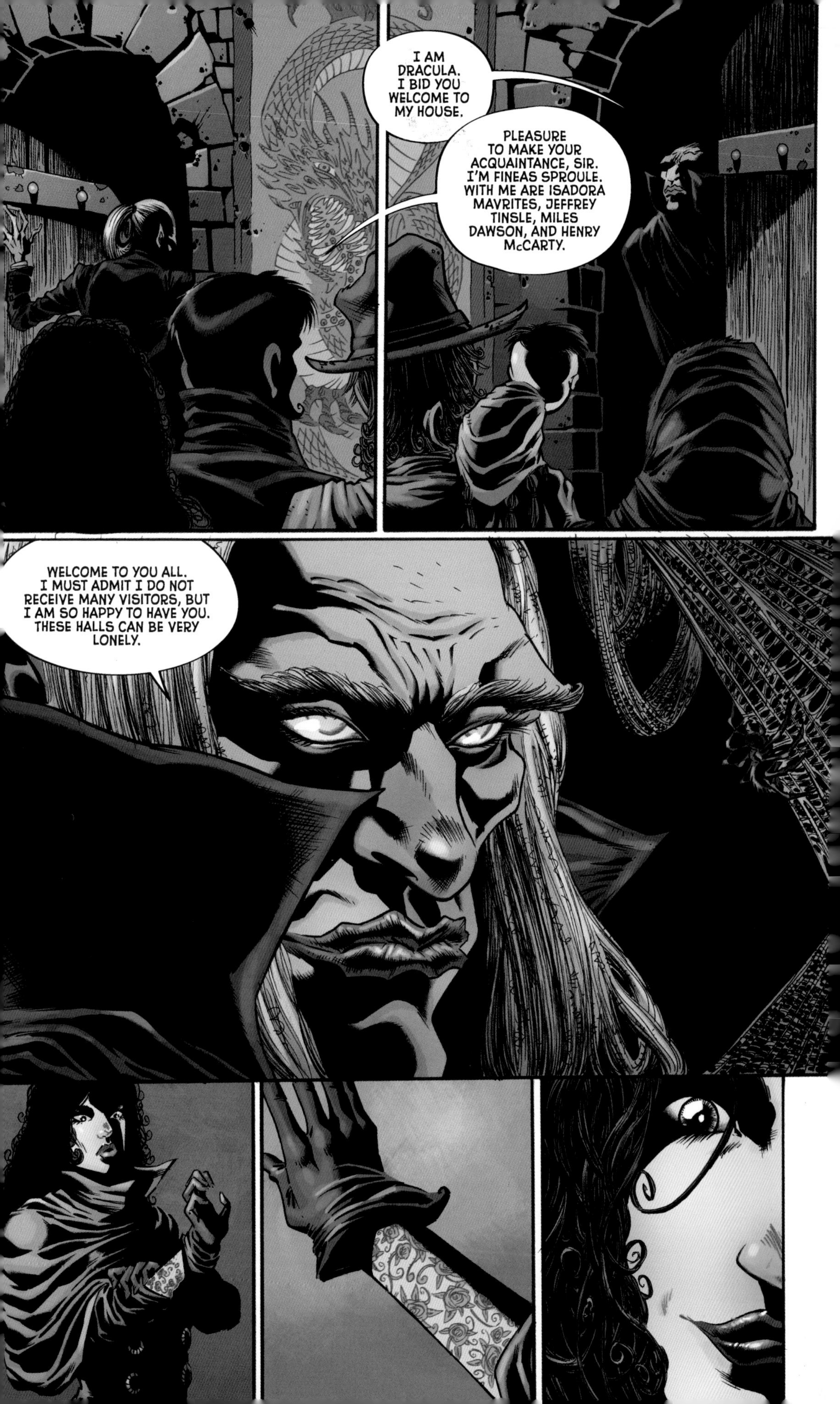
I AM DRACULA. I BID YOU WELCOME TO MY HOUSE.
PLEASURE TO MAKE YOUR ACQUAINTANCE, SIR. I'M FINEAS SPROULE. WITH ME ARE ISADORA MAVRITES, JEFFREY TINSLE, MILES DAWSON, AND HENRY McCARTY.
WELCOME TO YOU ALL. I MUST ADMIT I DO NOT RECEIVE MANY VISITORS, BUT I AM SO HAPPY TO HAVE YOU. THESE HALLS CAN BE VERY LONELY.

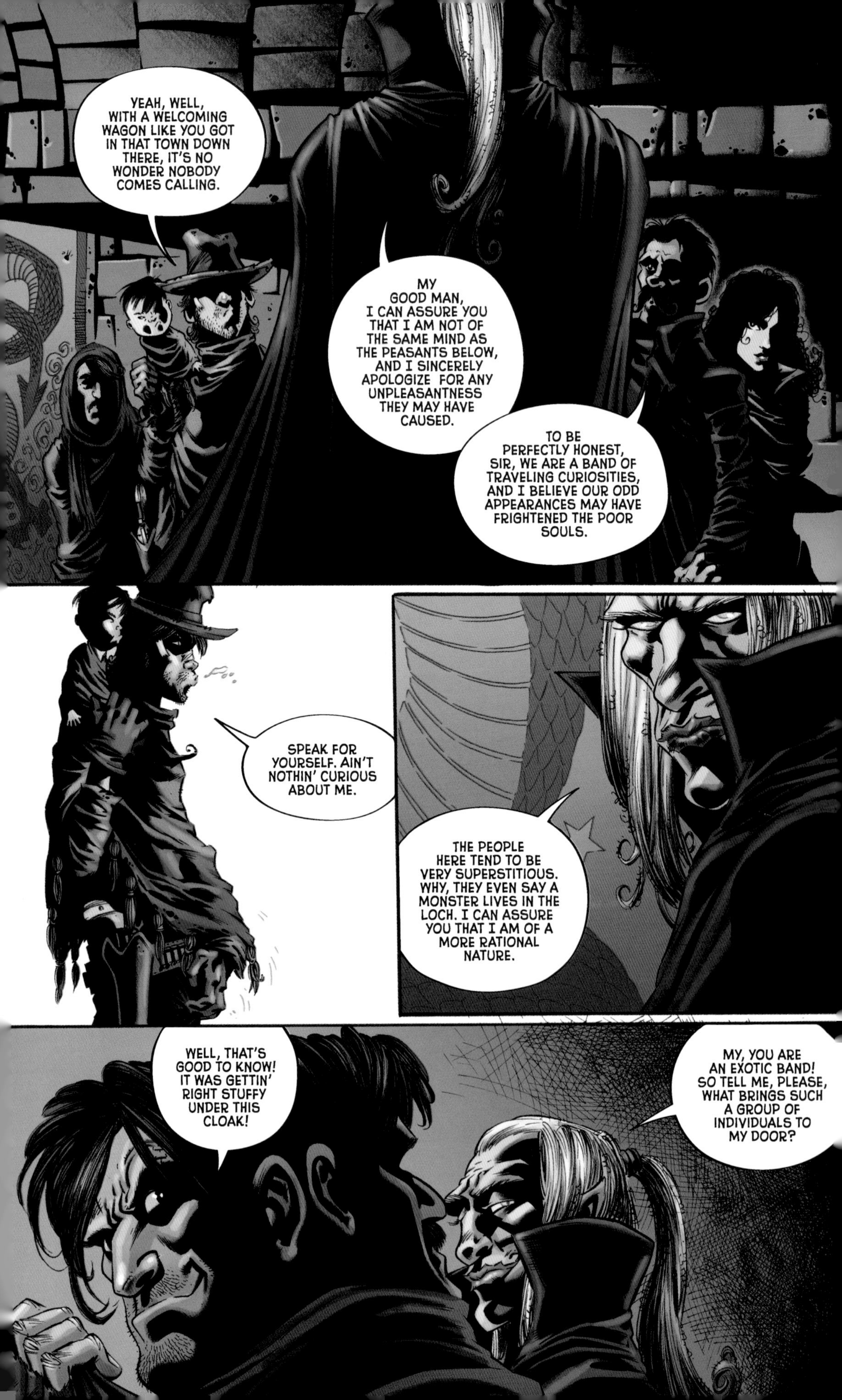
YEAH, WELL, WITH A WELCOMING WAGON LIKE YOU GOT IN THAT TOWN DOWN THERE, IT'S NO WONDER NOBODY COMES CALLING.
MY GOOD MAN, I CAN ASSURE YOU THAT I AM NOT OF THE SAME MIND AS THE PEASANTS BELOW, AND I SINCERELY APOLOGIZE FOR ANY UNPLEASANTNESS THEY MAY HAVE CAUSED.
TO BE PERFECTLY HONEST, SIR, WE ARE A BAND OF TRAVELING CURIOSITIES, AND I BELIEVE OUR ODD APPEARANCES MAY HAVE FRIGHTENED THE POOR SOULS.
SPEAK FOR YOURSELF. AIN'T NOTHIN' CURIOUS ABOUT ME.
THE PEOPLE HERE TEND TO BE VERY SUPERSTITIOUS. WHY, THEY EVEN SAY A MONSTER LIVES IN THE LOCH. I CAN ASSURE YOU THAT I AM OF A MORE RATIONAL NATURE.
WELL, THAT'S GOOD TO KNOW! IT WAS GETTIN' RIGHT STUFFY UNDER THIS CLOAK!
MY, YOU ARE AN EXOTIC BAND! SO TELL ME, PLEASE, WHAT BRINGS SUCH A GROUP OF INDIVIDUALS TO MY DOOR?

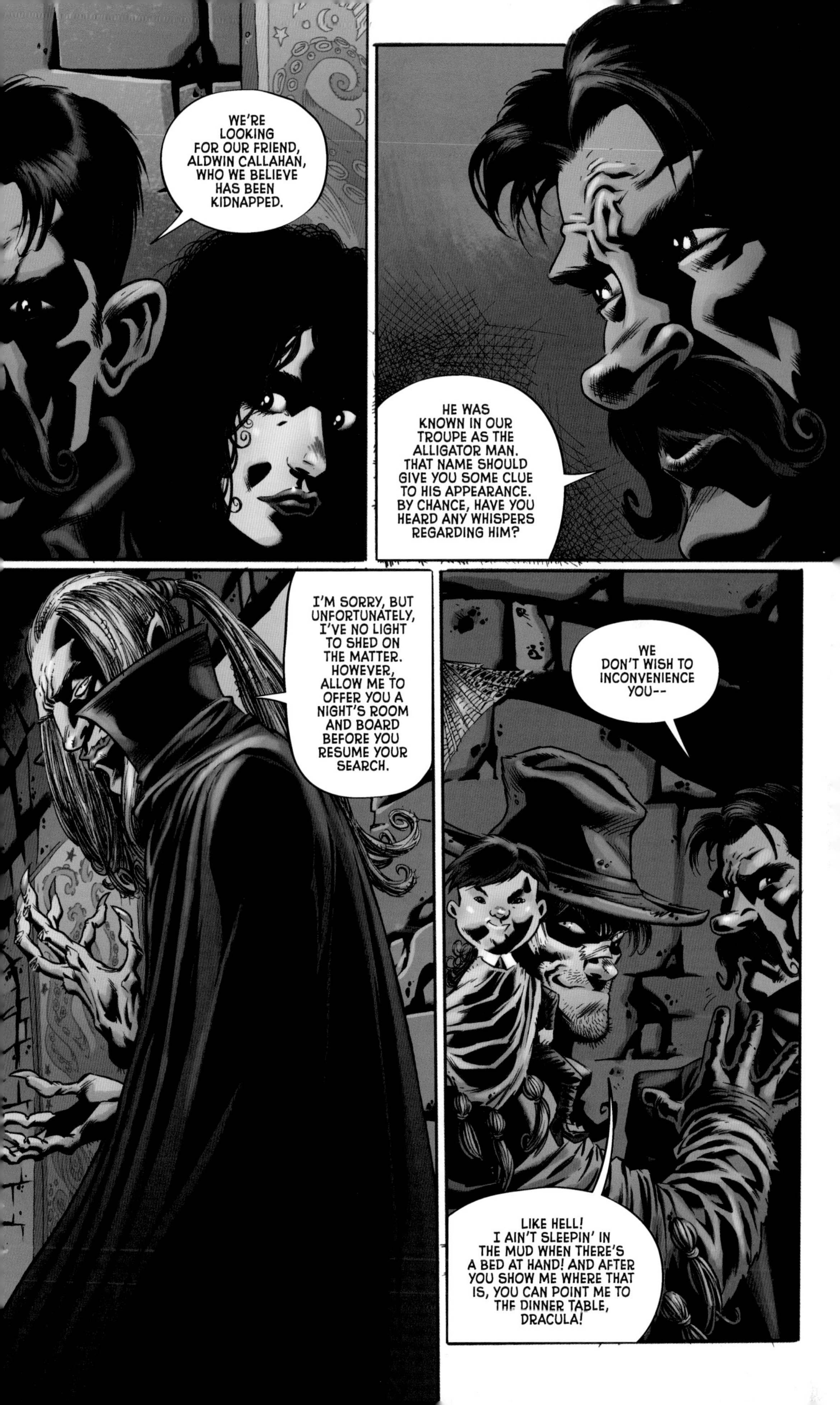
WE'RE LOOKING FOR OUR FRIEND, ALDWIN CALLAHAN, WHO WE BELIEVE HAS BEEN KIDNAPPED.
HE WAS KNOWN IN OUR TROUPE AS THE ALLIGATOR MAN. THAT NAME SHOULD GIVE YOU SOME CLUE TO HIS APPEARANCE. BY CHANCE, HAVE YOU HEARD ANY WHISPERS REGARDING HIM?
I'M SORRY, BUT UNFORTUNATELY, I'VE NO LIGHT TO SHED ON THE MATTER. HOWEVER, ALLOW ME TO OFFER YOU A NIGHT'S ROOM AND BOARD BEFORE YOU RESUME YOUR SEARCH.
WE DON'T WISH TO INCONVENIENCE YOU--
LIKE HELL! I AIN'T SLEEPIN' IN THE MUD WHEN THERE'S A BED AT HAND! AND AFTER YOU SHOW ME WHERE THAT IS, YOU CAN POINT ME TO THE DINNER TABLE, DRACULA!

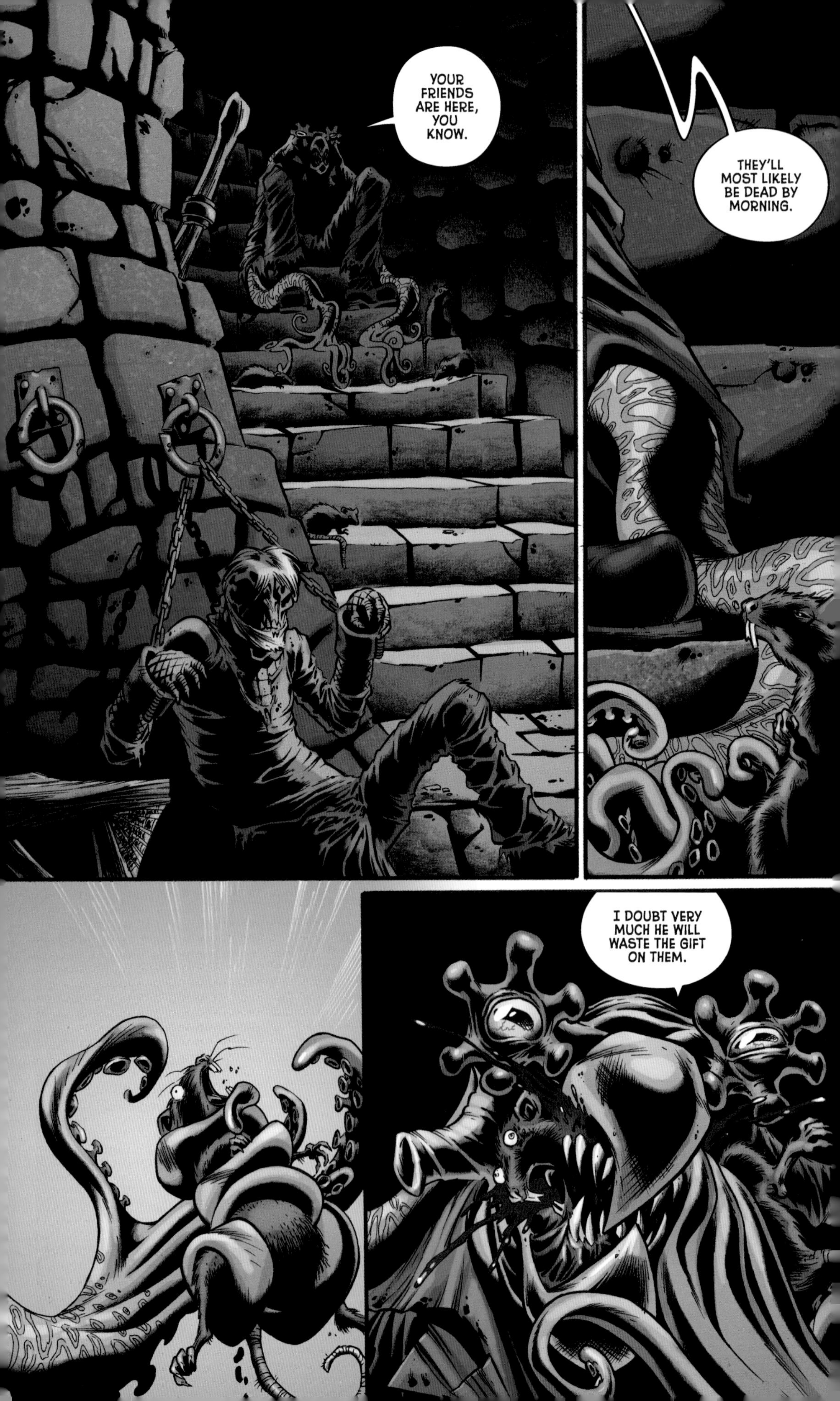

YOUR FRIENDS ARE HERE, YOU KNOW.
THEY'LL MOST LIKELY BE DEAD BY MORNING.
I DOUBT VERY MUCH HE WILL WASTE THE GIFT ON THEM.

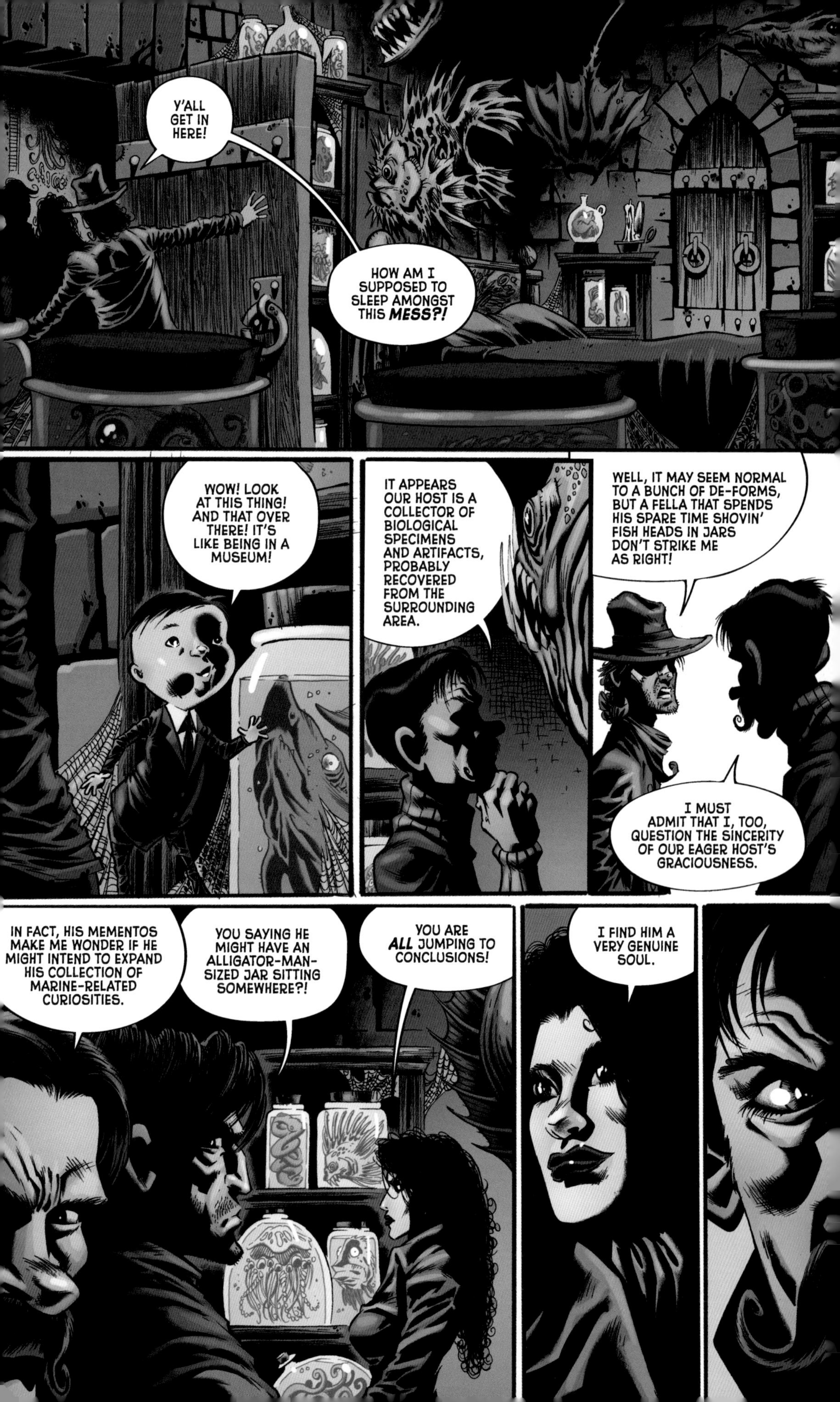
Y'ALL GET IN HERE!
HOW AM I SUPPOSED TO SLEEP AMONGST THIS *MESS?!*
WOW! LOOK AT THIS THING! AND THAT OVER THERE! IT'S LIKE BEING IN A MUSEUM!
IT APPEARS OUR HOST IS A COLLECTOR OF BIOLOGICAL SPECIMENS AND ARTIFACTS, PROBABLY RECOVERED FROM THE SURROUNDING AREA.
WELL, IT MAY SEEM NORMAL TO A BUNCH OF DE-FORMS, BUT A FELLA THAT SPENDS HIS SPARE TIME SHOVIN' FISH HEADS IN JARS DON'T STRIKE ME AS RIGHT!
I MUST ADMIT THAT I, TOO, QUESTION THE SINCERITY OF OUR EAGER HOST'S GRACIOUSNESS.
IN FACT, HIS MEMENTOS MAKE ME WONDER IF HE MIGHT INTEND TO EXPAND HIS COLLECTION OF MARINE-RELATED CURIOSITIES.
YOU SAYING HE MIGHT HAVE AN ALLIGATOR-MAN-SIZED JAR SITTING SOMEWHERE?!
YOU ARE *ALL* JUMPING TO CONCLUSIONS!
I FIND HIM A VERY GENUINE SOUL.

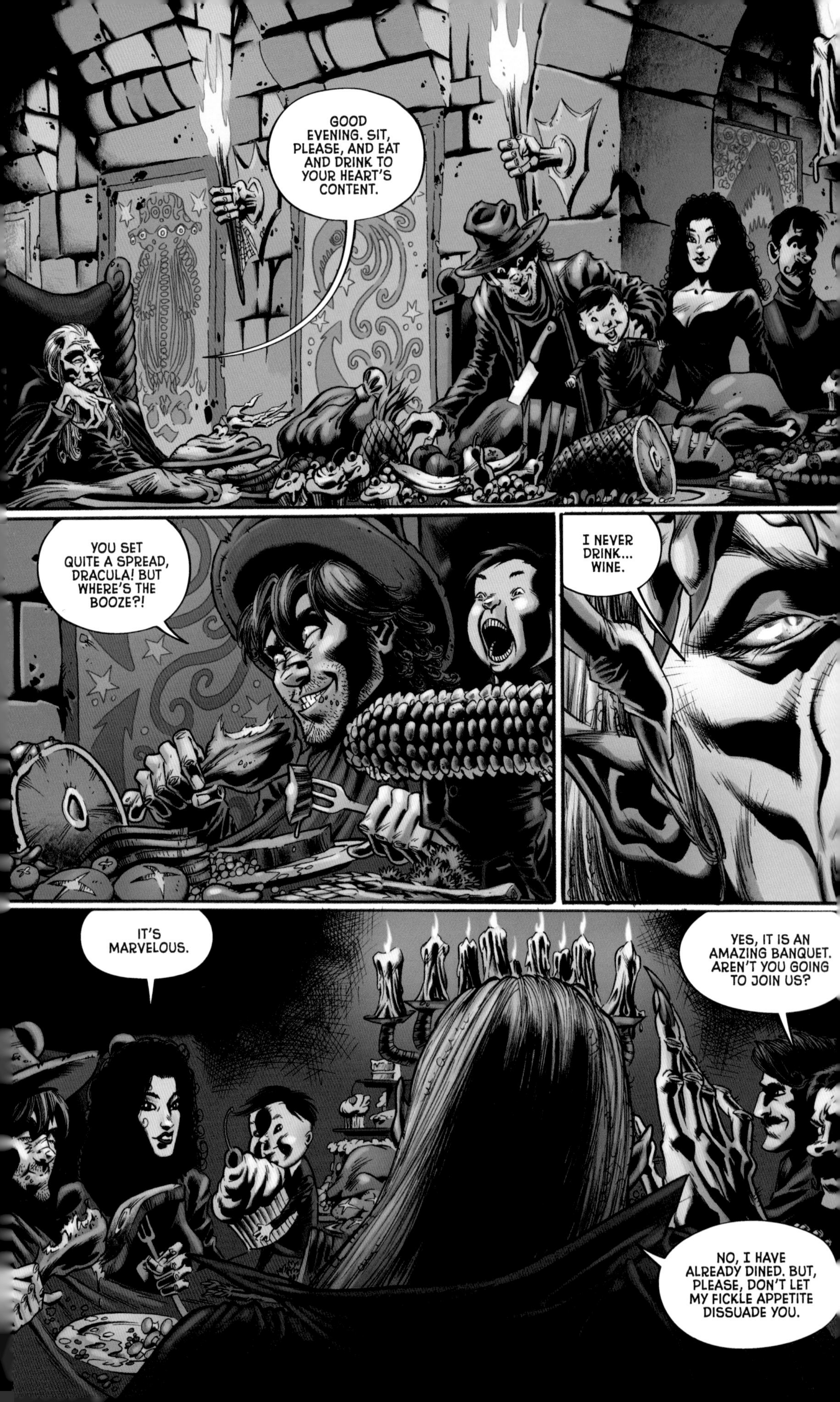
GOOD EVENING. SIT, PLEASE, AND EAT AND DRINK TO YOUR HEART'S CONTENT.
YOU SET QUITE A SPREAD, DRACULA! BUT WHERE'S THE BOOZE?!
I NEVER DRINK... WINE.
IT'S MARVELOUS.
YES, IT IS AN AMAZING BANQUET. AREN'T YOU GOING TO JOIN US?
NO, I HAVE ALREADY DINED. BUT, PLEASE, DON'T LET MY FICKLE APPETITE DISSUADE YOU.

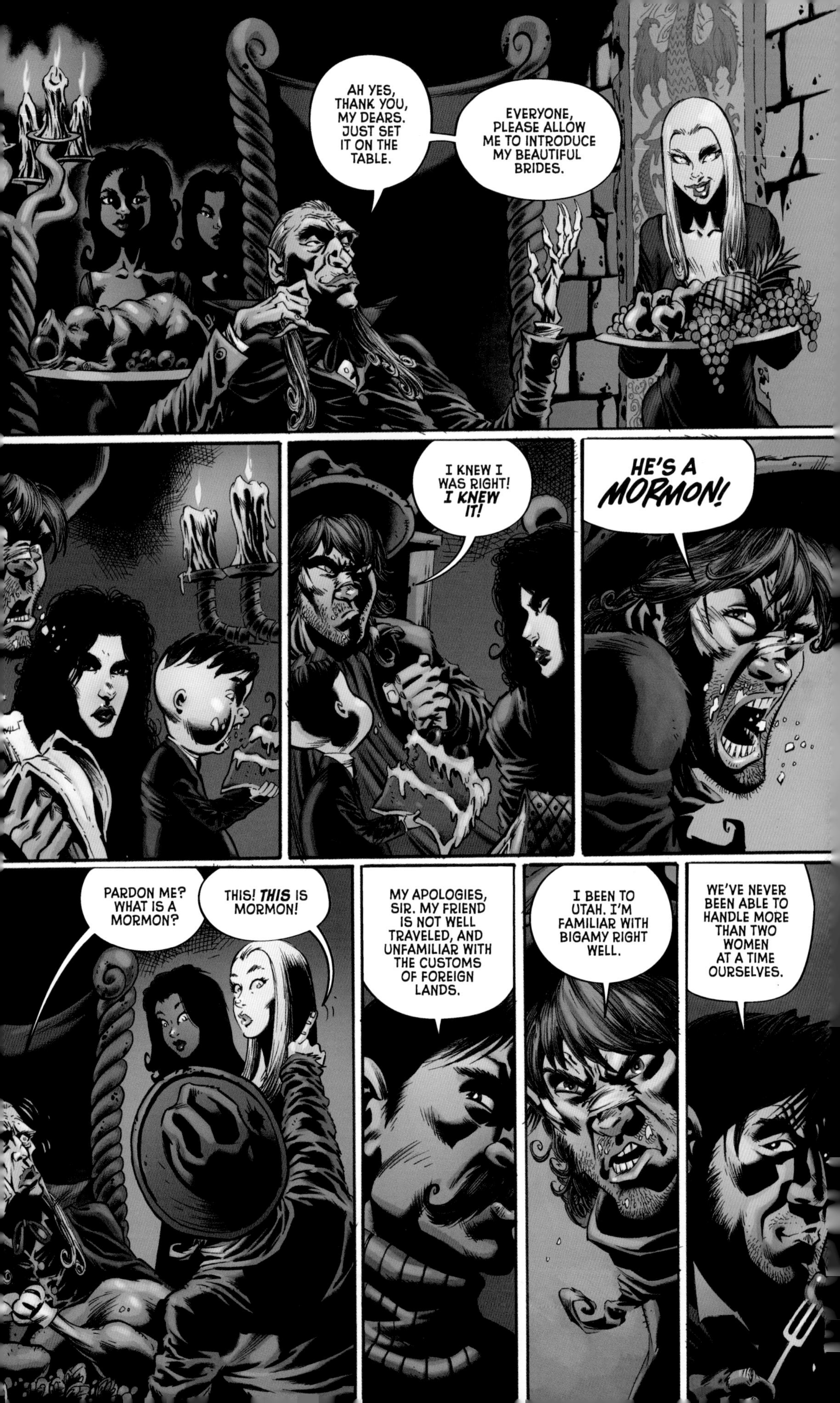
AH YES, THANK YOU, MY DEARS. JUST SET IT ON THE TABLE.
EVERYONE, PLEASE ALLOW ME TO INTRODUCE MY BEAUTIFUL BRIDES.
I KNEW I WAS RIGHT! I KNEW IT!
HE'S A MORMON!
PARDON ME? WHAT IS A MORMON?
THIS! THIS IS MORMON!
MY APOLOGIES, SIR. MY FRIEND IS NOT WELL TRAVELED, AND UNFAMILIAR WITH THE CUSTOMS OF FOREIGN LANDS.
I BEEN TO UTAH. I'M FAMILIAR WITH BIGAMY RIGHT WELL.
WE'VE NEVER BEEN ABLE TO HANDLE MORE THAN TWO WOMEN AT A TIME OURSELVES.

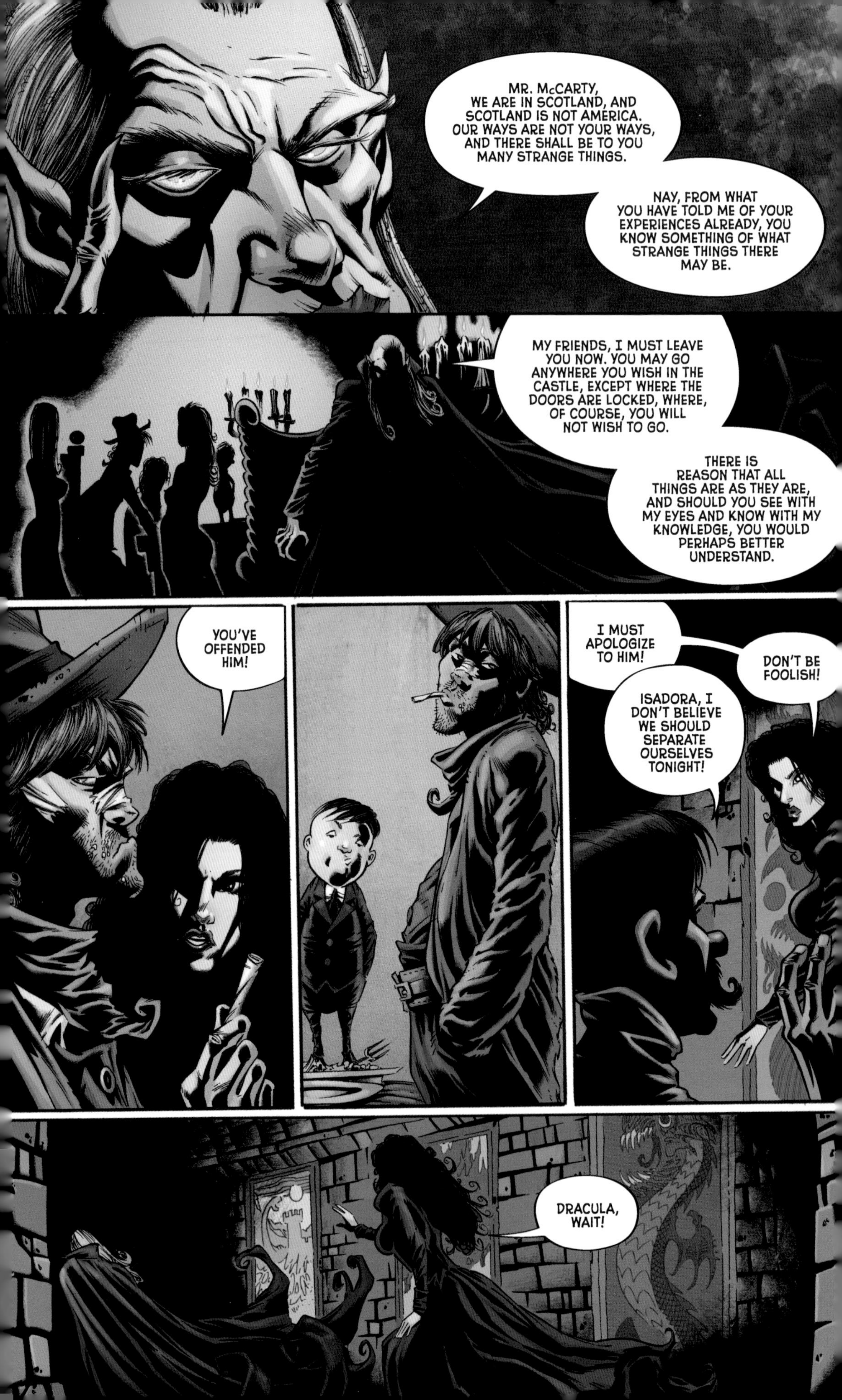
MR. McCARTY, WE ARE IN SCOTLAND, AND SCOTLAND IS NOT AMERICA. OUR WAYS ARE NOT YOUR WAYS, AND THERE SHALL BE TO YOU MANY STRANGE THINGS.
NAY, FROM WHAT YOU HAVE TOLD ME OF YOUR EXPERIENCES ALREADY, YOU KNOW SOMETHING OF WHAT STRANGE THINGS THERE MAY BE.
MY FRIENDS, I MUST LEAVE YOU NOW. YOU MAY GO ANYWHERE YOU WISH IN THE CASTLE, EXCEPT WHERE THE DOORS ARE LOCKED, WHERE, OF COURSE, YOU WILL NOT WISH TO GO.
THERE IS REASON THAT ALL THINGS ARE AS THEY ARE, AND SHOULD YOU SEE WITH MY EYES AND KNOW WITH MY KNOWLEDGE, YOU WOULD PERHAPS BETTER UNDERSTAND.
YOU'VE OFFENDED HIM!
I MUST APOLOGIZE TO HIM!
DON'T BE FOOLISH!
ISADORA, I DON'T BELIEVE WE SHOULD SEPARATE OURSELVES TONIGHT!
DRACULA, WAIT!

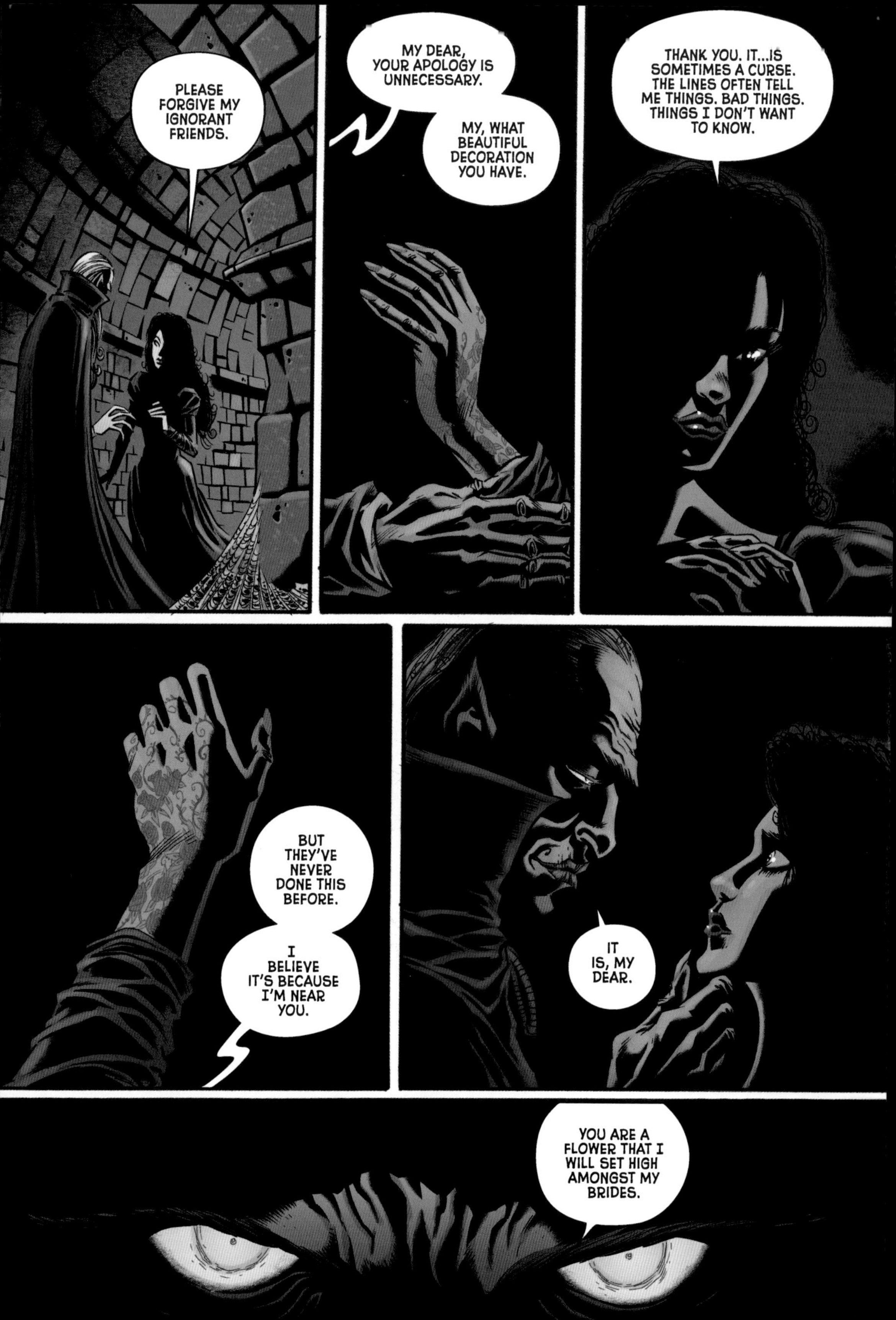
PLEASE FORGIVE MY IGNORANT FRIENDS.
MY DEAR, YOUR APOLOGY IS UNNECESSARY.
MY, WHAT BEAUTIFUL DECORATION YOU HAVE.
THANK YOU. IT...IS SOMETIMES A CURSE. THE LINES OFTEN TELL ME THINGS. BAD THINGS. THINGS I DON'T WANT TO KNOW.
BUT THEY'VE NEVER DONE THIS BEFORE.
I BELIEVE IT'S BECAUSE I'M NEAR YOU.
IT IS, MY DEAR.
YOU ARE A FLOWER THAT I WILL SET HIGH AMONGST MY BRIDES.

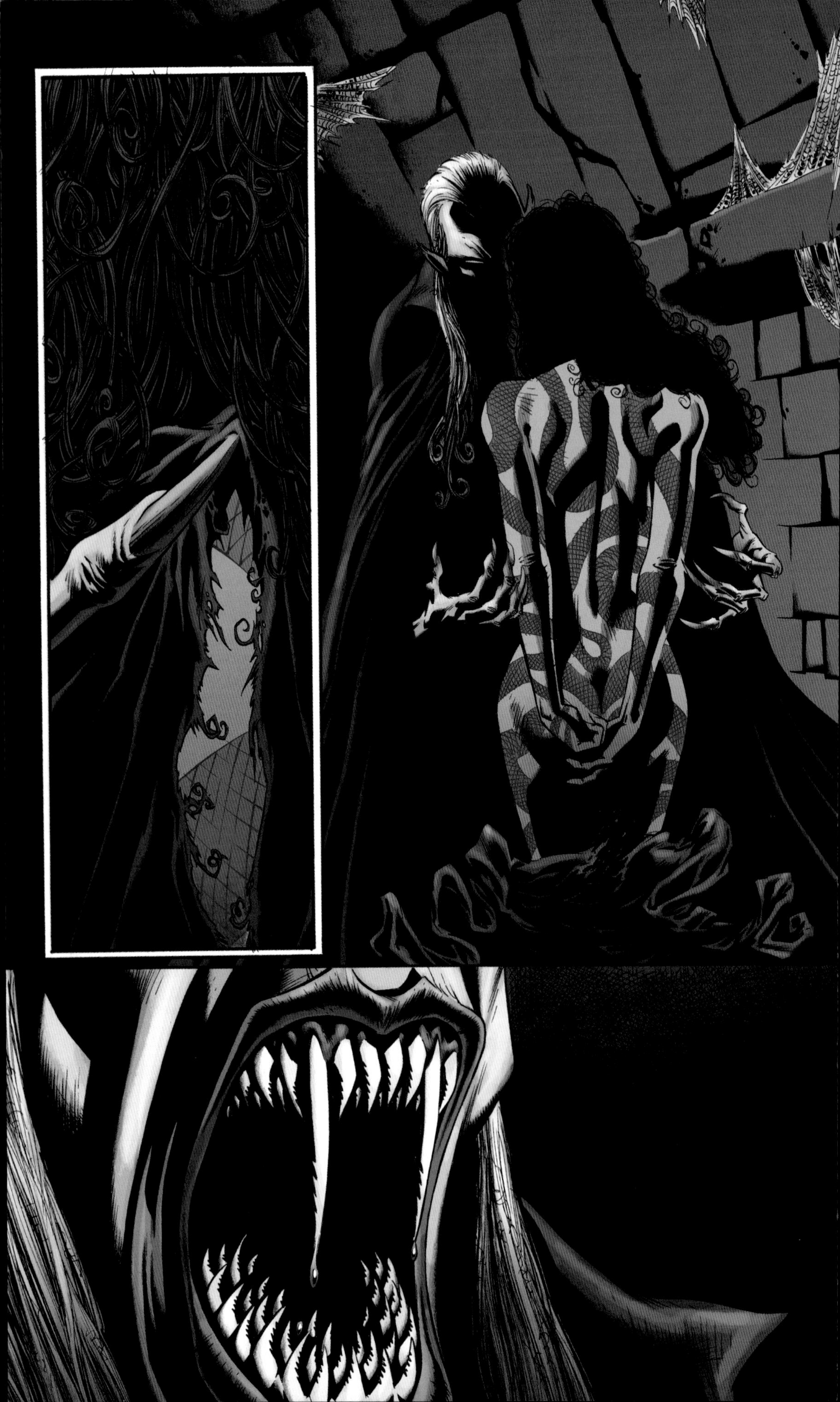

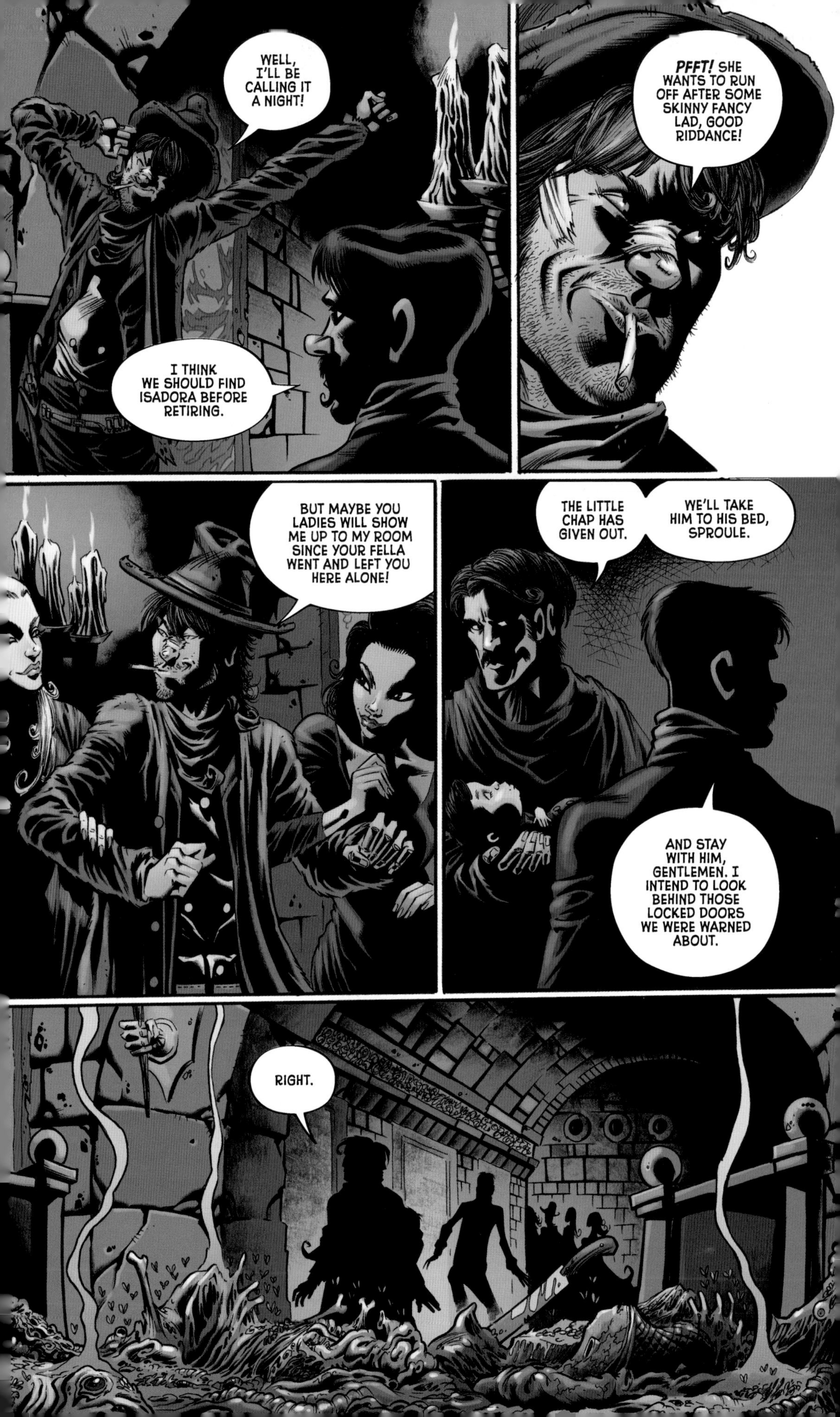
WELL, I'LL BE CALLING IT A NIGHT!
I THINK WE SHOULD FIND ISADORA BEFORE RETIRING.
PFFT! SHE WANTS TO RUN OFF AFTER SOME SKINNY FANCY LAD, GOOD RIDDANCE!
BUT MAYBE YOU LADIES WILL SHOW ME UP TO MY ROOM SINCE YOUR FELLA WENT AND LEFT YOU HERE ALONE!
THE LITTLE CHAP HAS GIVEN OUT.
WE'LL TAKE HIM TO HIS BED, SPROULE.
AND STAY WITH HIM, GENTLEMEN. I INTEND TO LOOK BEHIND THOSE LOCKED DOORS WE WERE WARNED ABOUT.
RIGHT.

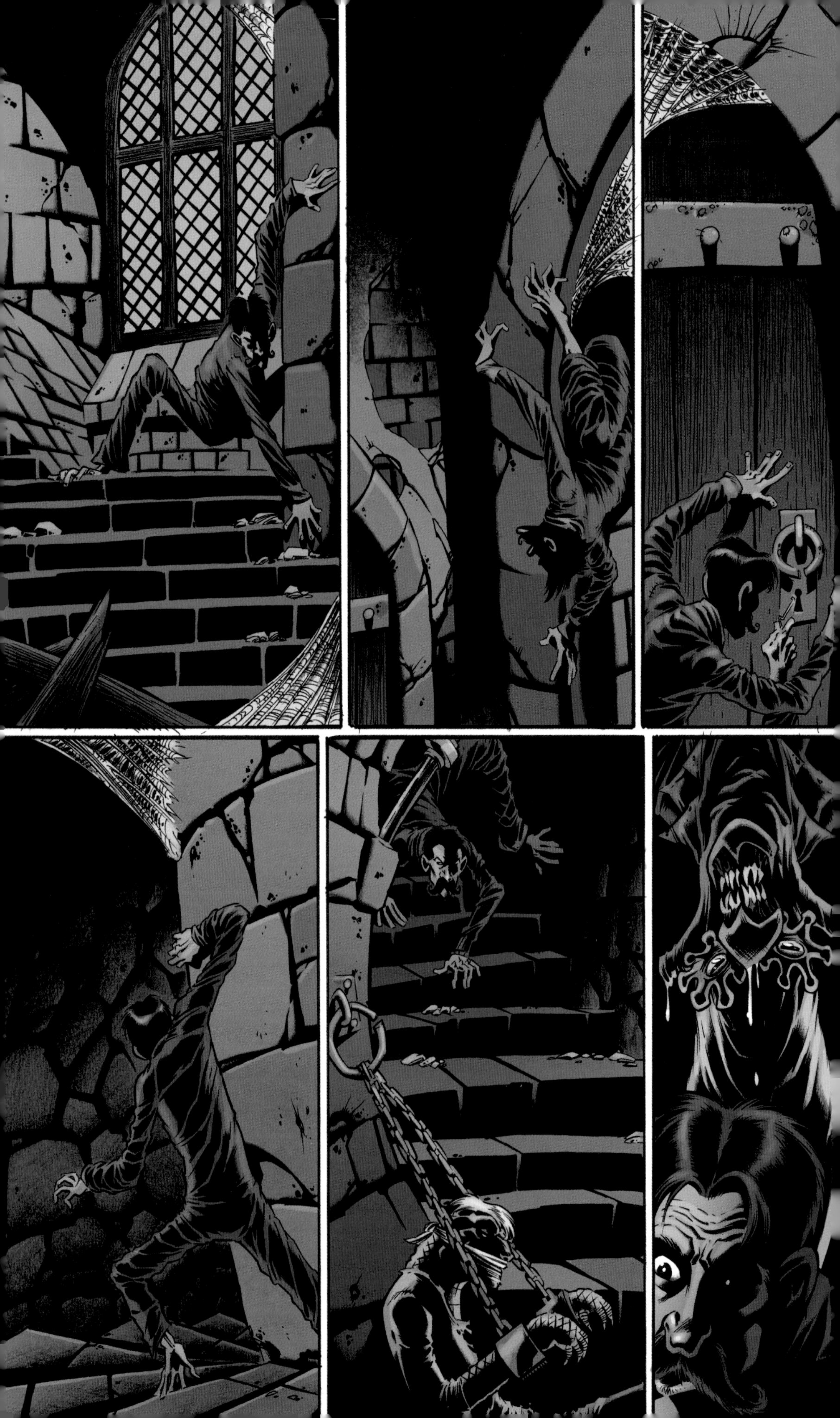

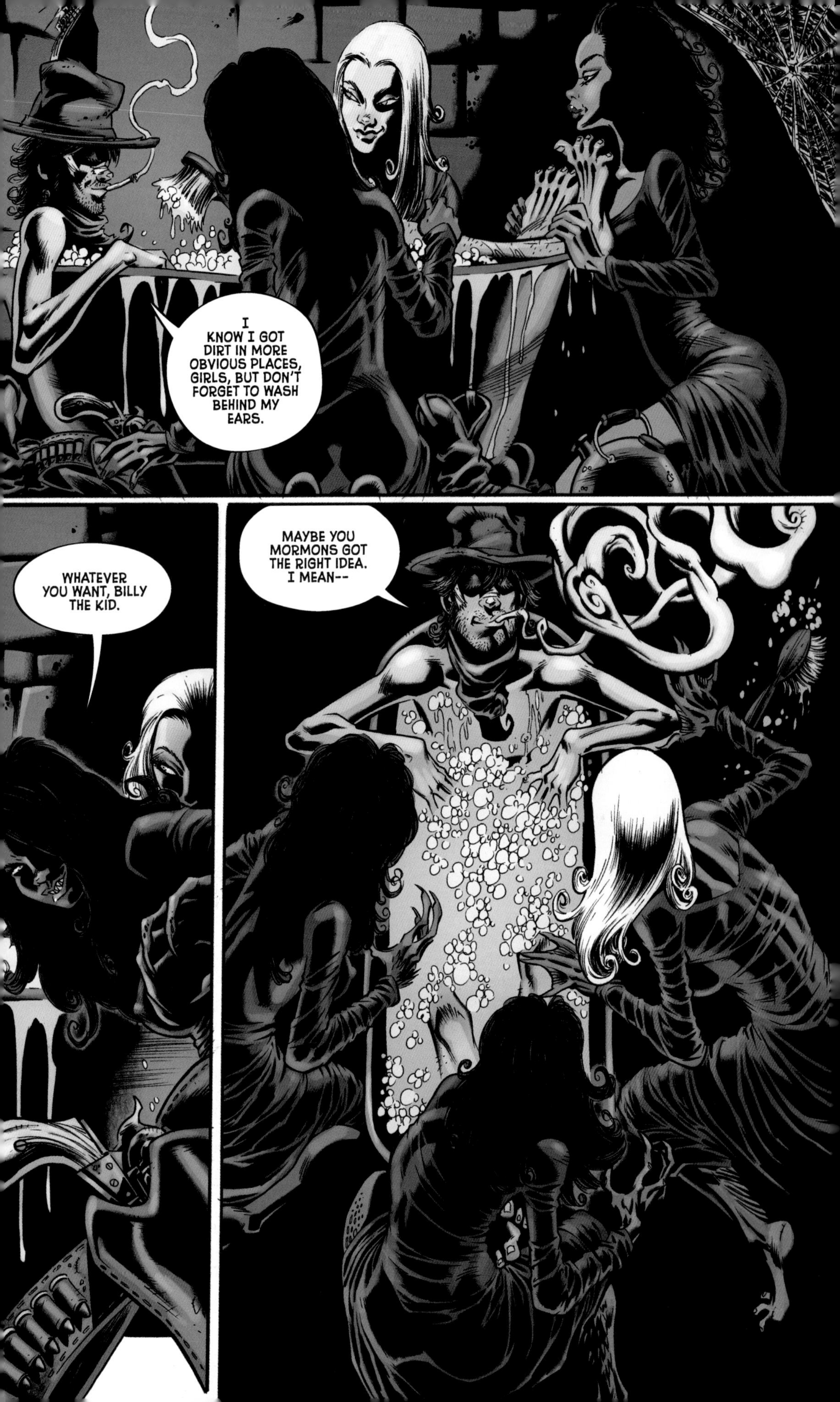
I KNOW I GOT DIRT IN MORE OBVIOUS PLACES, GIRLS, BUT DON'T FORGET TO WASH BEHIND MY EARS.
WHATEVER YOU WANT, BILLY THE KID.
MAYBE YOU MORMONS GOT THE RIGHT IDEA. I MEAN--

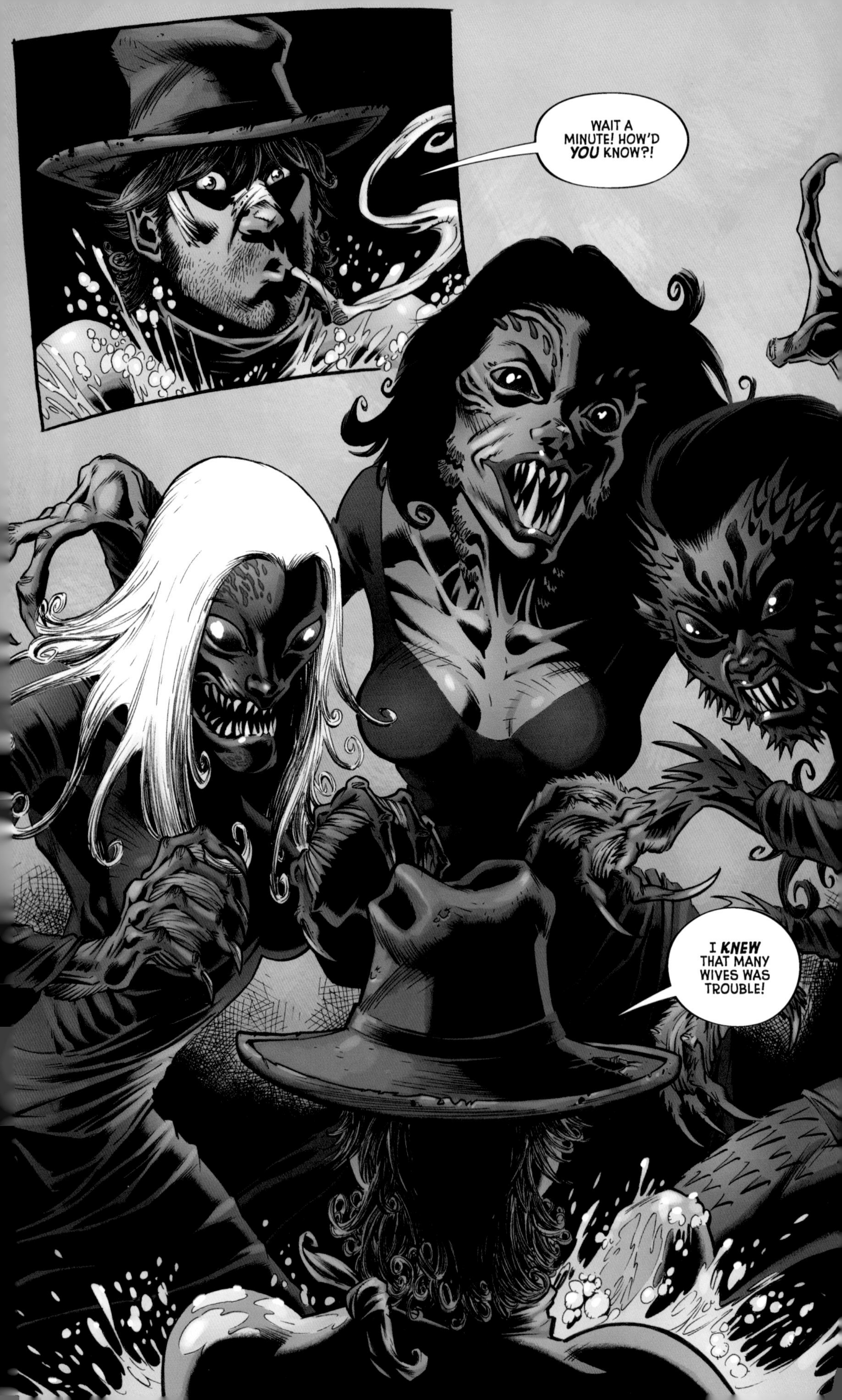
WAIT A MINUTE! HOW'D YOU KNOW?!
I KNEW THAT MANY WIVES WAS TROUBLE!

CHAPTER THREE

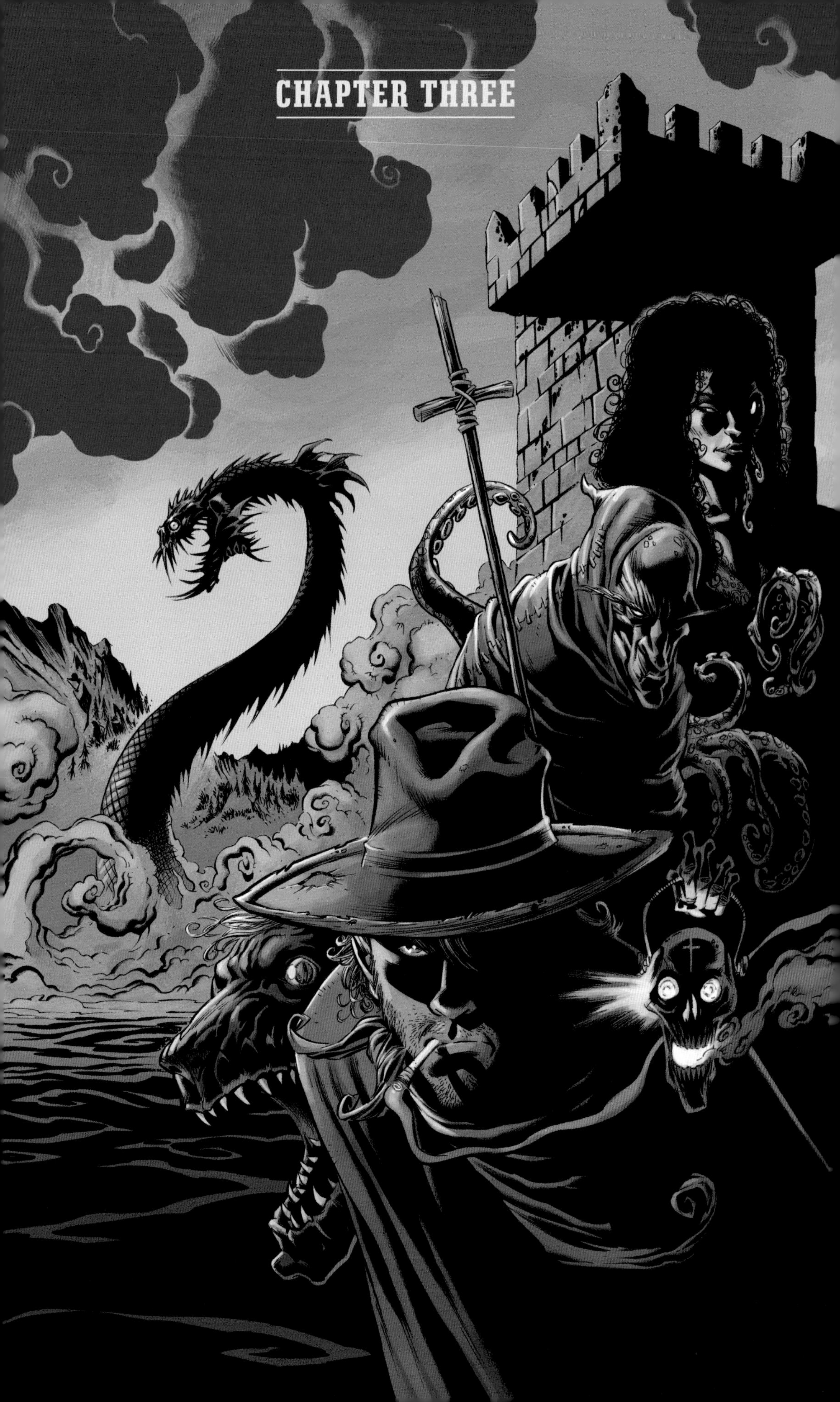

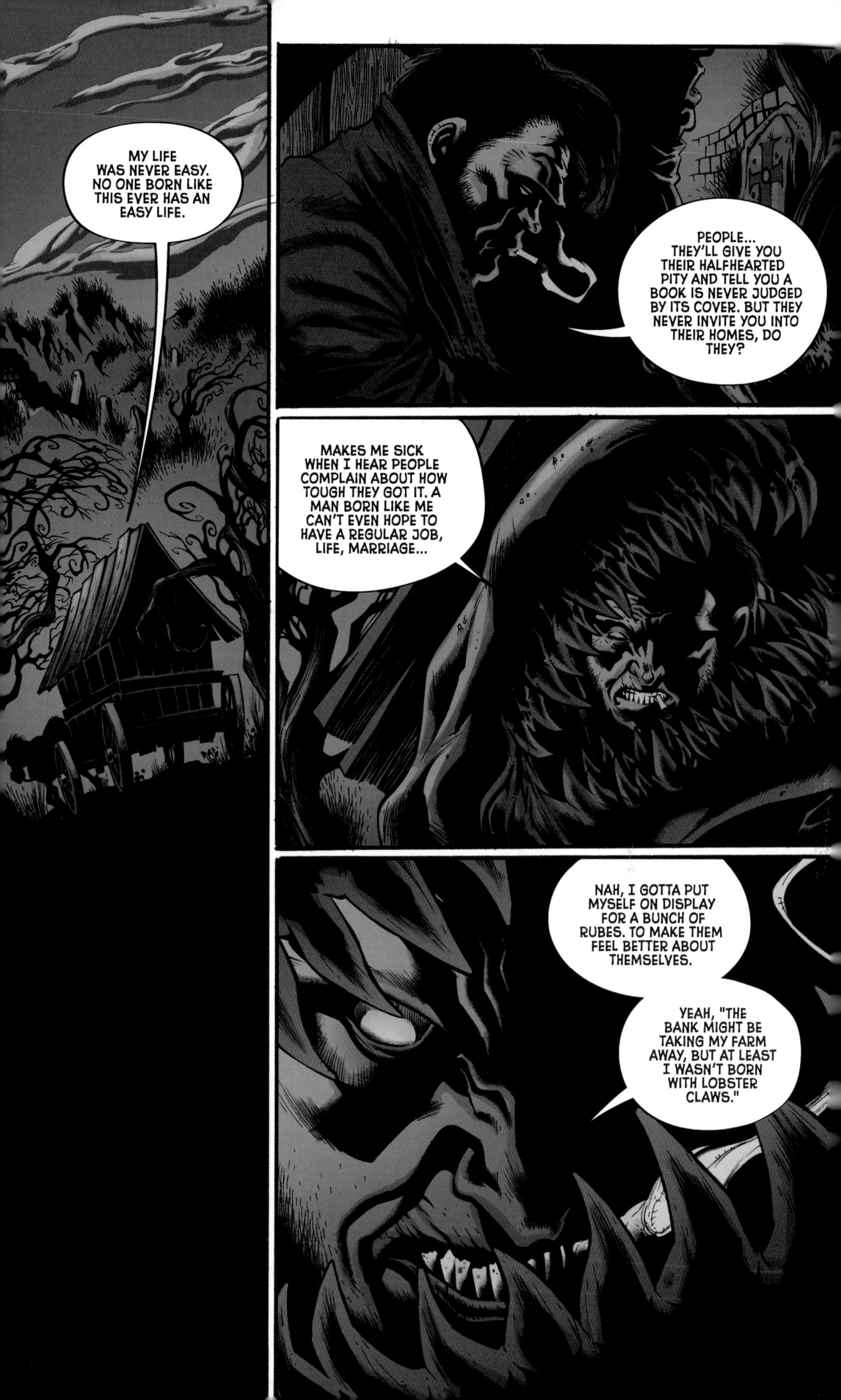
MY LIFE WAS NEVER EASY. NO ONE BORN LIKE THIS EVER HAS AN EASY LIFE.
PEOPLE... THEY'LL GIVE YOU THEIR HALFHEARTED PITY AND TELL YOU A BOOK IS NEVER JUDGED BY ITS COVER. BUT THEY NEVER INVITE YOU INTO THEIR HOMES, DO THEY?
MAKES ME SICK WHEN I HEAR PEOPLE COMPLAIN ABOUT HOW TOUGH THEY GOT IT. A MAN BORN LIKE ME CAN'T EVEN HOPE TO HAVE A REGULAR JOB, LIFE, MARRIAGE...
NAH, I GOTTA PUT MYSELF ON DISPLAY FOR A BUNCH OF RUBES. TO MAKE THEM FEEL BETTER ABOUT THEMSELVES.
YEAH, "THE BANK MIGHT BE TAKING MY FARM AWAY, BUT AT LEAST I WASN'T BORN WITH LOBSTER CLAWS."

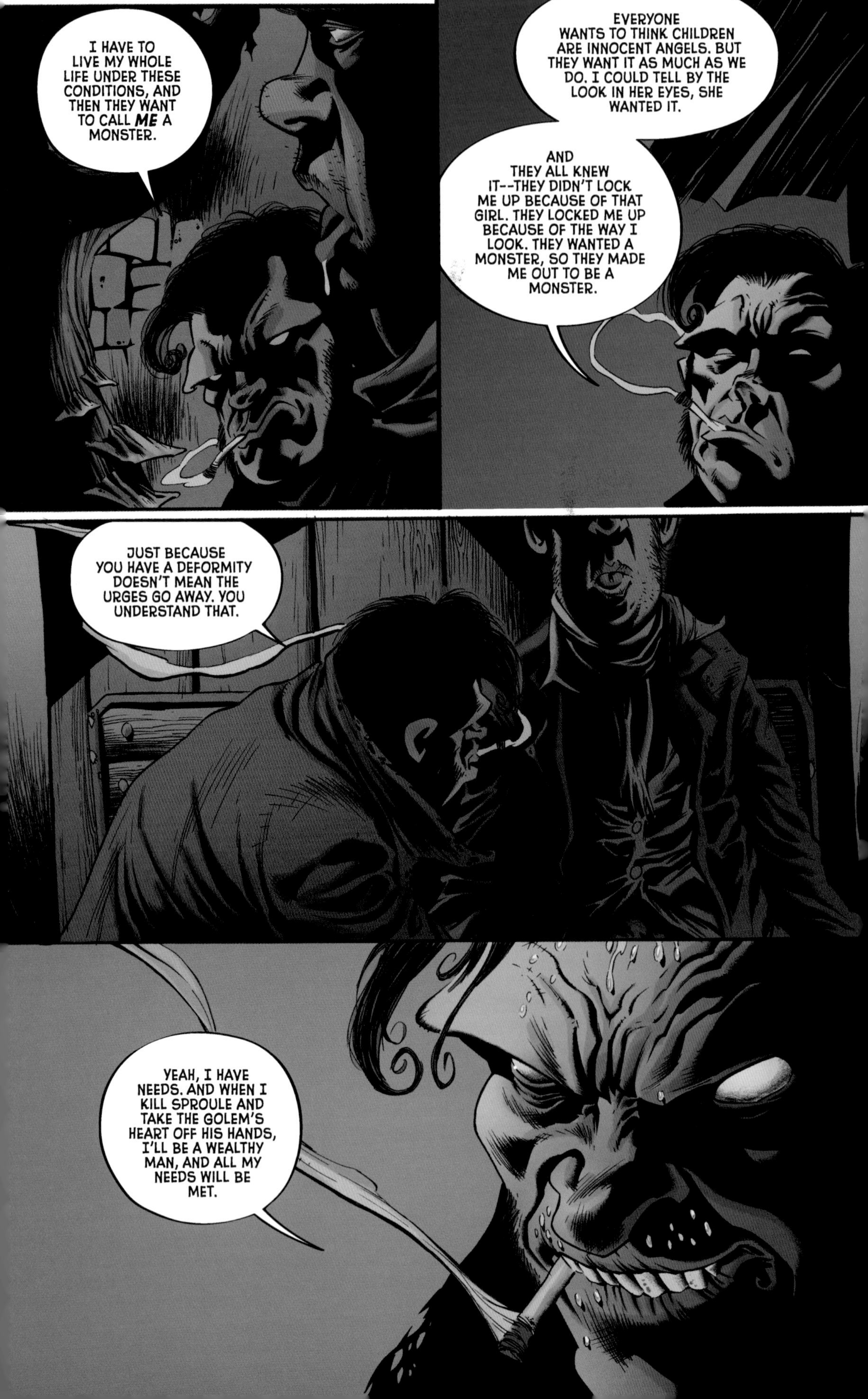

I HAVE TO LIVE MY WHOLE LIFE UNDER THESE CONDITIONS, AND THEN THEY WANT TO CALL *ME* A MONSTER.
EVERYONE WANTS TO THINK CHILDREN ARE INNOCENT ANGELS. BUT THEY WANT IT AS MUCH AS WE DO. I COULD TELL BY THE LOOK IN HER EYES, SHE WANTED IT.
AND THEY ALL KNEW IT--THEY DIDN'T LOCK ME UP BECAUSE OF THAT GIRL. THEY LOCKED ME UP BECAUSE OF THE WAY I LOOK. THEY WANTED A MONSTER, SO THEY MADE ME OUT TO BE A MONSTER.
JUST BECAUSE YOU HAVE A DEFORMITY DOESN'T MEAN THE URGES GO AWAY. YOU UNDERSTAND THAT.
YEAH, I HAVE NEEDS. AND WHEN I KILL SPROULE AND TAKE THE GOLEM'S HEART OFF HIS HANDS, I'LL BE A WEALTHY MAN, AND ALL MY NEEDS WILL BE MET.

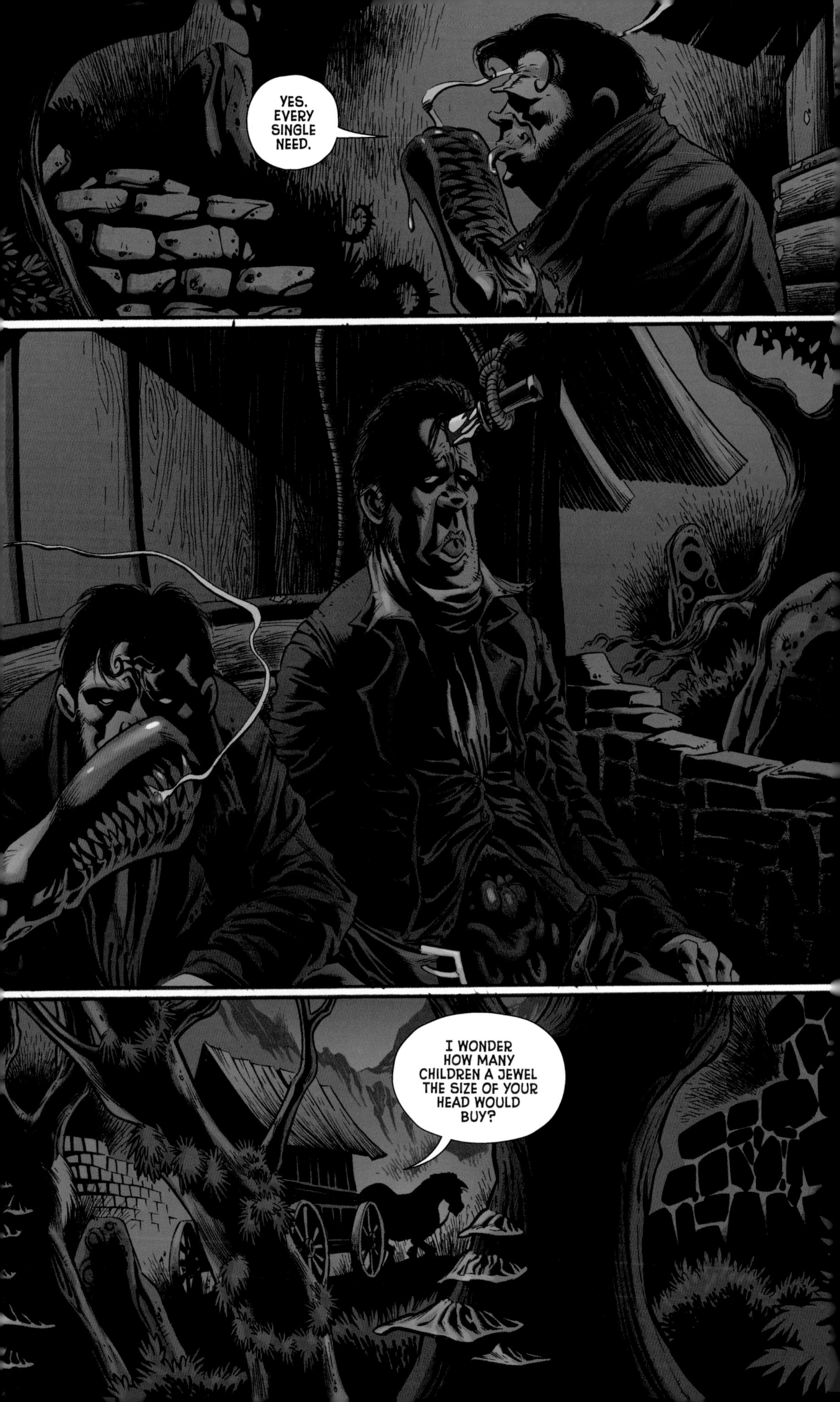
YES. EVERY SINGLE NEED.
I WONDER HOW MANY CHILDREN A JEWEL THE SIZE OF YOUR HEAD WOULD BUY?

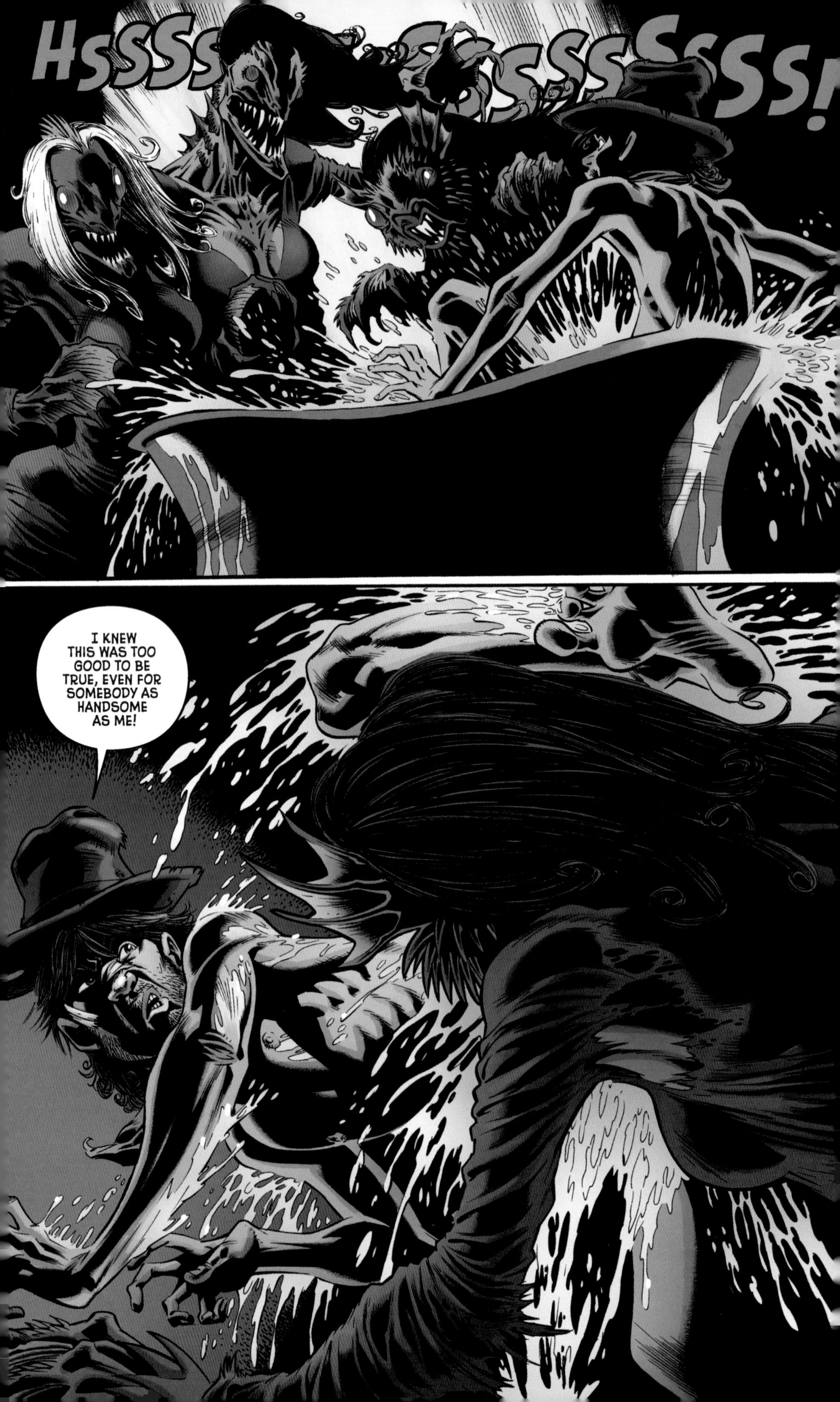
HsSSsSSsSSsSSsSSs!
I KNEW THIS WAS TOO GOOD TO BE TRUE, EVEN FOR SOMEBODY AS HANDSOME AS ME!

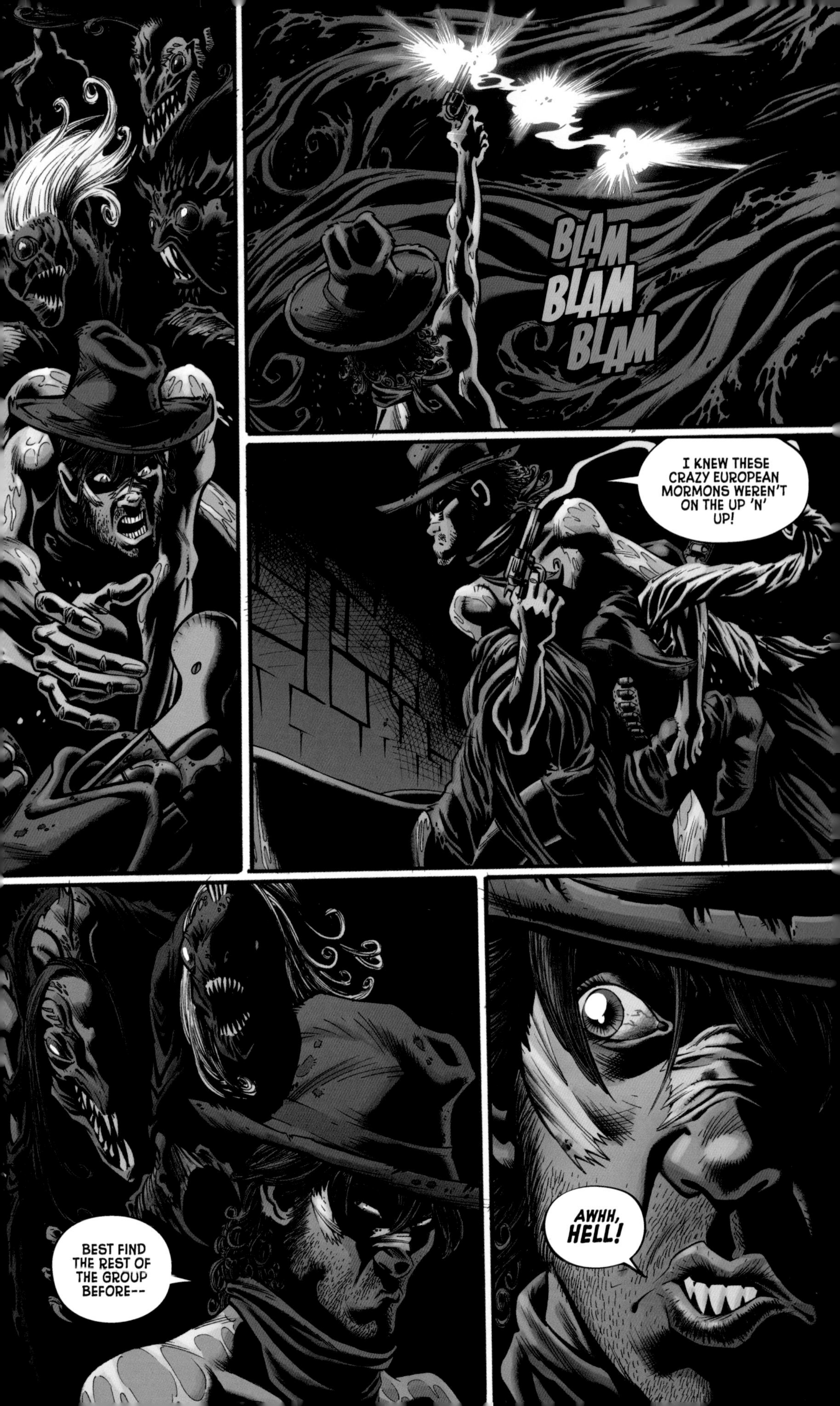
BLAM
BLAM
BLAM
I KNEW THESE CRAZY EUROPEAN MORMONS WEREN'T ON THE UP 'N' UP!
BEST FIND THE REST OF THE GROUP BEFORE--
AWHH, HELL!

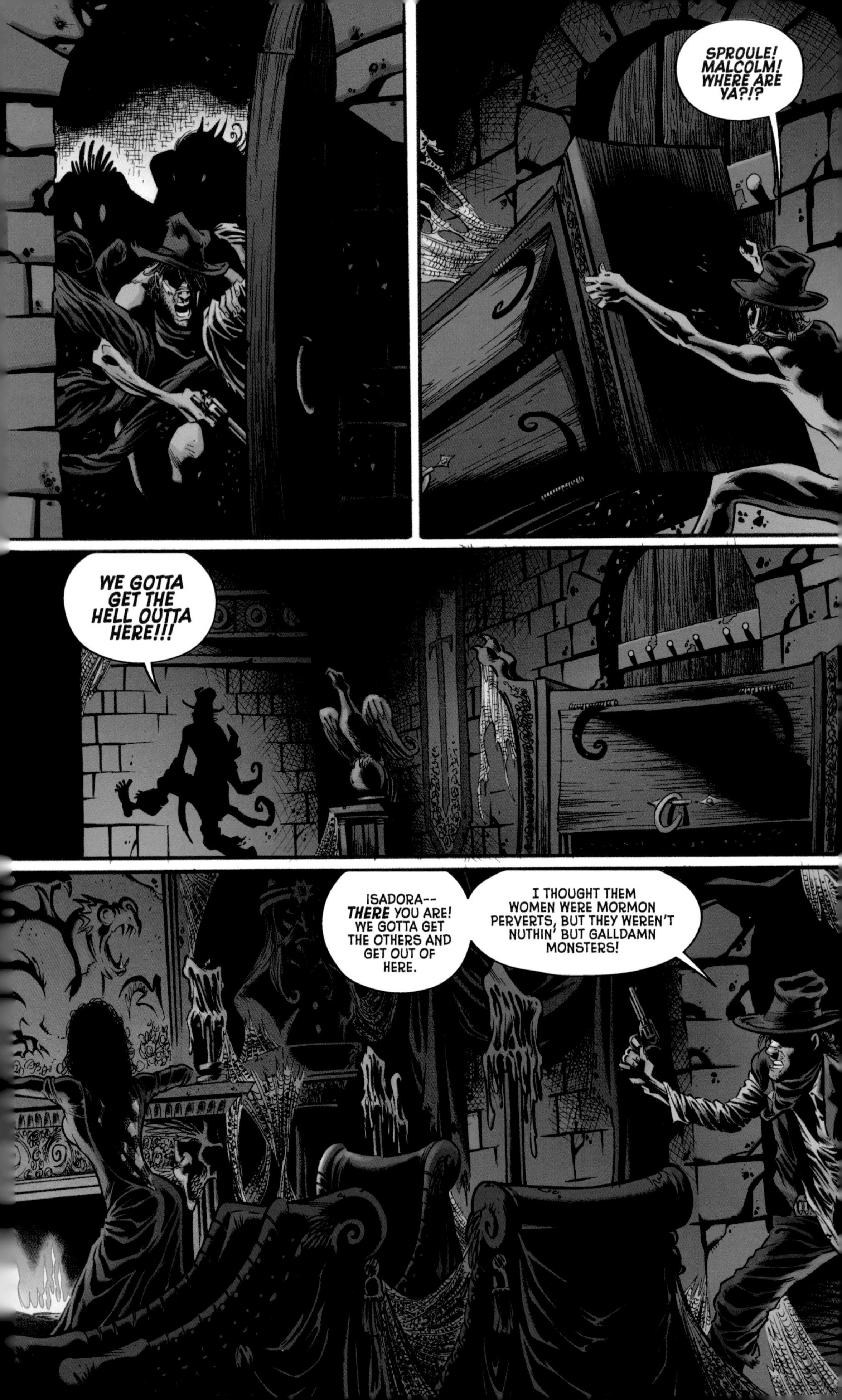
SPROULE! MALCOLM! WHERE ARE YA?!?
WE GOTTA GET THE HELL OUTTA HERE!!!
ISADORA-- THERE YOU ARE! WE GOTTA GET THE OTHERS AND GET OUT OF HERE.
I THOUGHT THEM WOMEN WERE MORMON PERVERTS, BUT THEY WEREN'T NUTHIN' BUT GALLDAMN MONSTERS!

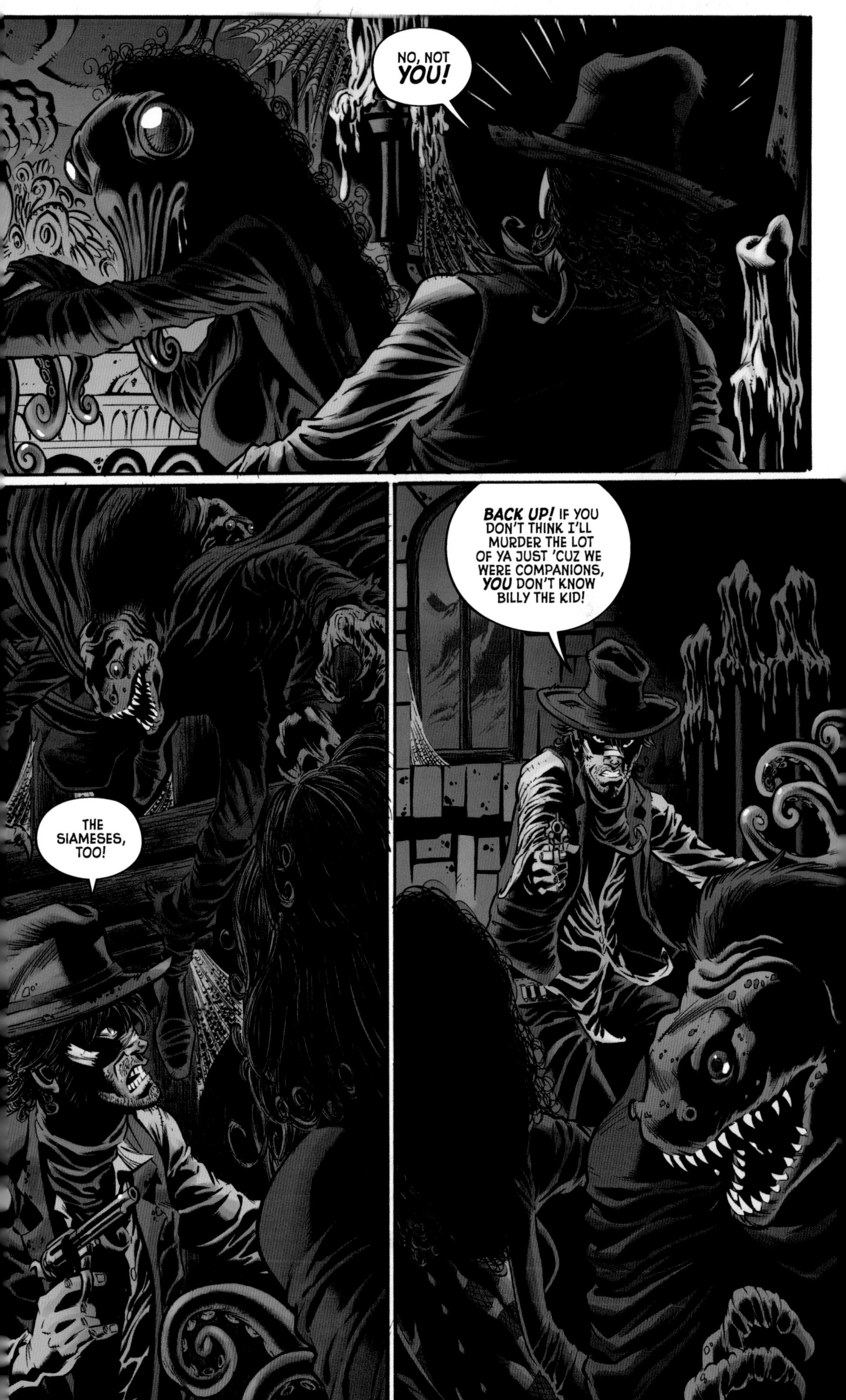
NO, NOT *YOU!*
THE SIAMESES, TOO!
BACK UP! IF YOU DON'T THINK I'LL MURDER THE LOT OF YA JUST 'CUZ WE WERE COMPANIONS, *YOU* DON'T KNOW BILLY THE KID!

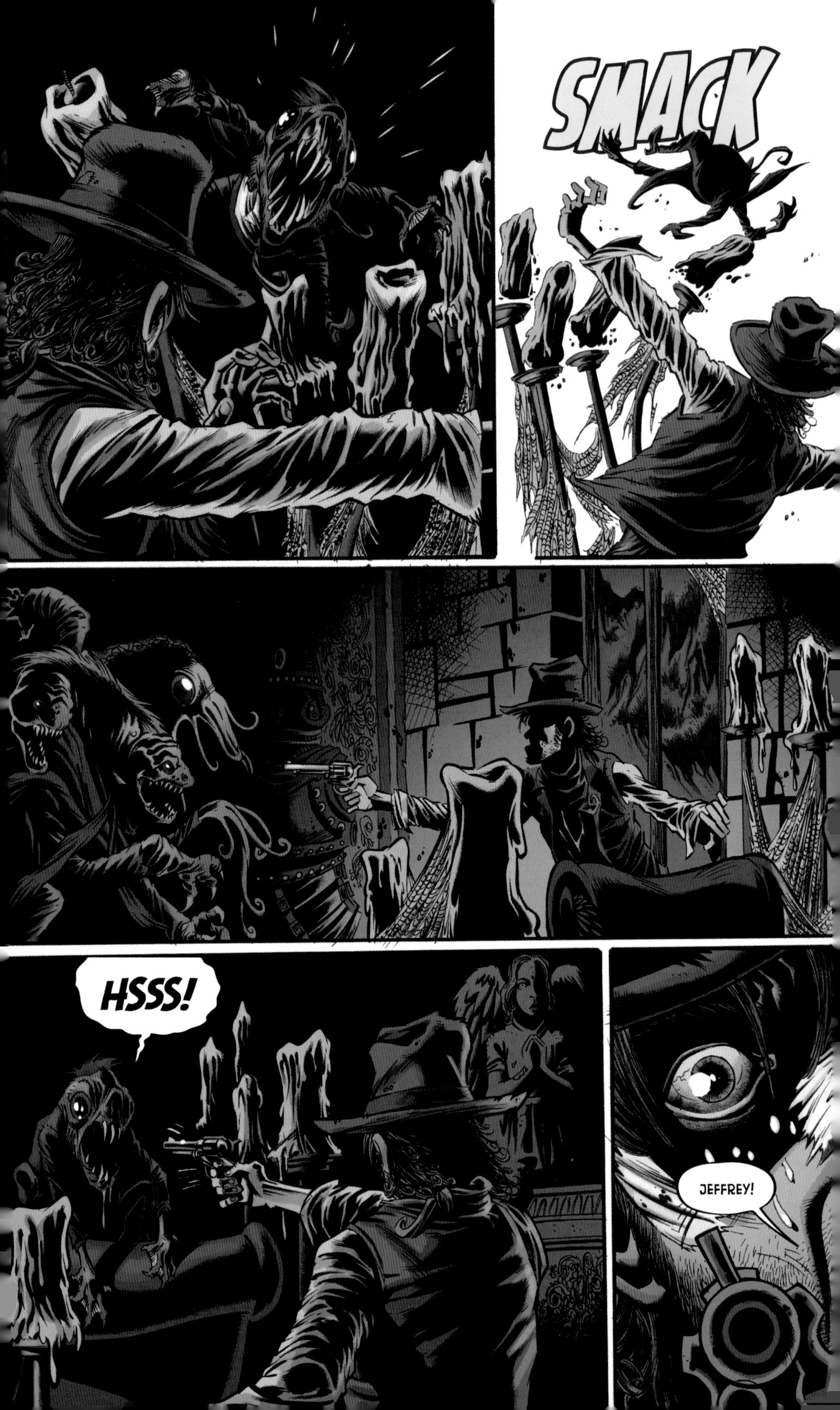
SMACK
HSSS!
JEFFREY!

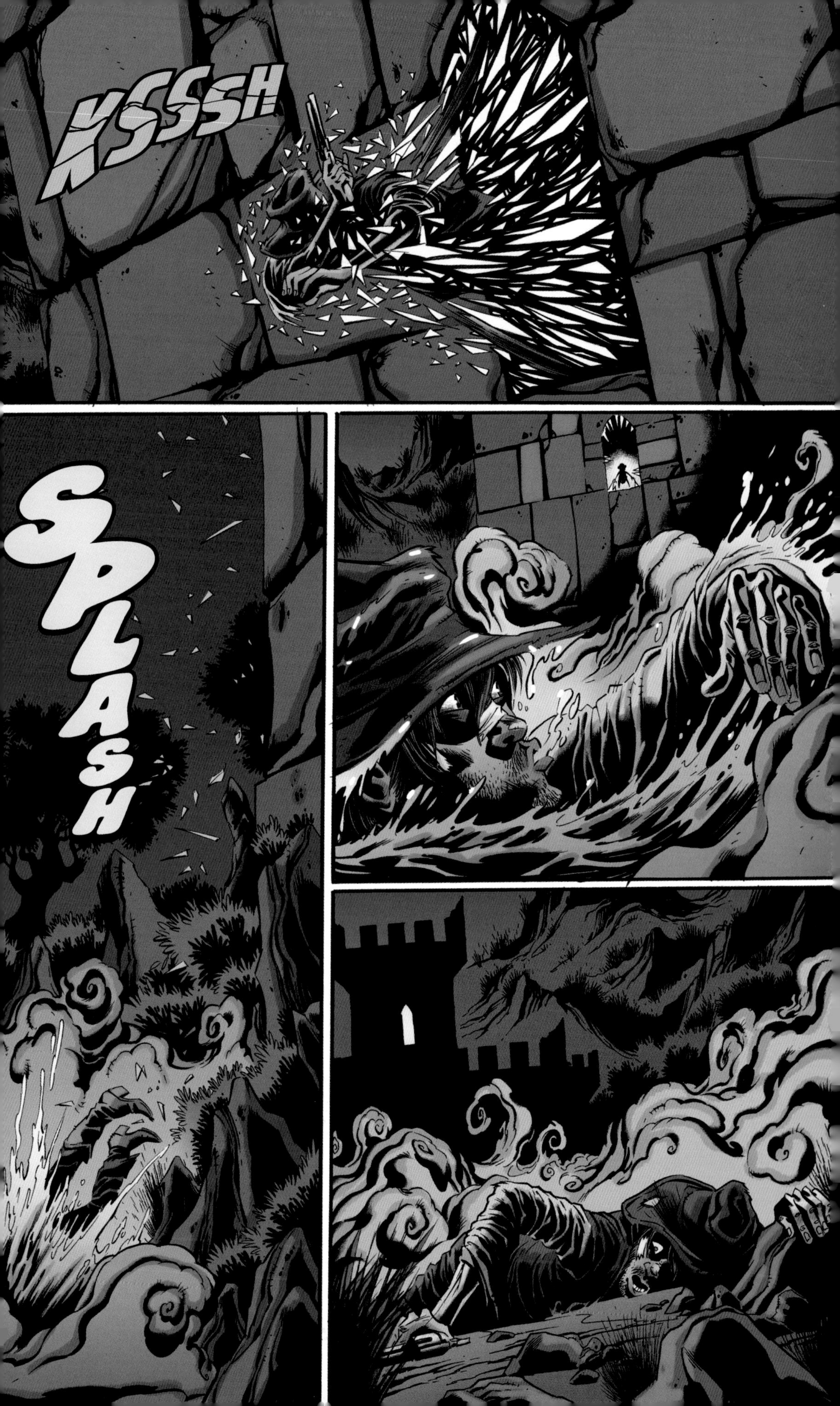
KSSSH
SPLASH

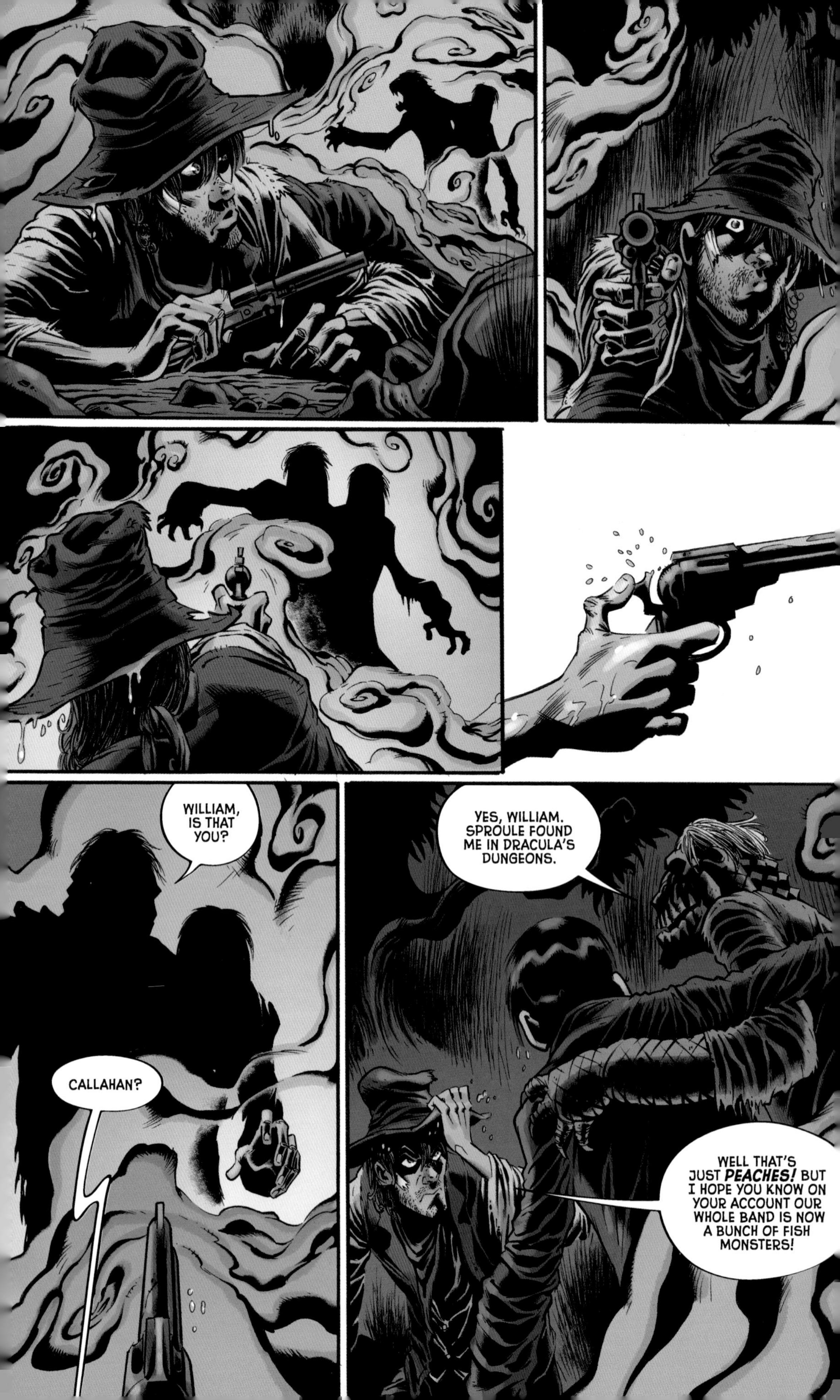
WILLIAM, IS THAT YOU?
CALLAHAN?
YES, WILLIAM. SPROULE FOUND ME IN DRACULA'S DUNGEONS.
WELL THAT'S JUST PEACHES! BUT I HOPE YOU KNOW ON YOUR ACCOUNT OUR WHOLE BAND IS NOW A BUNCH OF FISH MONSTERS!

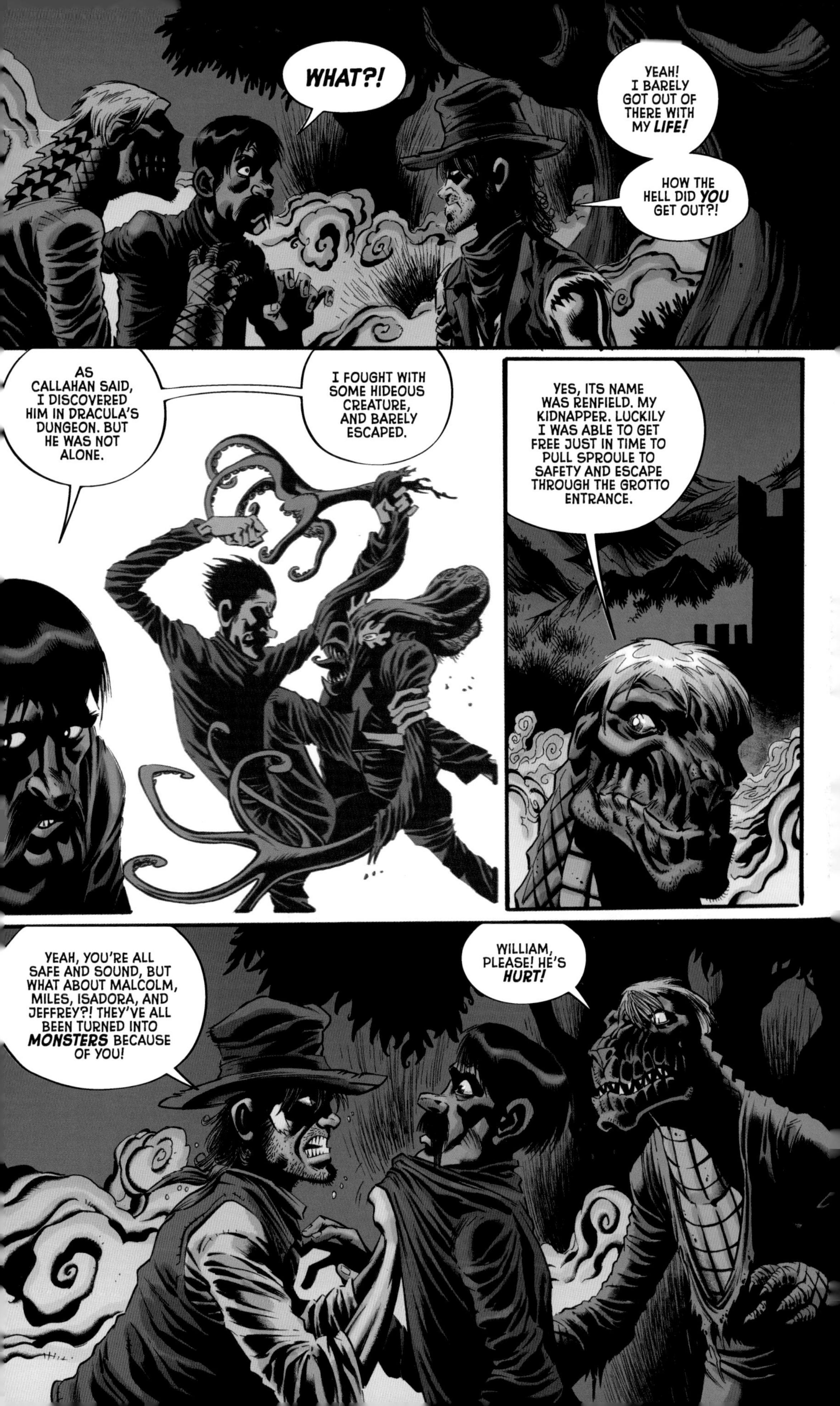
WHAT?!
YEAH! I BARELY GOT OUT OF THERE WITH MY *LIFE!*
HOW THE HELL DID *YOU* GET OUT?!
AS CALLAHAN SAID, I DISCOVERED HIM IN DRACULA'S DUNGEON. BUT HE WAS NOT ALONE.
I FOUGHT WITH SOME HIDEOUS CREATURE, AND BARELY ESCAPED.
YES, ITS NAME WAS RENFIELD. MY KIDNAPPER. LUCKILY I WAS ABLE TO GET FREE JUST IN TIME TO PULL SPROULE TO SAFETY AND ESCAPE THROUGH THE GROTTO ENTRANCE.
YEAH, YOU'RE ALL SAFE AND SOUND, BUT WHAT ABOUT MALCOLM, MILES, ISADORA, AND JEFFREY?! THEY'VE ALL BEEN TURNED INTO **MONSTERS** BECAUSE OF YOU!
WILLIAM, PLEASE! HE'S *HURT!*

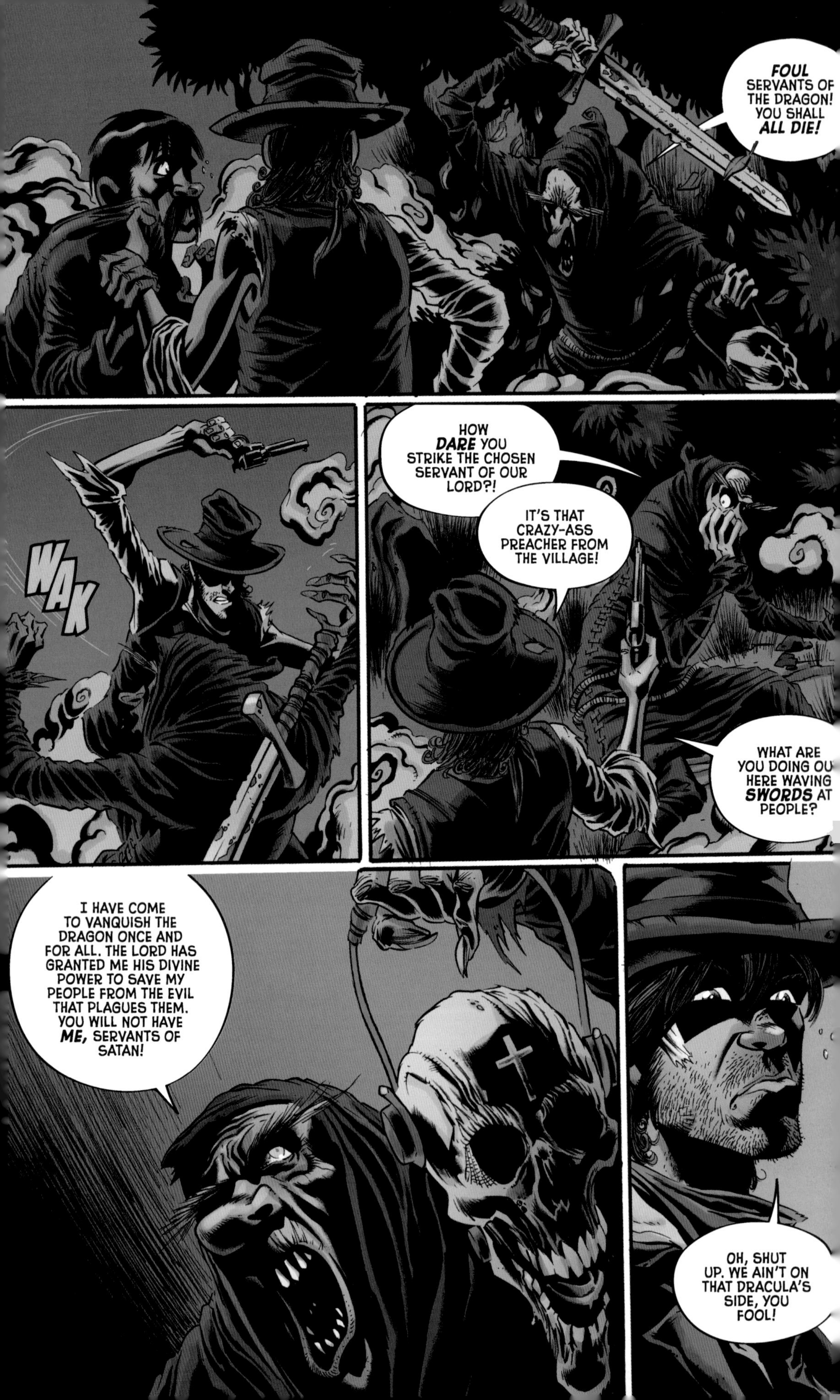
FOUL SERVANTS OF THE DRAGON! YOU SHALL ALL DIE!
WAK
HOW DARE YOU STRIKE THE CHOSEN SERVANT OF OUR LORD?!
IT'S THAT CRAZY-ASS PREACHER FROM THE VILLAGE!
WHAT ARE YOU DOING OU HERE WAVING SWORDS AT PEOPLE?
I HAVE COME TO VANQUISH THE DRAGON ONCE AND FOR ALL. THE LORD HAS GRANTED ME HIS DIVINE POWER TO SAVE MY PEOPLE FROM THE EVIL THAT PLAGUES THEM. YOU WILL NOT HAVE ME, SERVANTS OF SATAN!
OH, SHUT UP. WE AIN'T ON THAT DRACULA'S SIDE, YOU FOOL!

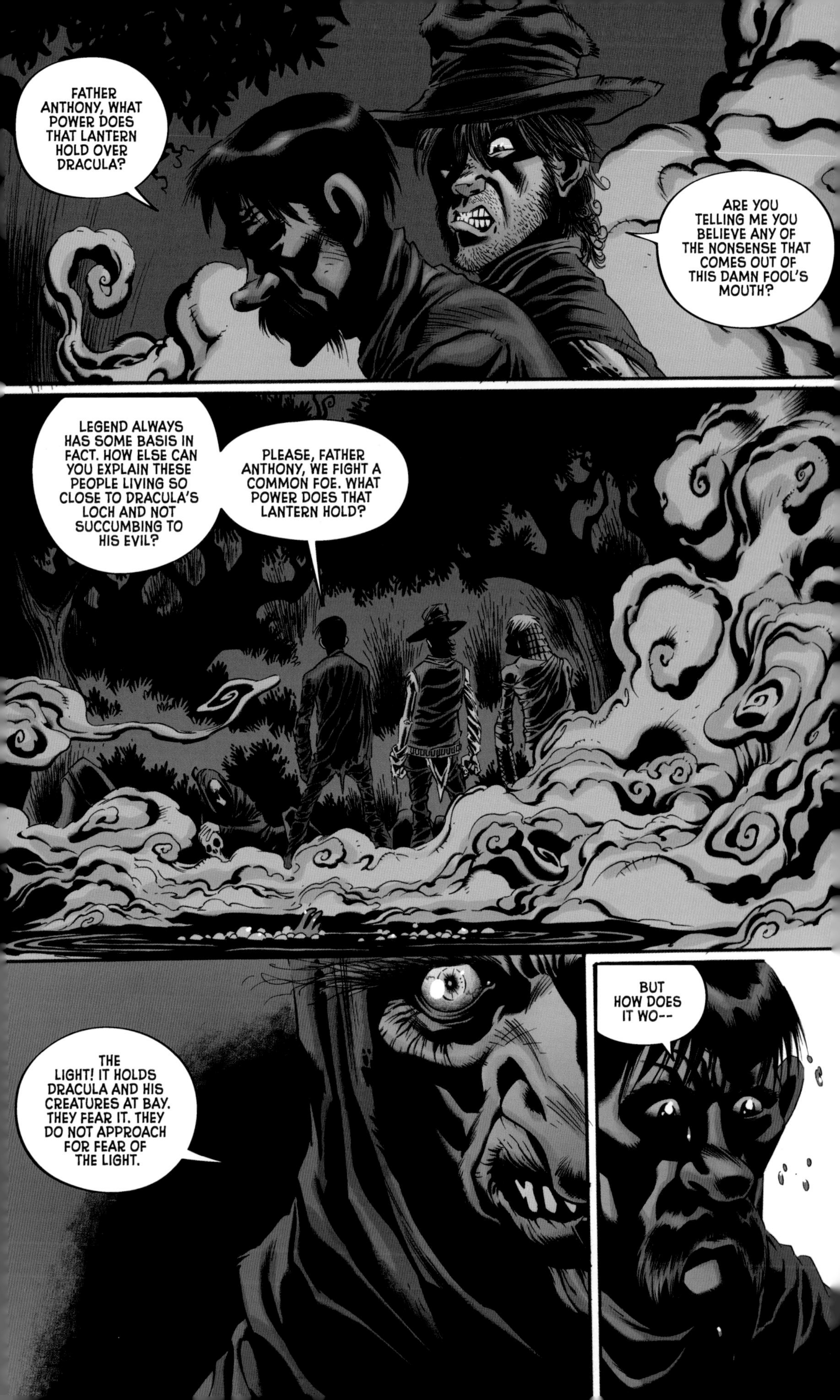
FATHER ANTHONY, WHAT POWER DOES THAT LANTERN HOLD OVER DRACULA?
ARE YOU TELLING ME YOU BELIEVE ANY OF THE NONSENSE THAT COMES OUT OF THIS DAMN FOOL'S MOUTH?
LEGEND ALWAYS HAS SOME BASIS IN FACT. HOW ELSE CAN YOU EXPLAIN THESE PEOPLE LIVING SO CLOSE TO DRACULA'S LOCH AND NOT SUCCUMBING TO HIS EVIL?
PLEASE, FATHER ANTHONY, WE FIGHT A COMMON FOE. WHAT POWER DOES THAT LANTERN HOLD?
THE LIGHT! IT HOLDS DRACULA AND HIS CREATURES AT BAY. THEY FEAR IT. THEY DO NOT APPROACH FOR FEAR OF THE LIGHT.
BUT HOW DOES IT WO--

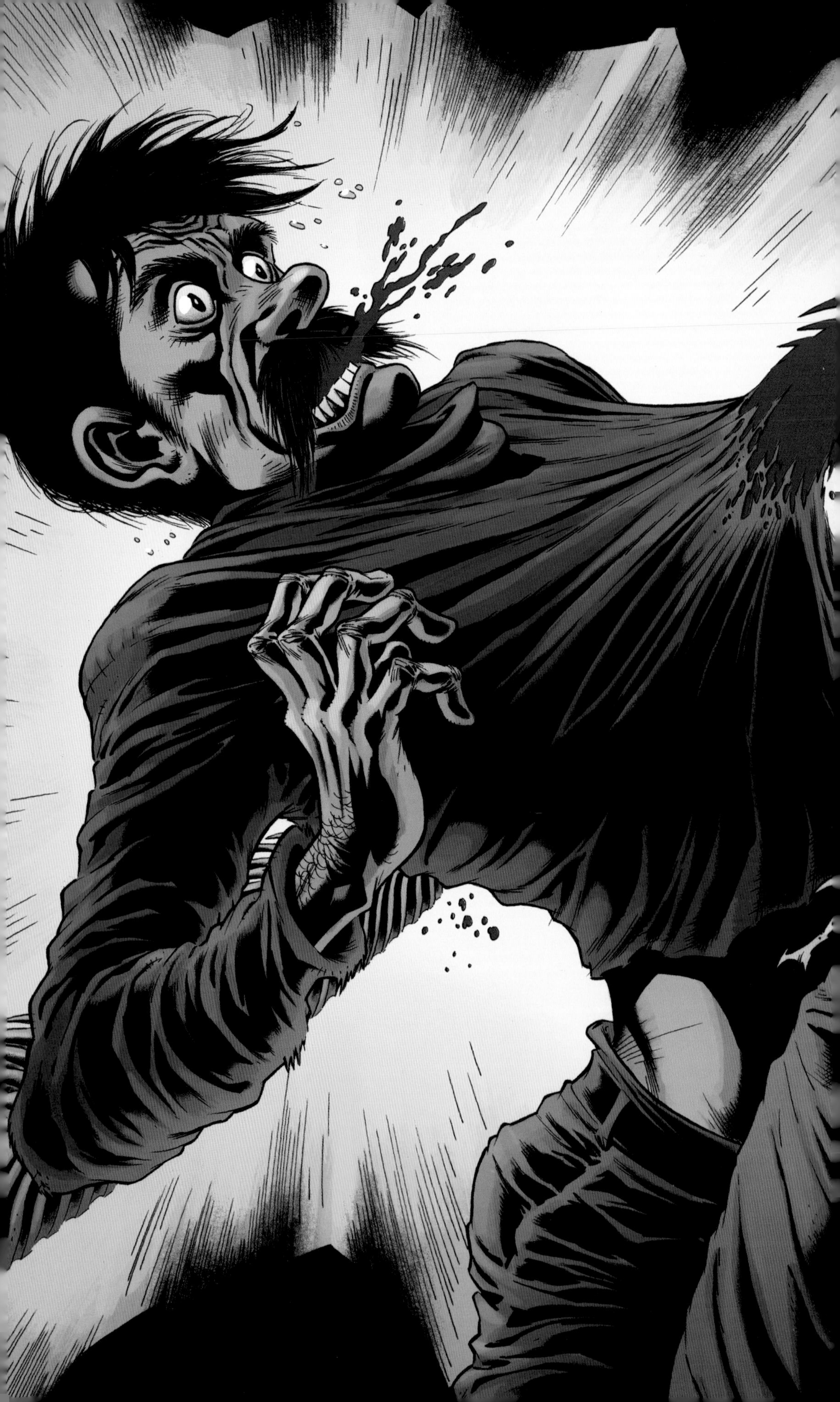

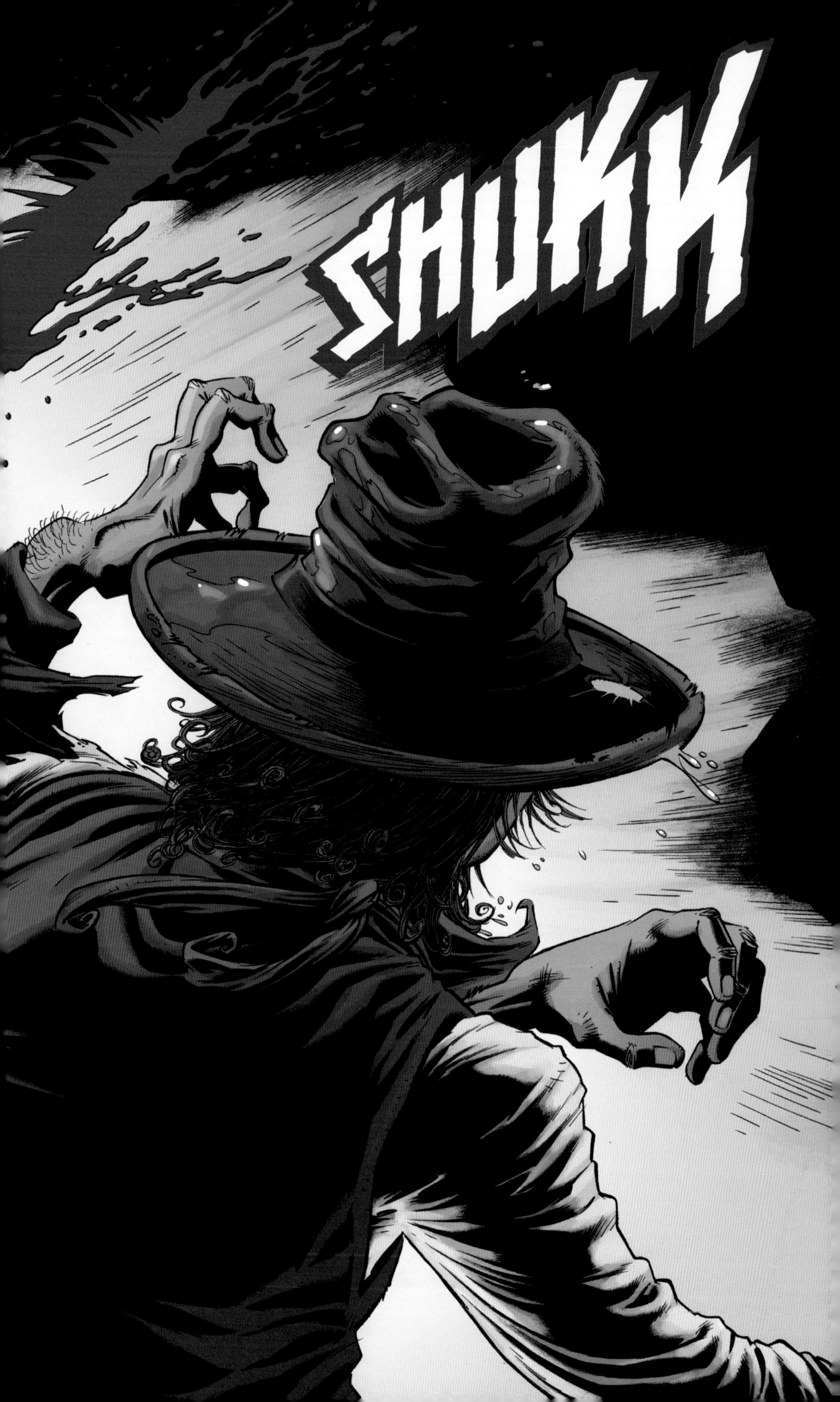
SHUKK

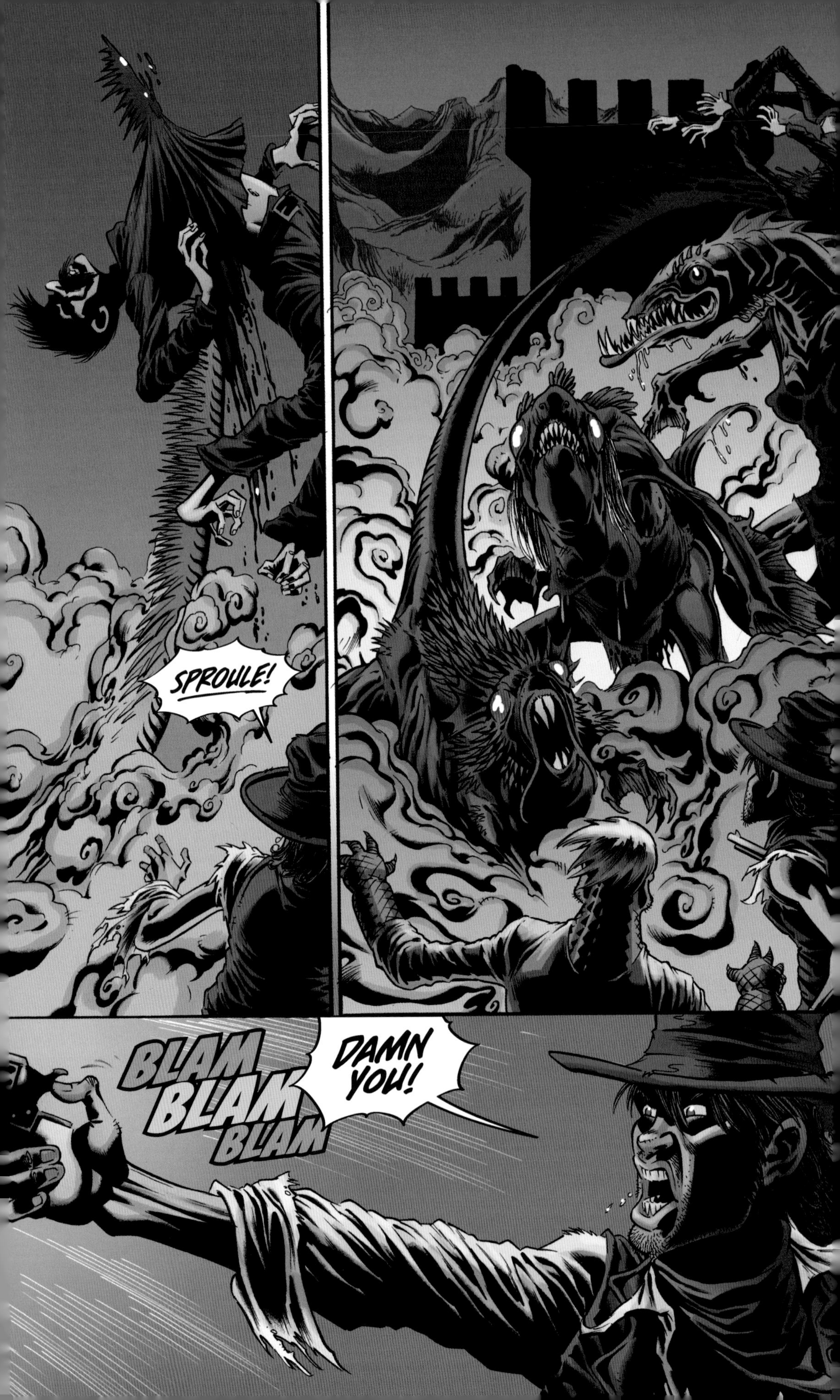
SPROULE!
BLAM
BLAM
BLAM
DAMN YOU!

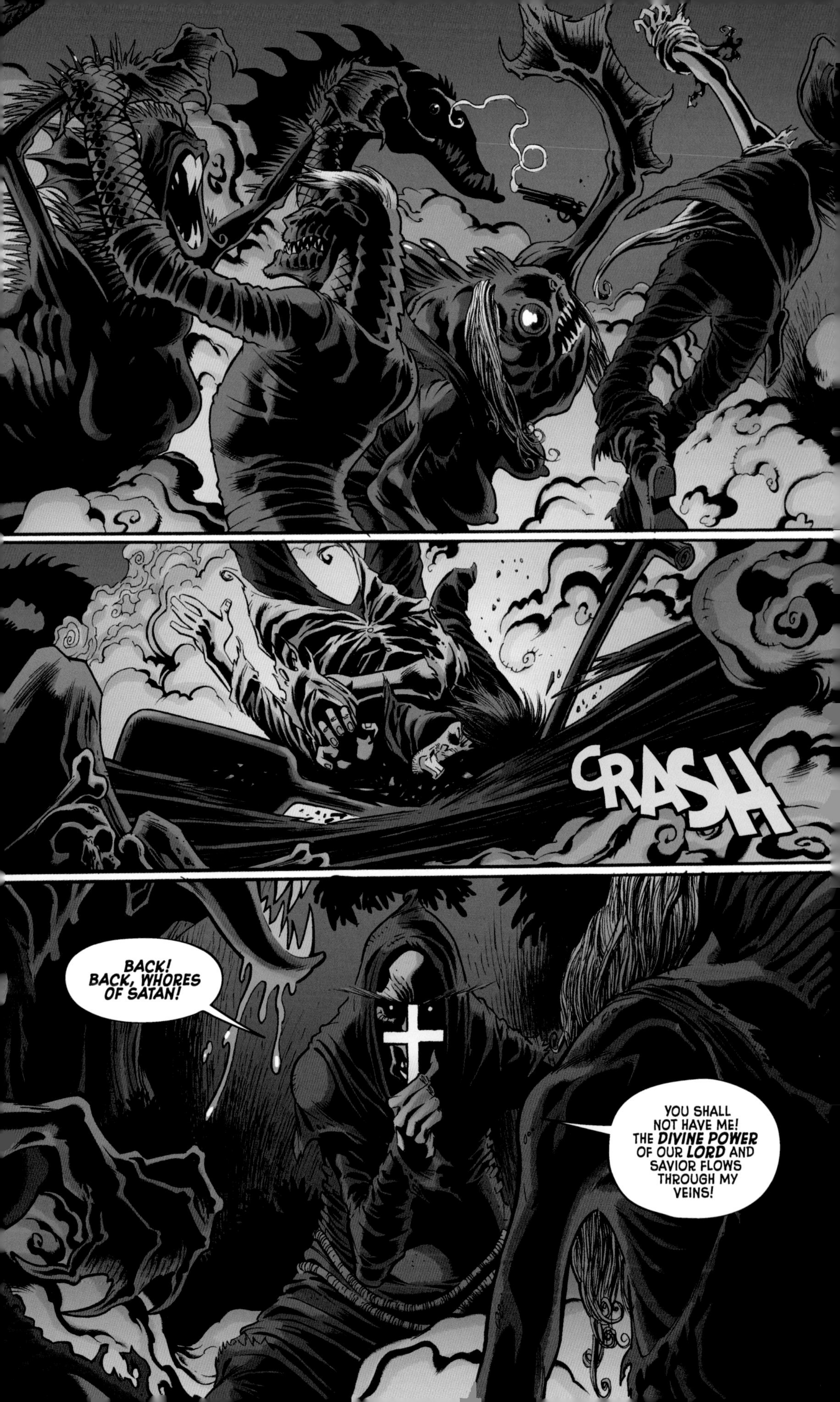
CRASH
BACK! BACK, WHORES OF SATAN!
YOU SHALL NOT HAVE ME! THE DIVINE POWER OF OUR LORD AND SAVIOR FLOWS THROUGH MY VEINS!

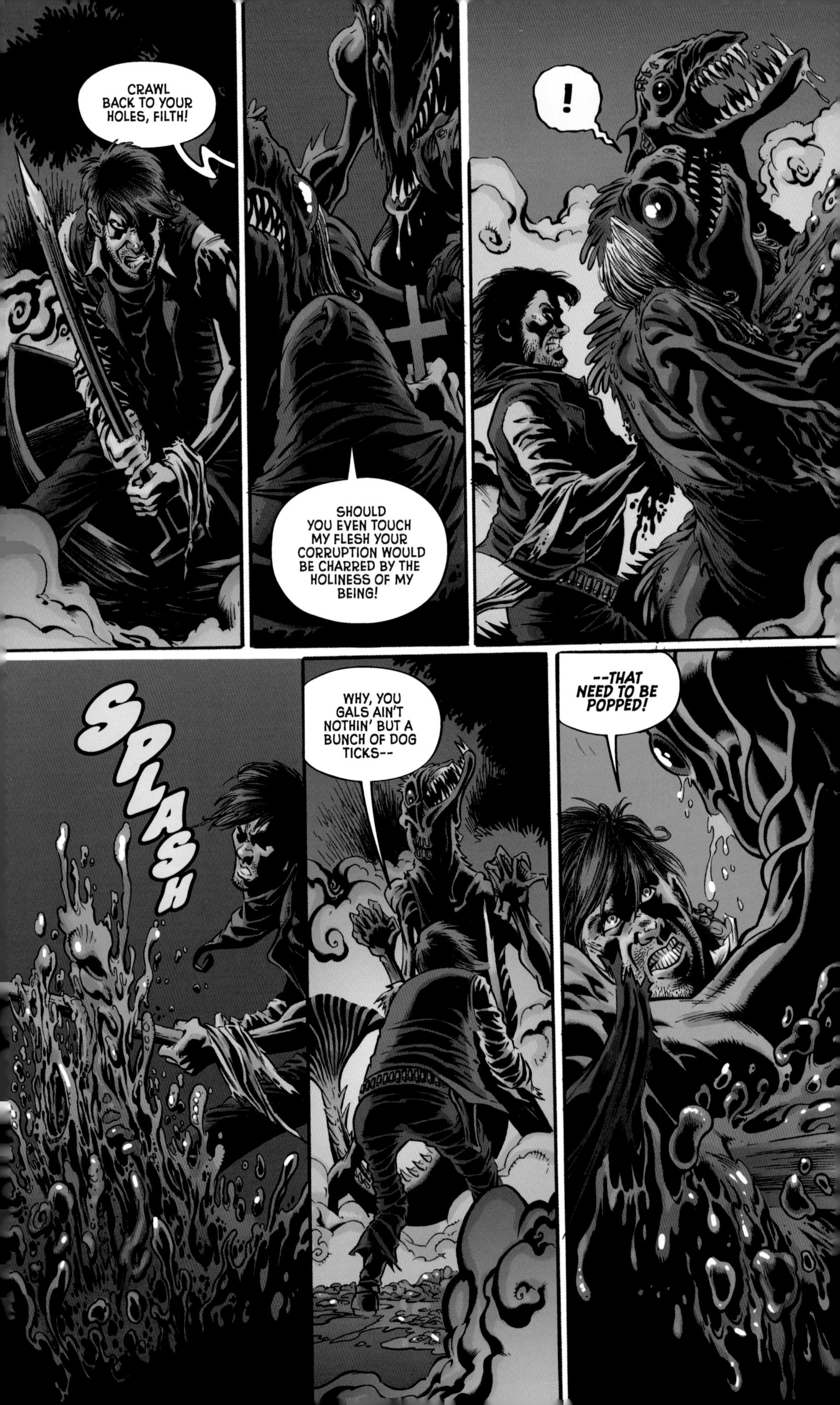
CRAWL BACK TO YOUR HOLES, FILTH!
SHOULD YOU EVEN TOUCH MY FLESH YOUR CORRUPTION WOULD BE CHARRED BY THE HOLINESS OF MY BEING!
!
SPLASH
WHY, YOU GALS AIN'T NOTHIN' BUT A BUNCH OF DOG TICKS--
--THAT NEED TO BE POPPED!

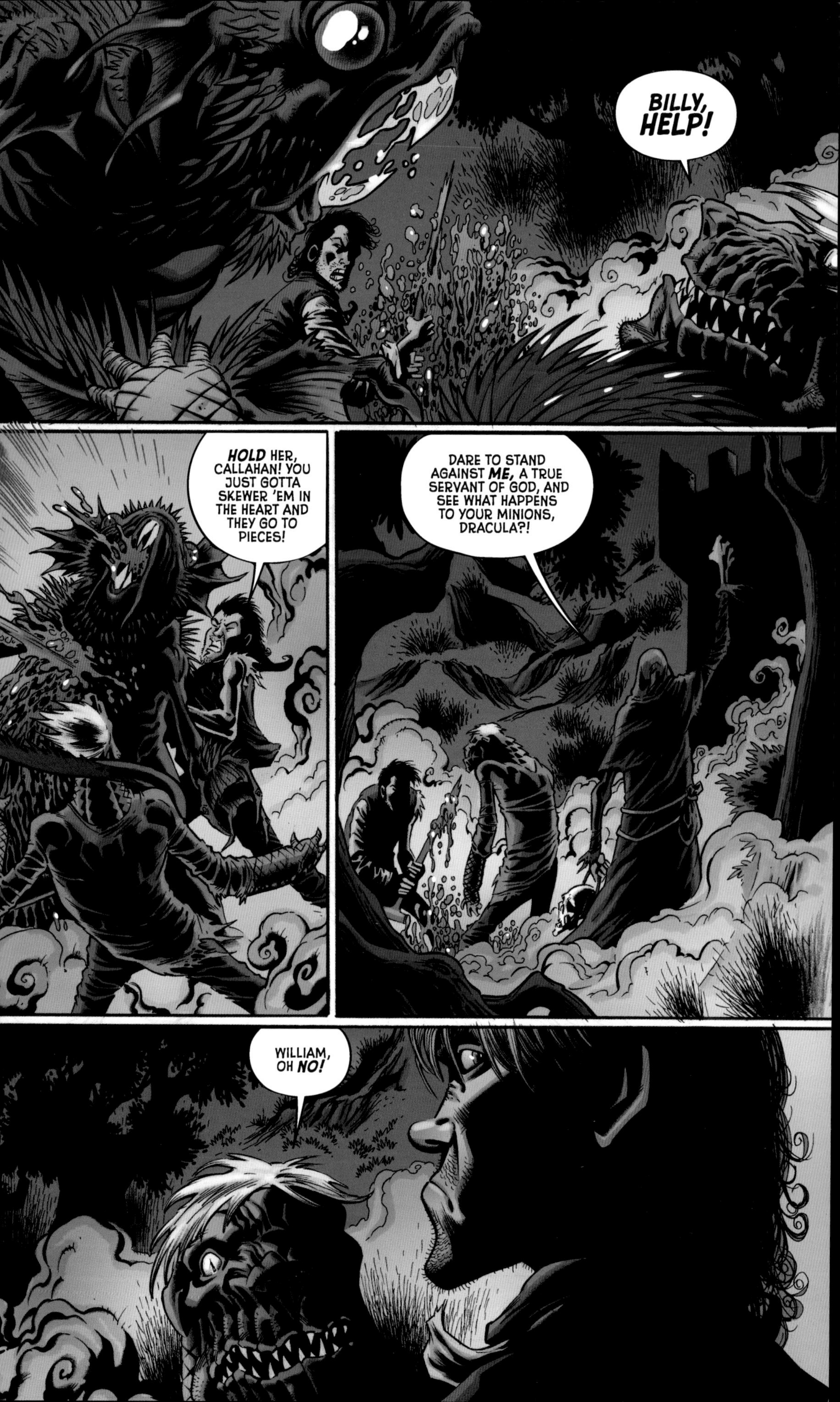

BILLY, HELP!
HOLD HER, CALLAHAN! YOU JUST GOTTA SKEWER 'EM IN THE HEART AND THEY GO TO PIECES!
DARE TO STAND AGAINST ME, A TRUE SERVANT OF GOD, AND SEE WHAT HAPPENS TO YOUR MINIONS, DRACULA?!
WILLIAM, OH NO!

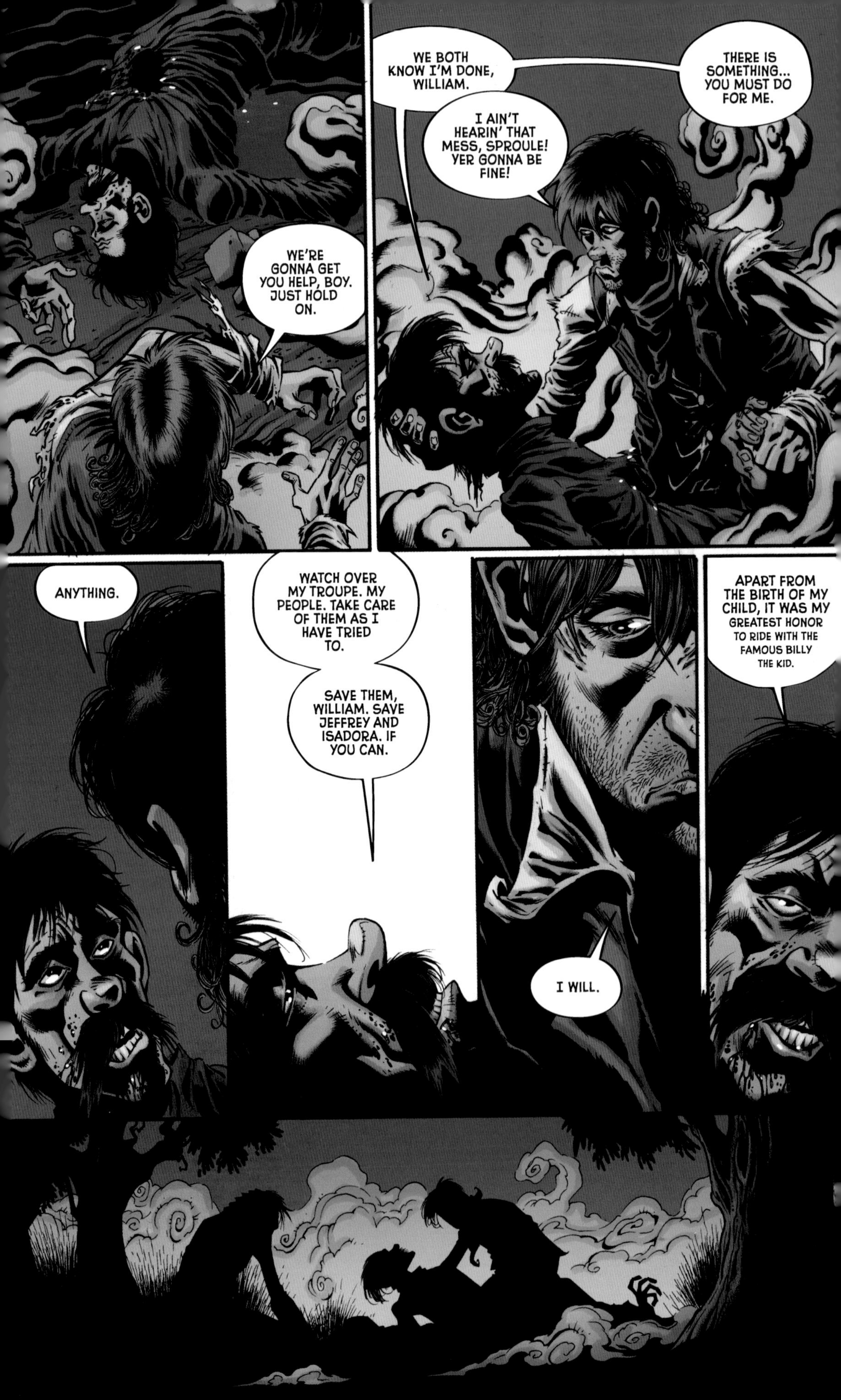
WE'RE GONNA GET YOU HELP, BOY. JUST HOLD ON.
WE BOTH KNOW I'M DONE, WILLIAM.
THERE IS SOMETHING... YOU MUST DO FOR ME.
I AIN'T HEARIN' THAT MESS, SPROULE! YER GONNA BE FINE!
ANYTHING.
WATCH OVER MY TROUPE. MY PEOPLE. TAKE CARE OF THEM AS I HAVE TRIED TO.
SAVE THEM, WILLIAM. SAVE JEFFREY AND ISADORA. IF YOU CAN.
I WILL.
APART FROM THE BIRTH OF MY CHILD, IT WAS MY GREATEST HONOR TO RIDE WITH THE FAMOUS BILLY THE KID.

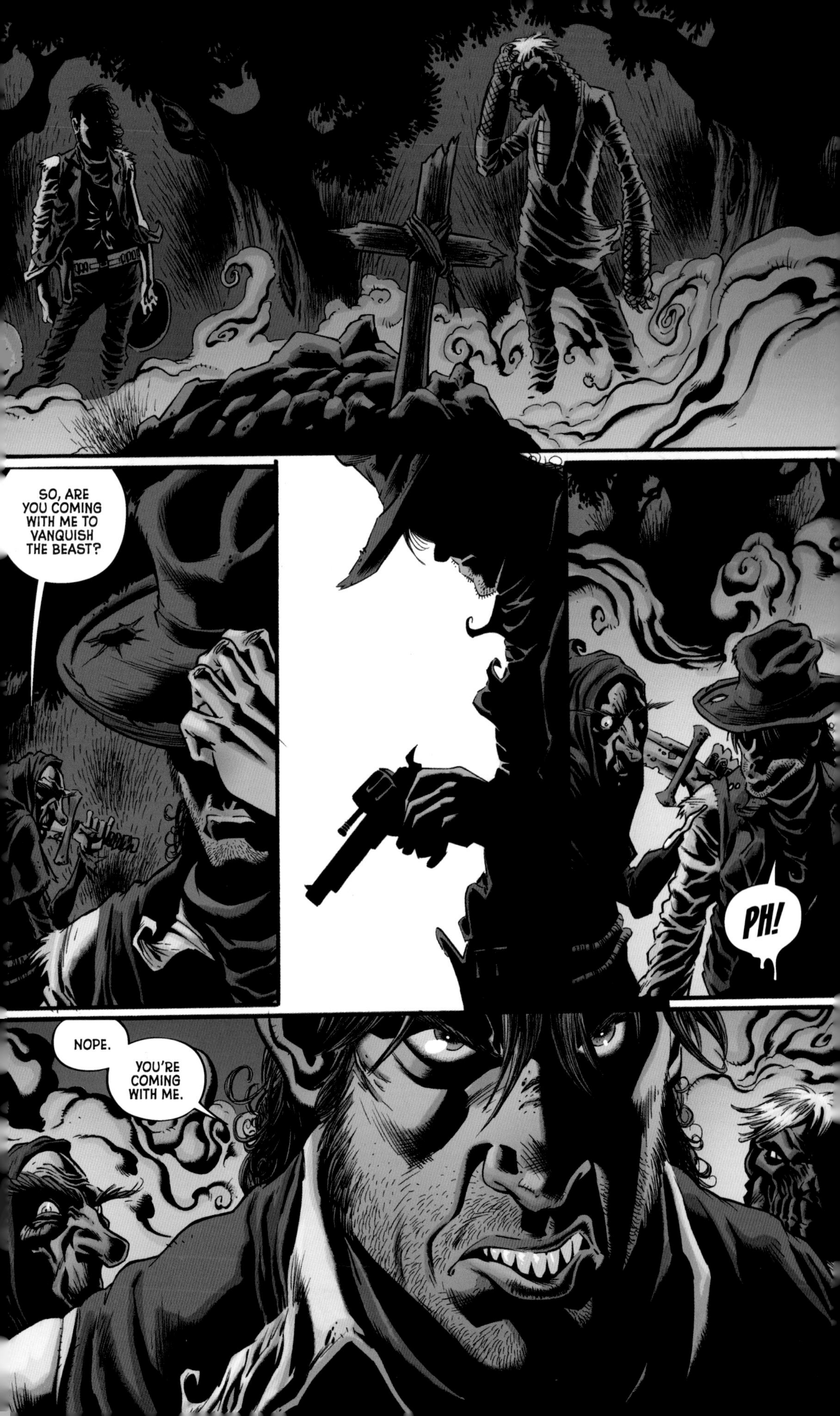
SO, ARE YOU COMING WITH ME TO VANQUISH THE BEAST?
PH!
NOPE.
YOU'RE COMING WITH ME.

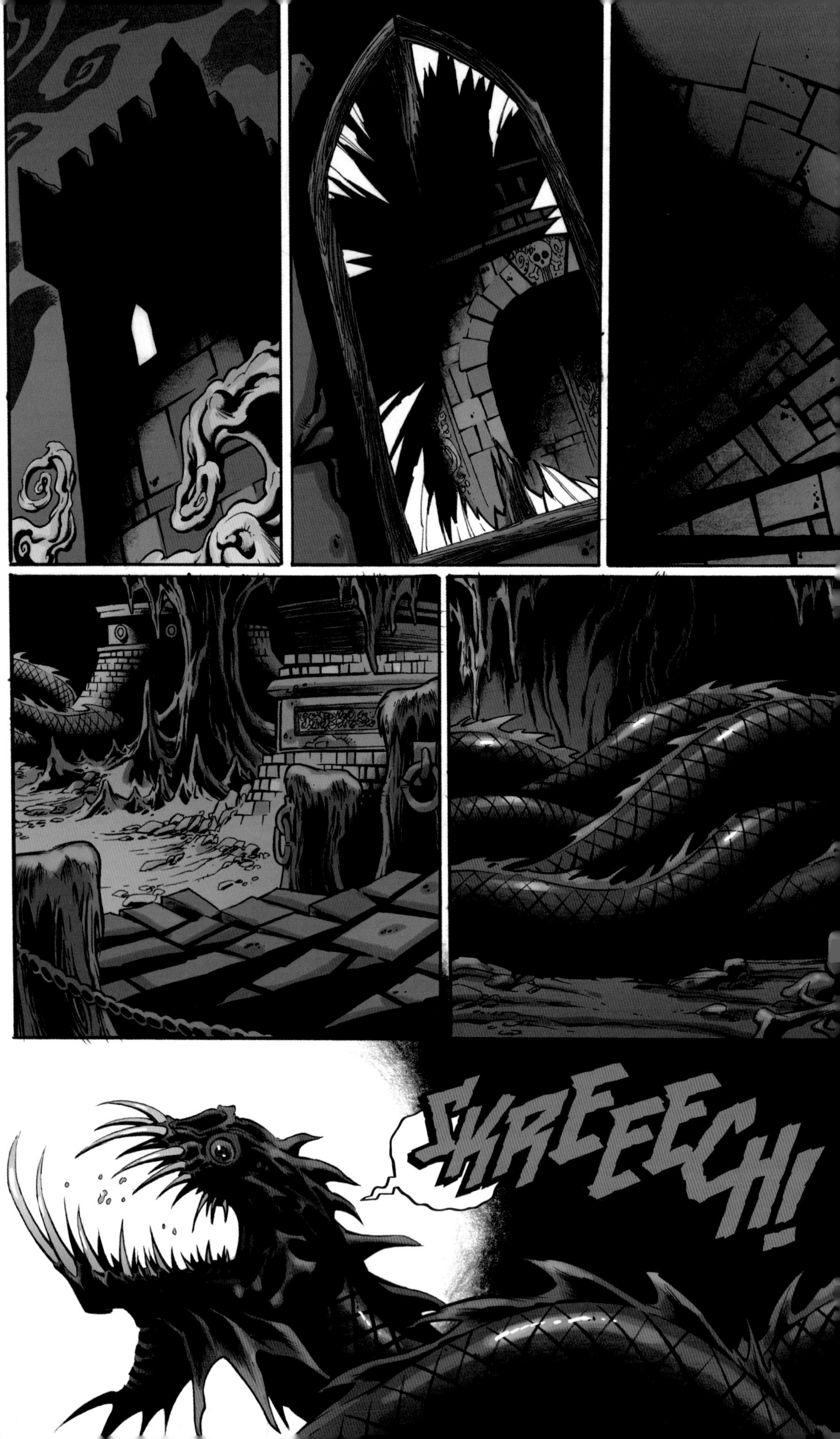
SKREEECH!

CHAPTER FOUR

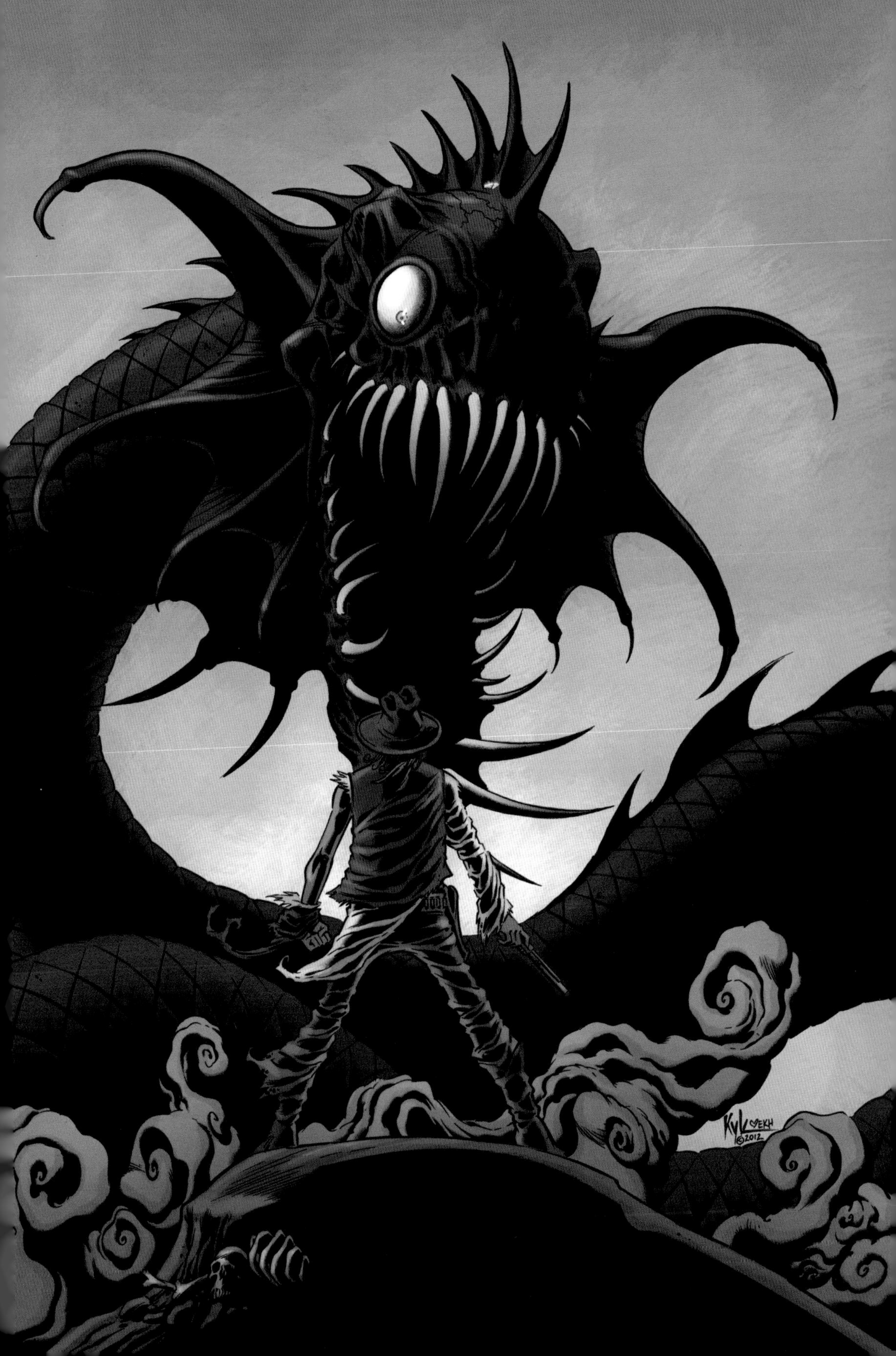

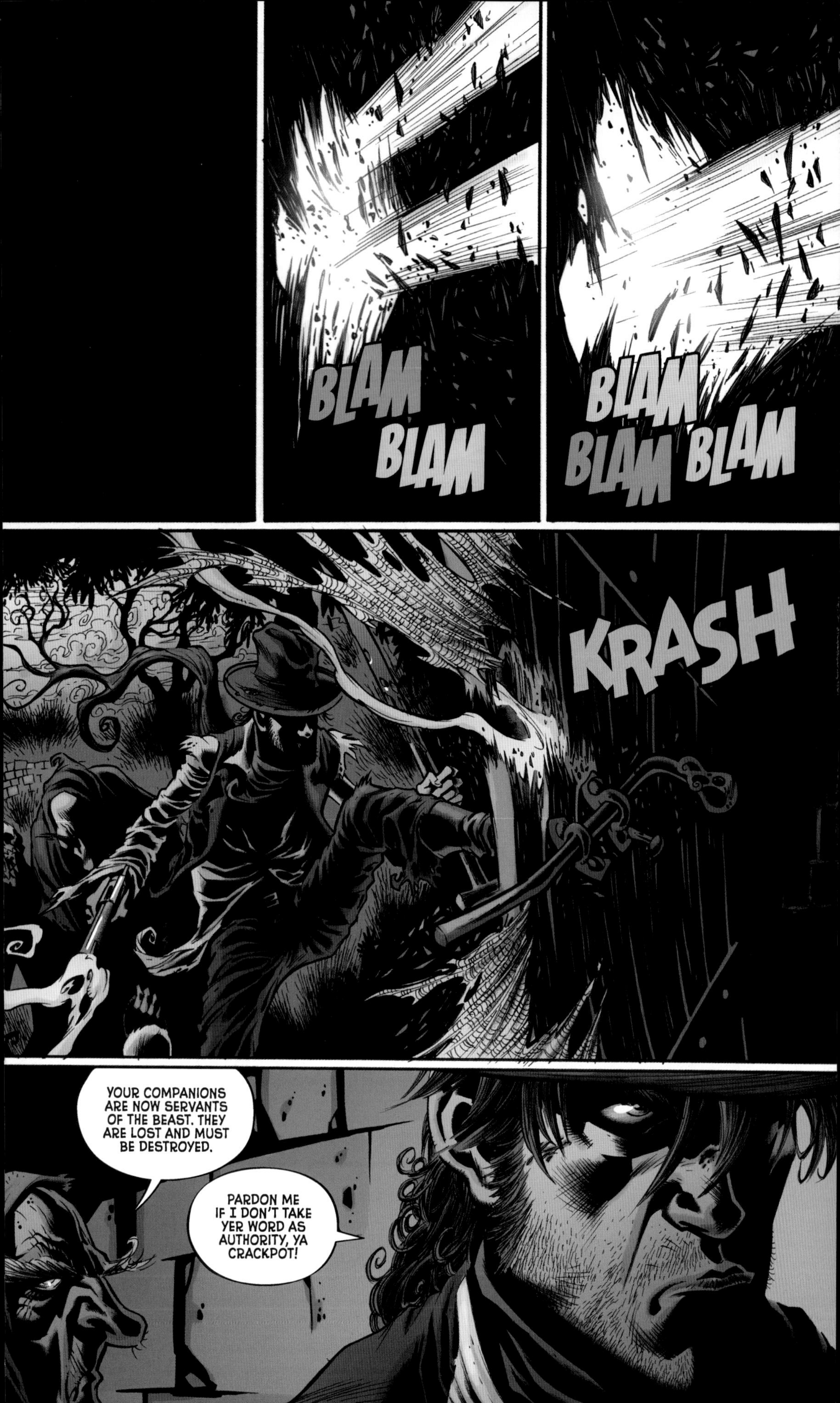
BLAM
BLAM
BLAM
BLAM BLAM
KRASH
YOUR COMPANIONS ARE NOW SERVANTS OF THE BEAST. THEY ARE LOST AND MUST BE DESTROYED.
PARDON ME IF I DON'T TAKE YER WORD AS AUTHORITY, YA CRACKPOT!

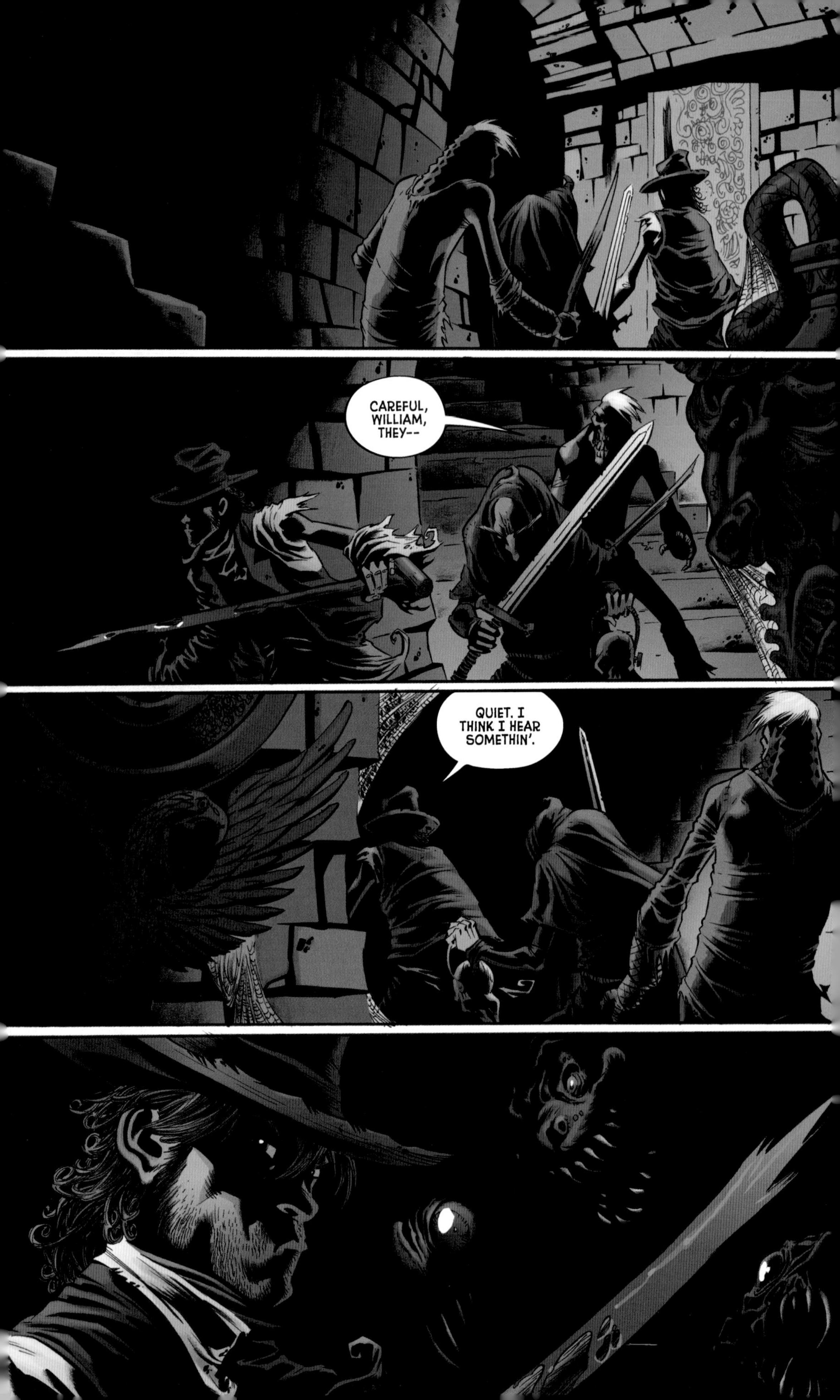
CAREFUL, WILLIAM, THEY--
QUIET. I THINK I HEAR SOMETHIN'.

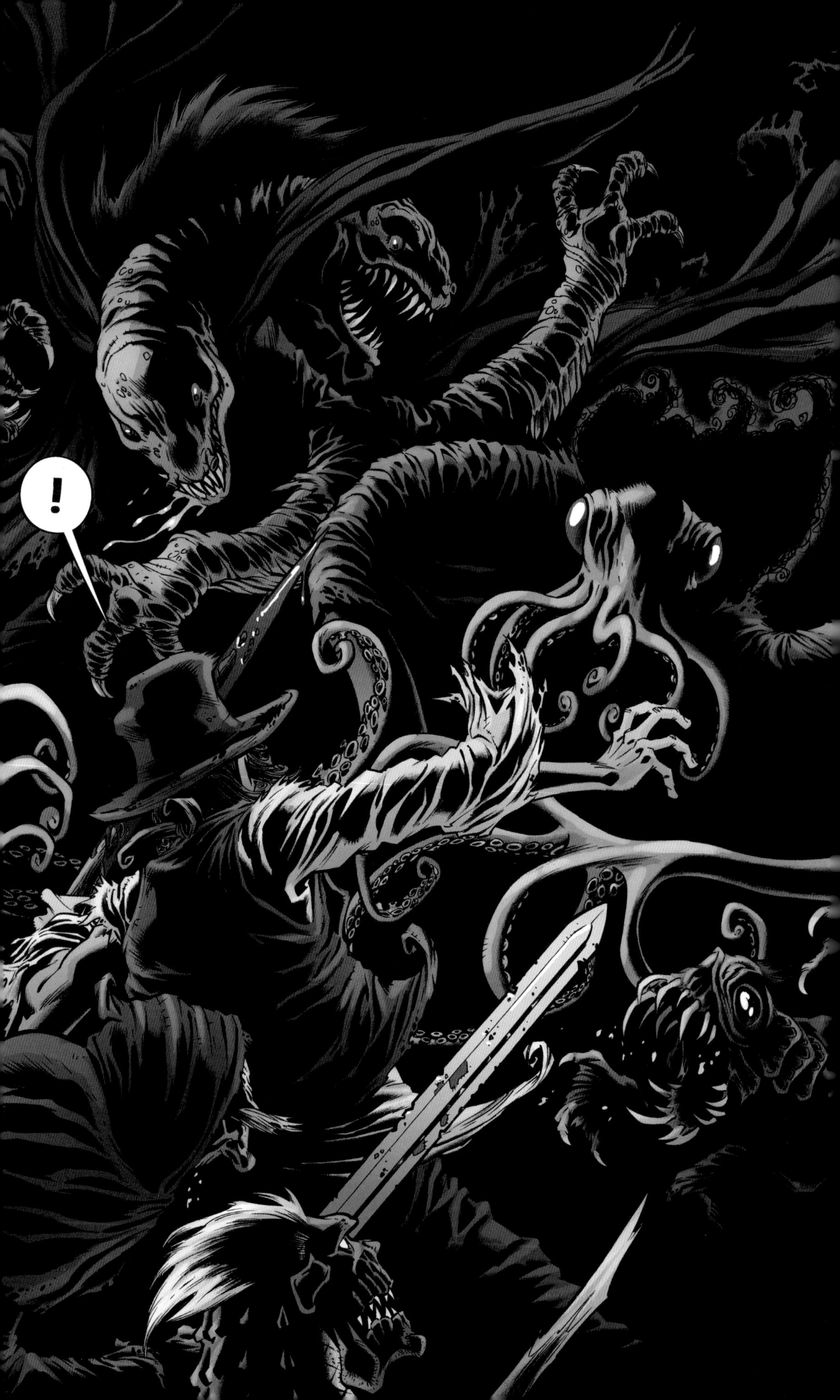
!

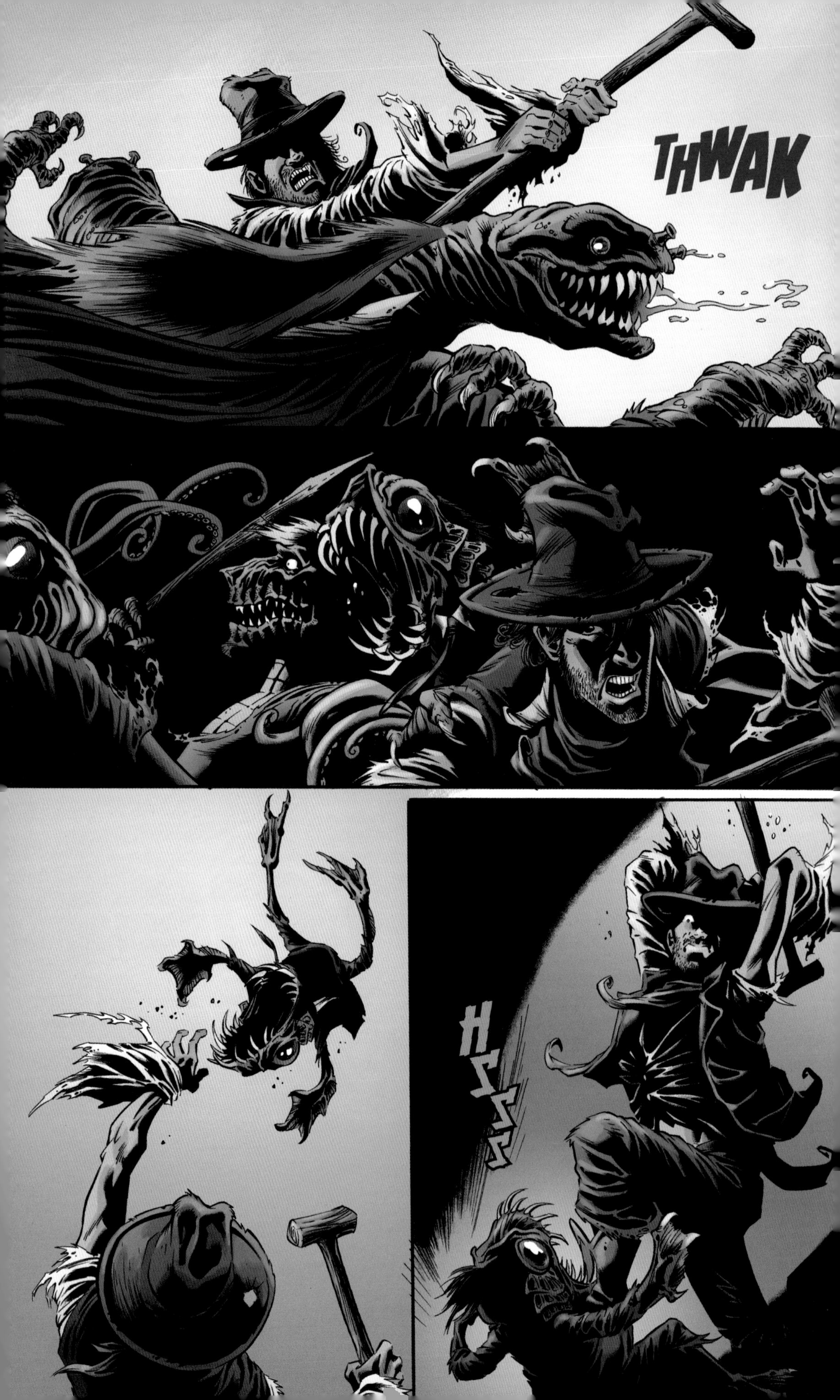
THWAK
HSSS

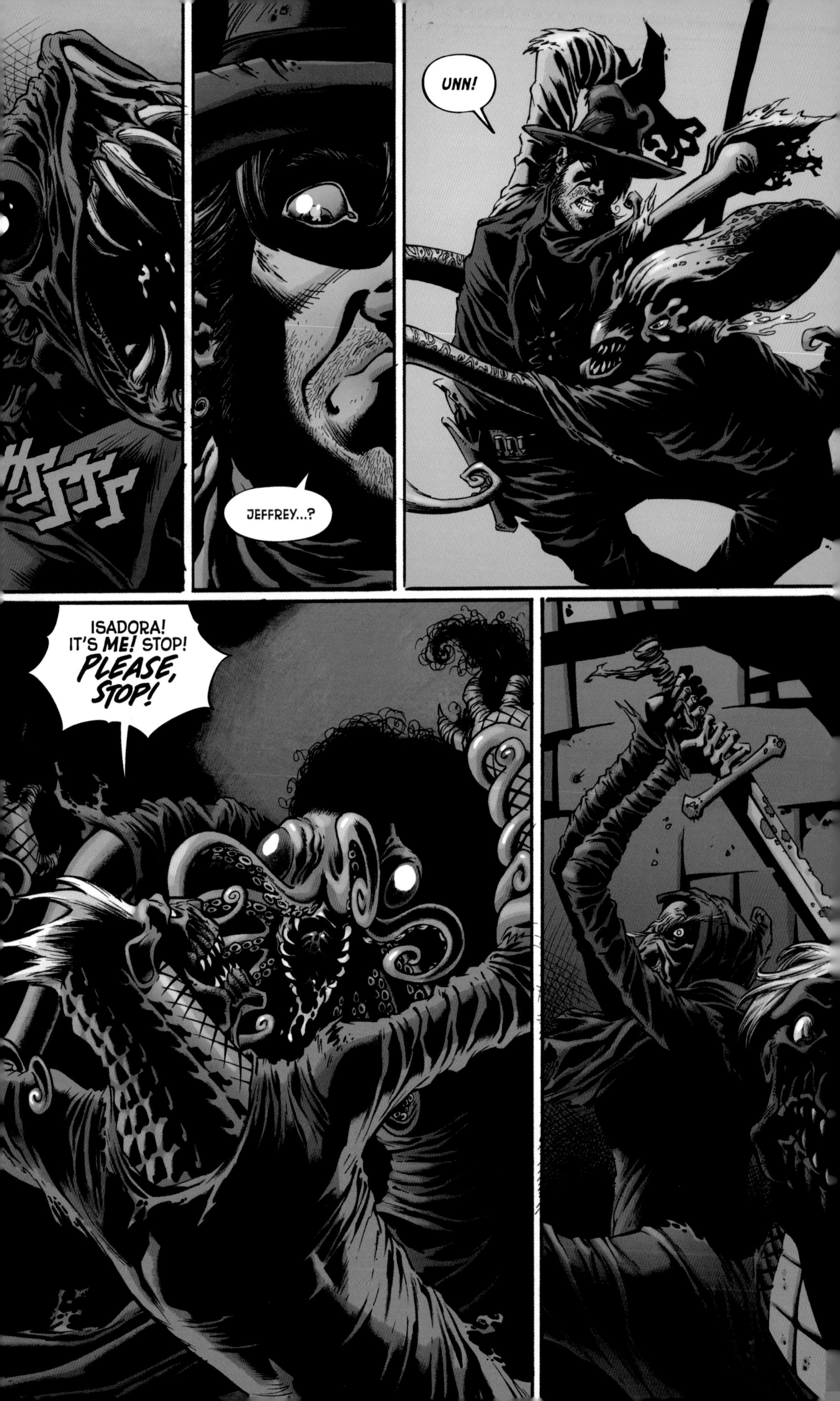
JEFFREY...?
UNN!
ISADORA! IT'S **ME!** STOP! ***PLEASE, STOP!***

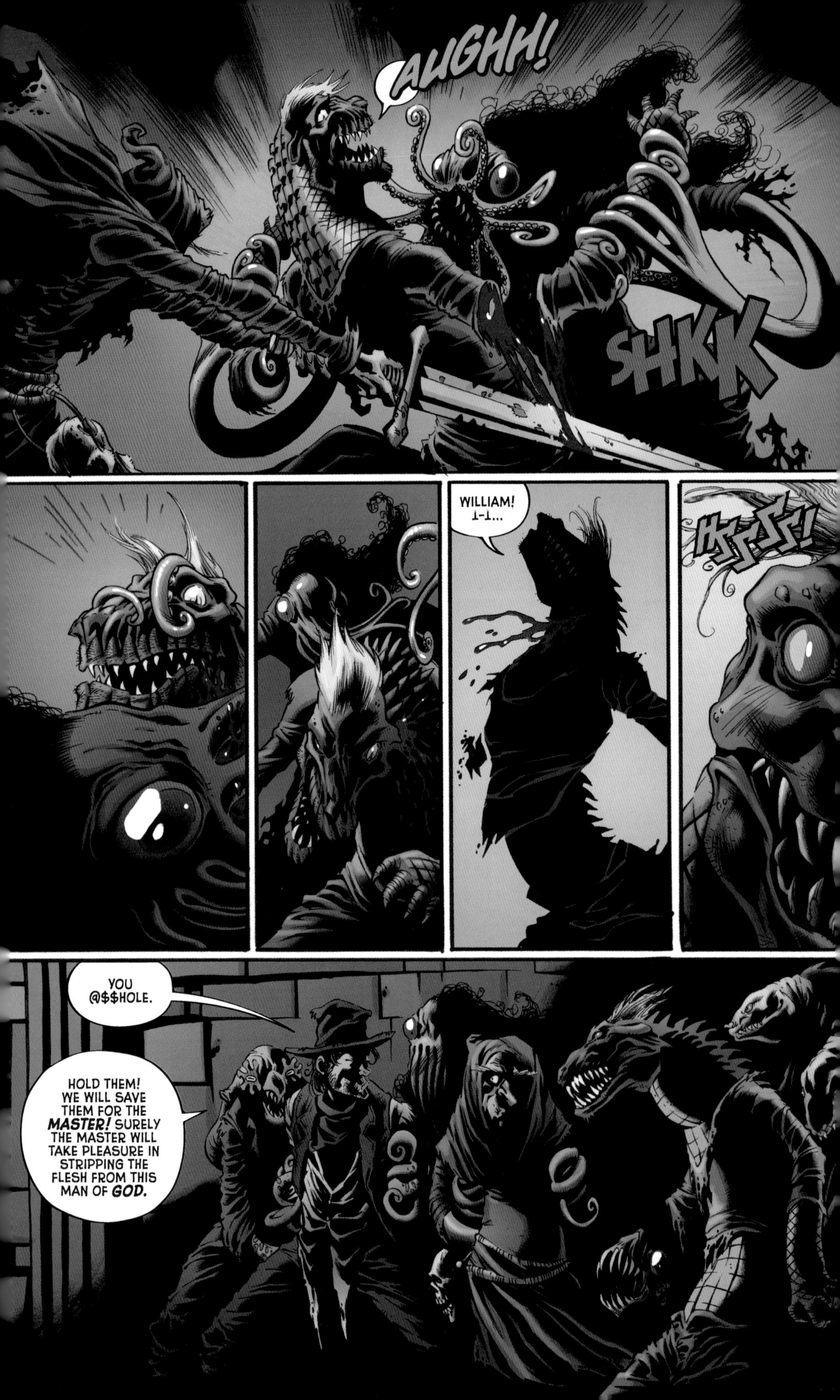
AUGHH!
SHKK
WILLIAM! I-I...
HYSSS!
YOU @$$HOLE.
HOLD THEM! WE WILL SAVE THEM FOR THE **MASTER!** SURELY THE MASTER WILL TAKE PLEASURE IN STRIPPING THE FLESH FROM THIS MAN OF **GOD.**

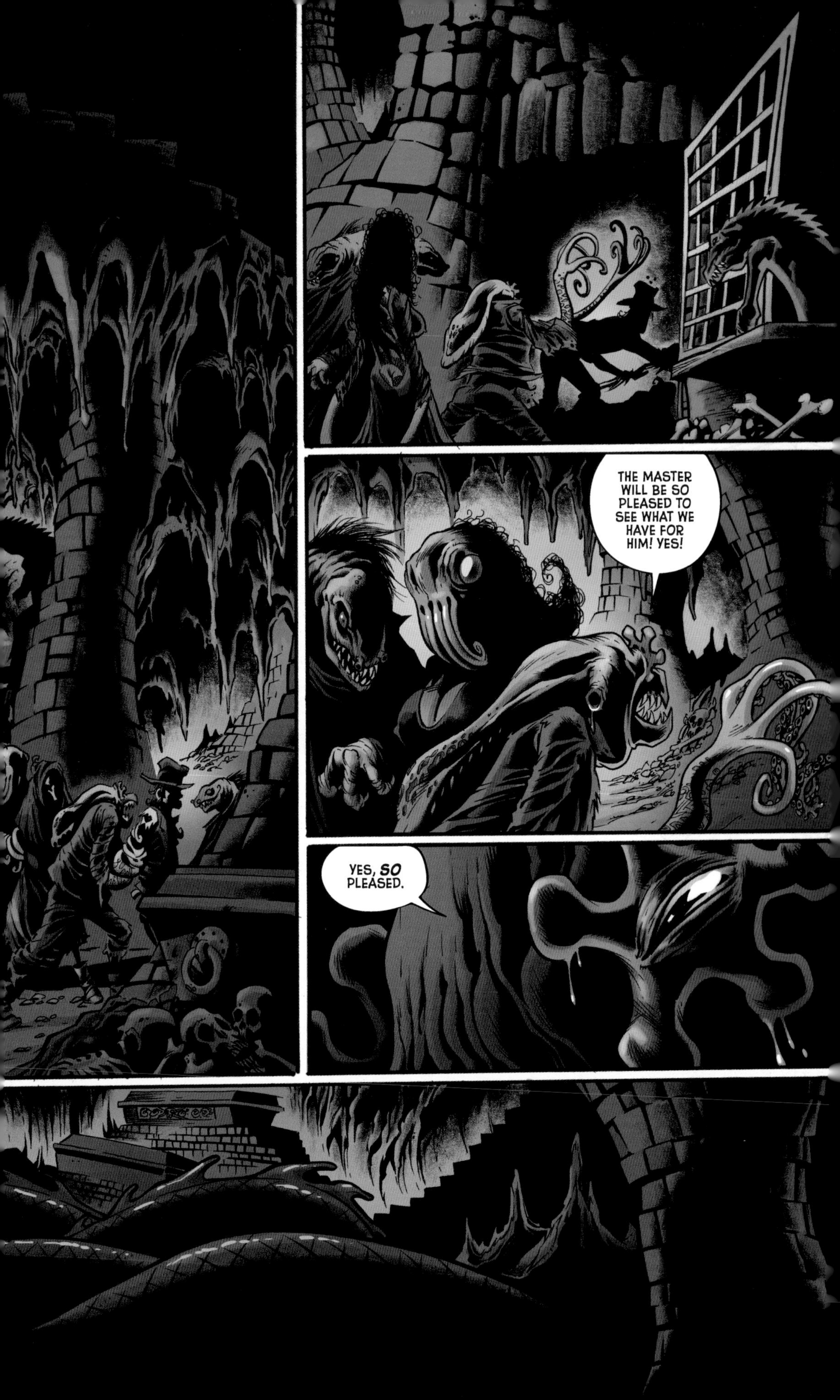
THE MASTER WILL BE SO PLEASED TO SEE WHAT WE HAVE FOR HIM! YES!
YES, SO PLEASED.

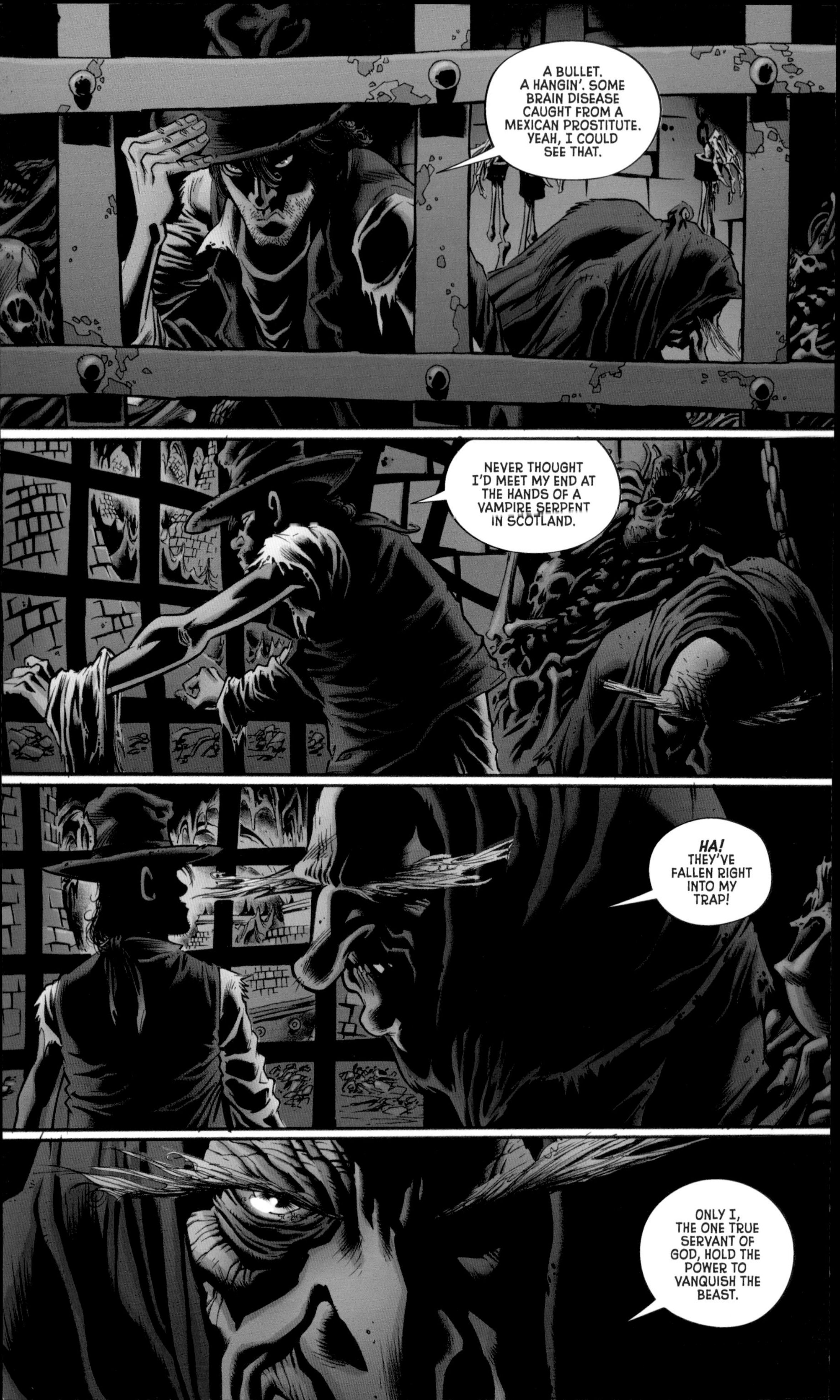
A BULLET. A HANGIN'. SOME BRAIN DISEASE CAUGHT FROM A MEXICAN PROSTITUTE. YEAH, I COULD SEE THAT.
NEVER THOUGHT I'D MEET MY END AT THE HANDS OF A VAMPIRE SERPENT IN SCOTLAND.
HA! THEY'VE FALLEN RIGHT INTO MY TRAP!
ONLY I, THE ONE TRUE SERVANT OF GOD, HOLD THE POWER TO VANQUISH THE BEAST.

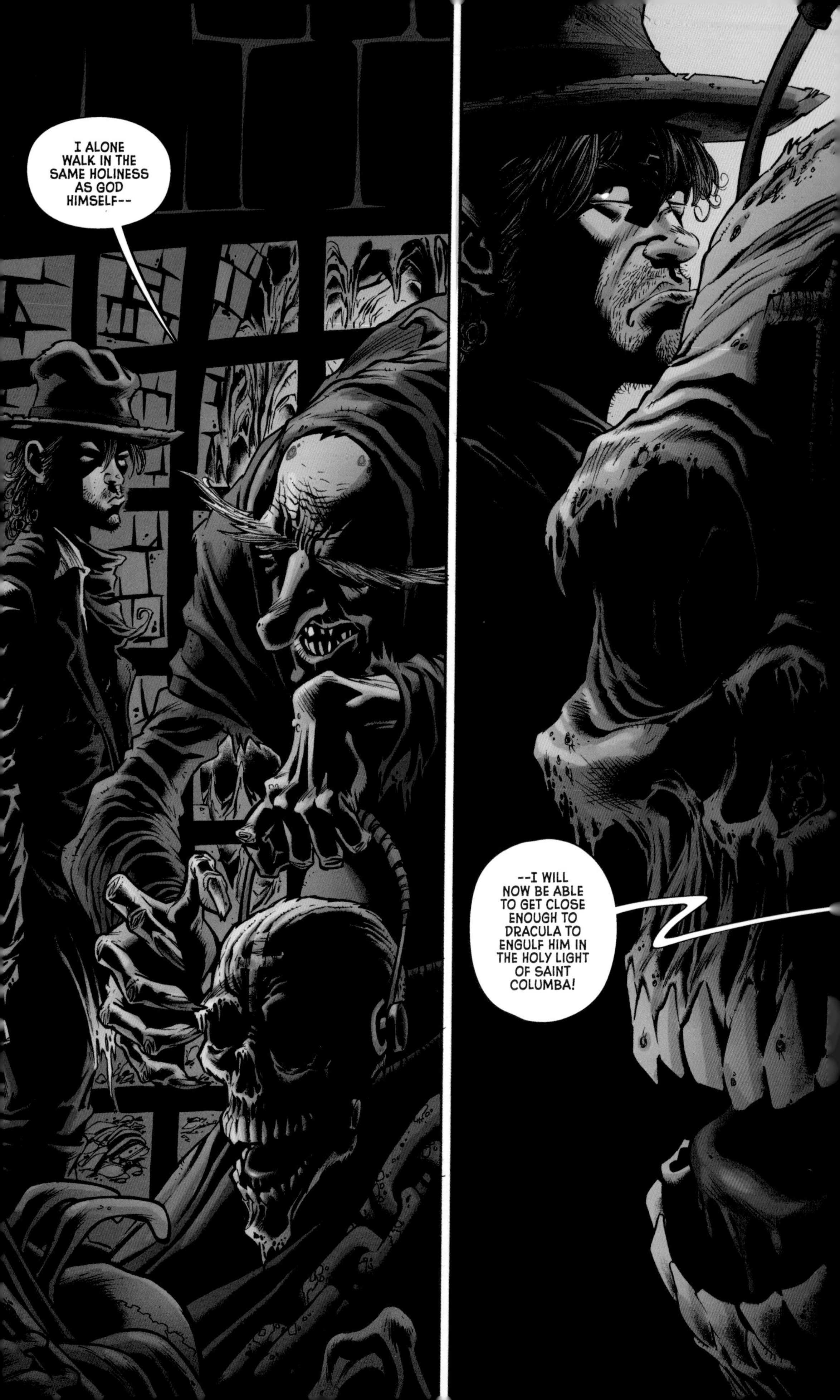
I ALONE WALK IN THE SAME HOLINESS AS GOD HIMSELF--
--I WILL NOW BE ABLE TO GET CLOSE ENOUGH TO DRACULA TO ENGULF HIM IN THE HOLY LIGHT OF SAINT COLUMBA!

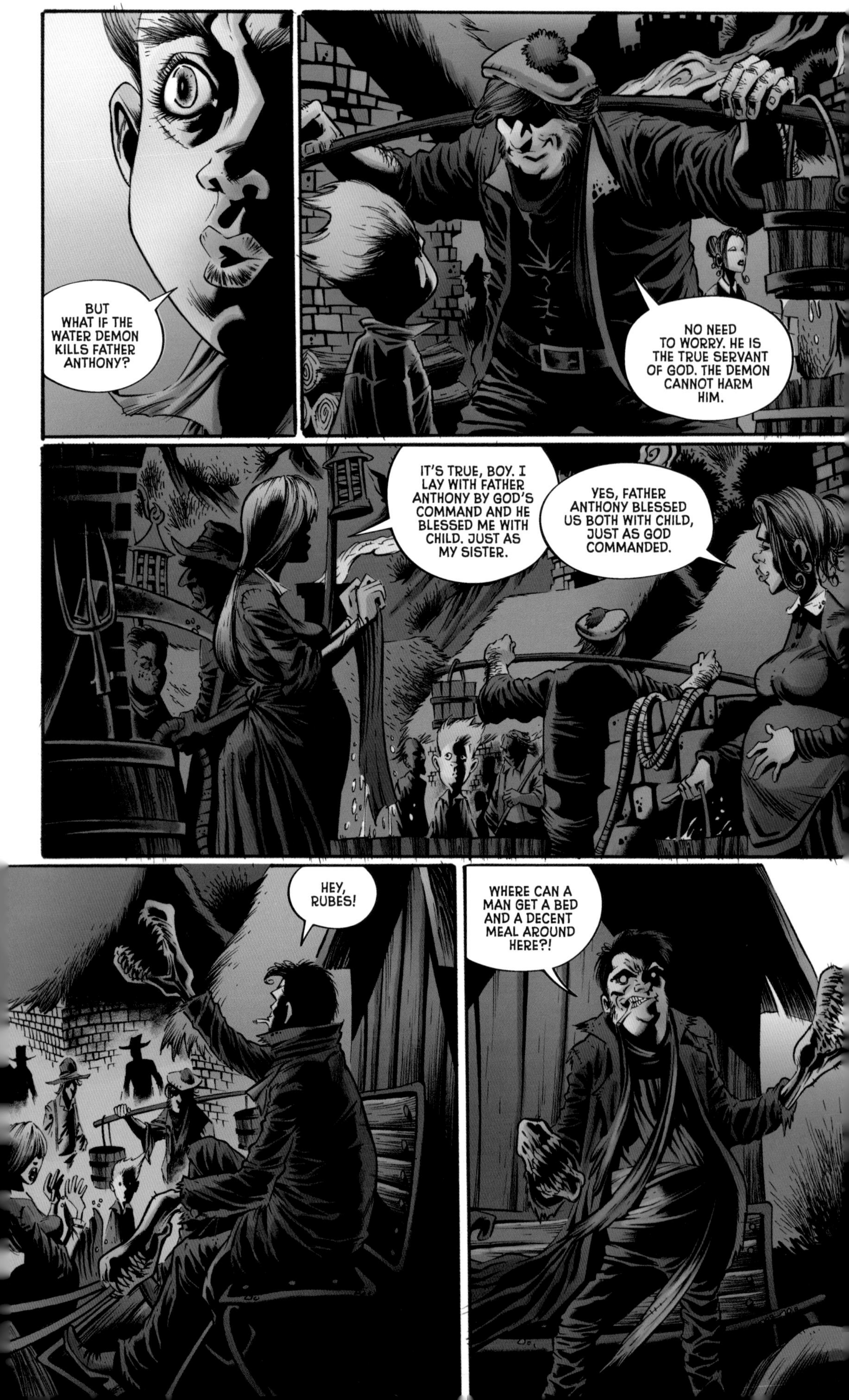
BUT WHAT IF THE WATER DEMON KILLS FATHER ANTHONY?
NO NEED TO WORRY. HE IS THE TRUE SERVANT OF GOD. THE DEMON CANNOT HARM HIM.
IT'S TRUE, BOY. I LAY WITH FATHER ANTHONY BY GOD'S COMMAND AND HE BLESSED ME WITH CHILD. JUST AS MY SISTER.
YES, FATHER ANTHONY BLESSED US BOTH WITH CHILD, JUST AS GOD COMMANDED.
HEY, RUBES!
WHERE CAN A MAN GET A BED AND A DECENT MEAL AROUND HERE?!

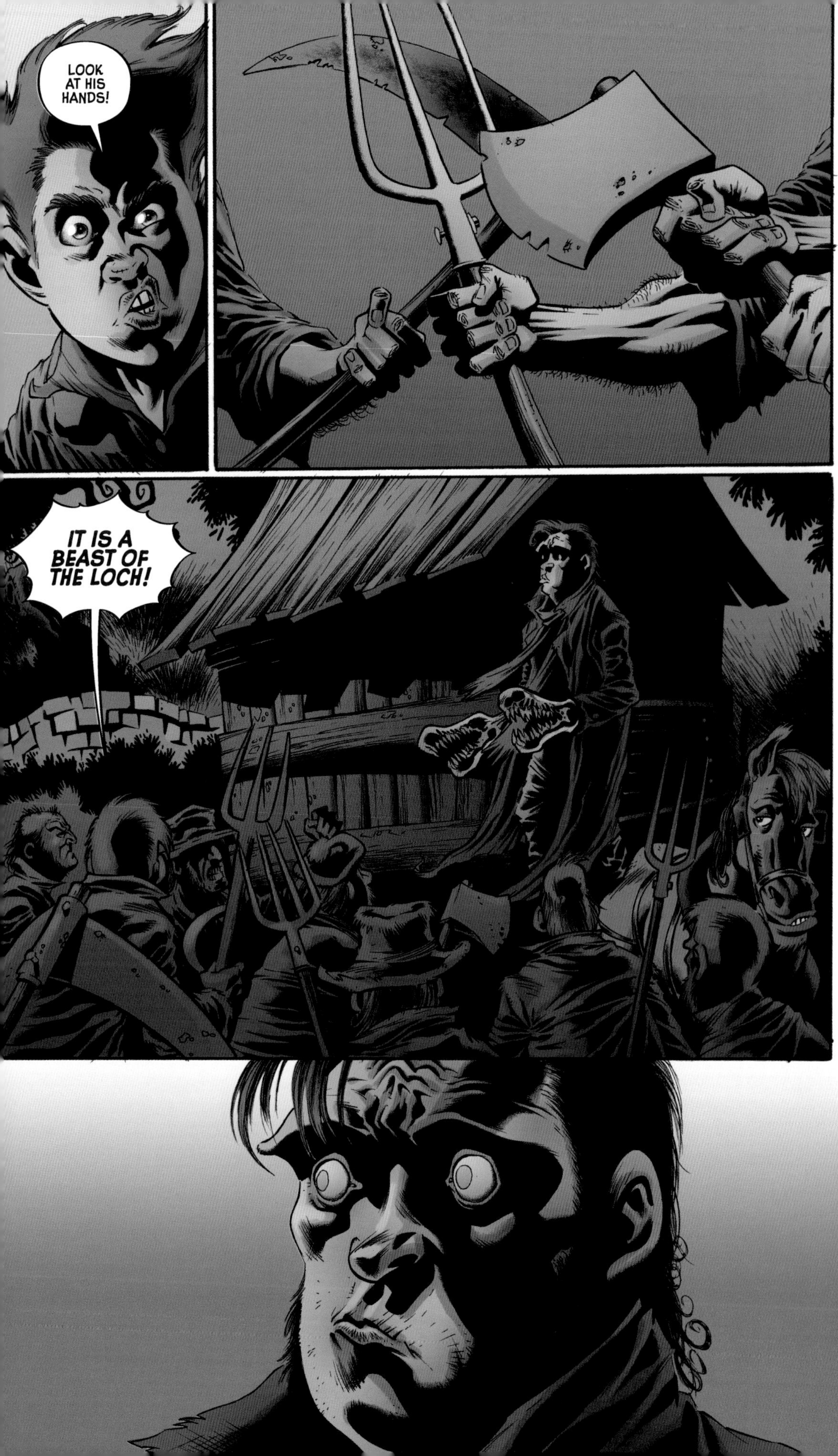
LOOK AT HIS HANDS!
IT IS A BEAST OF THE LOCH!

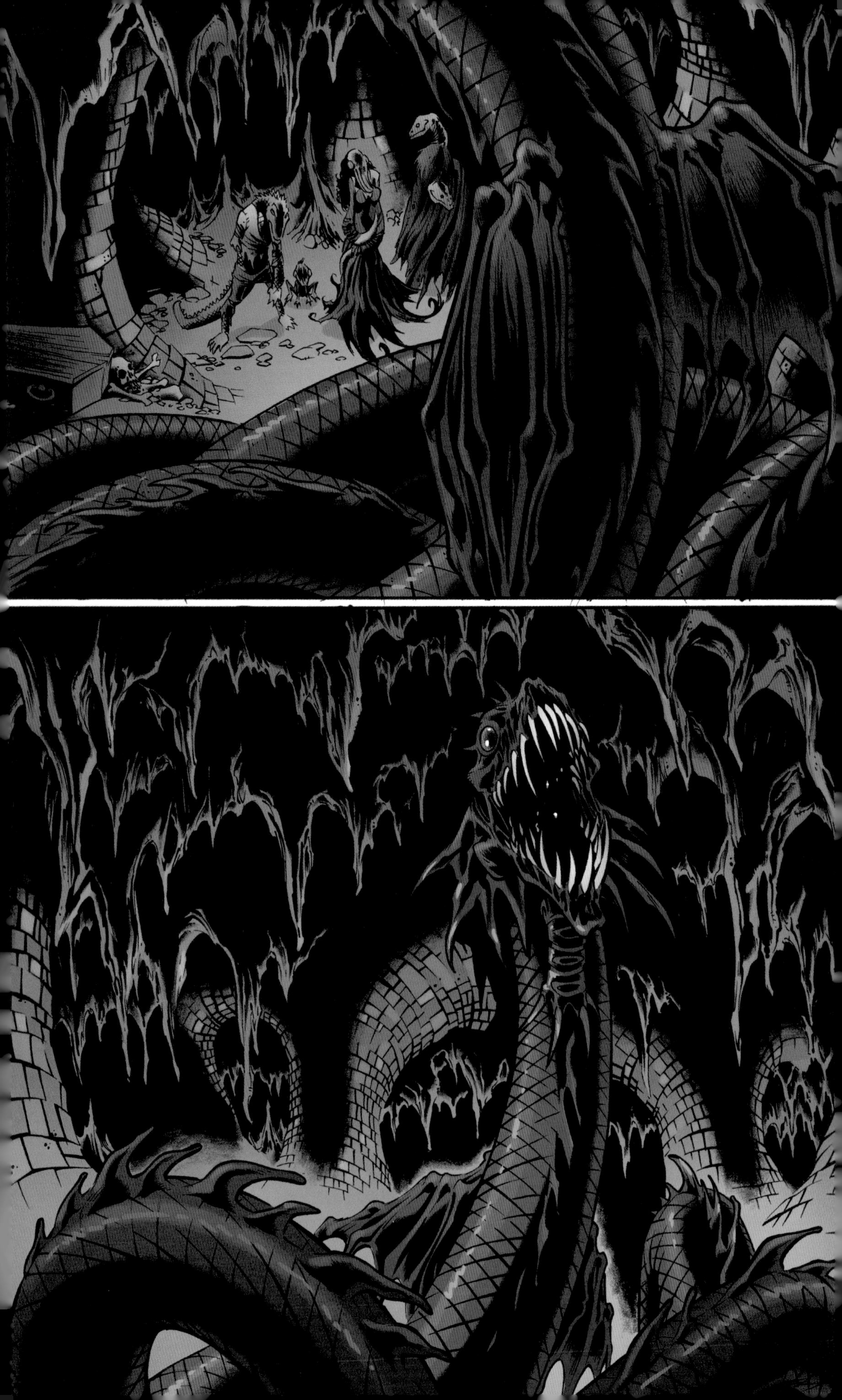

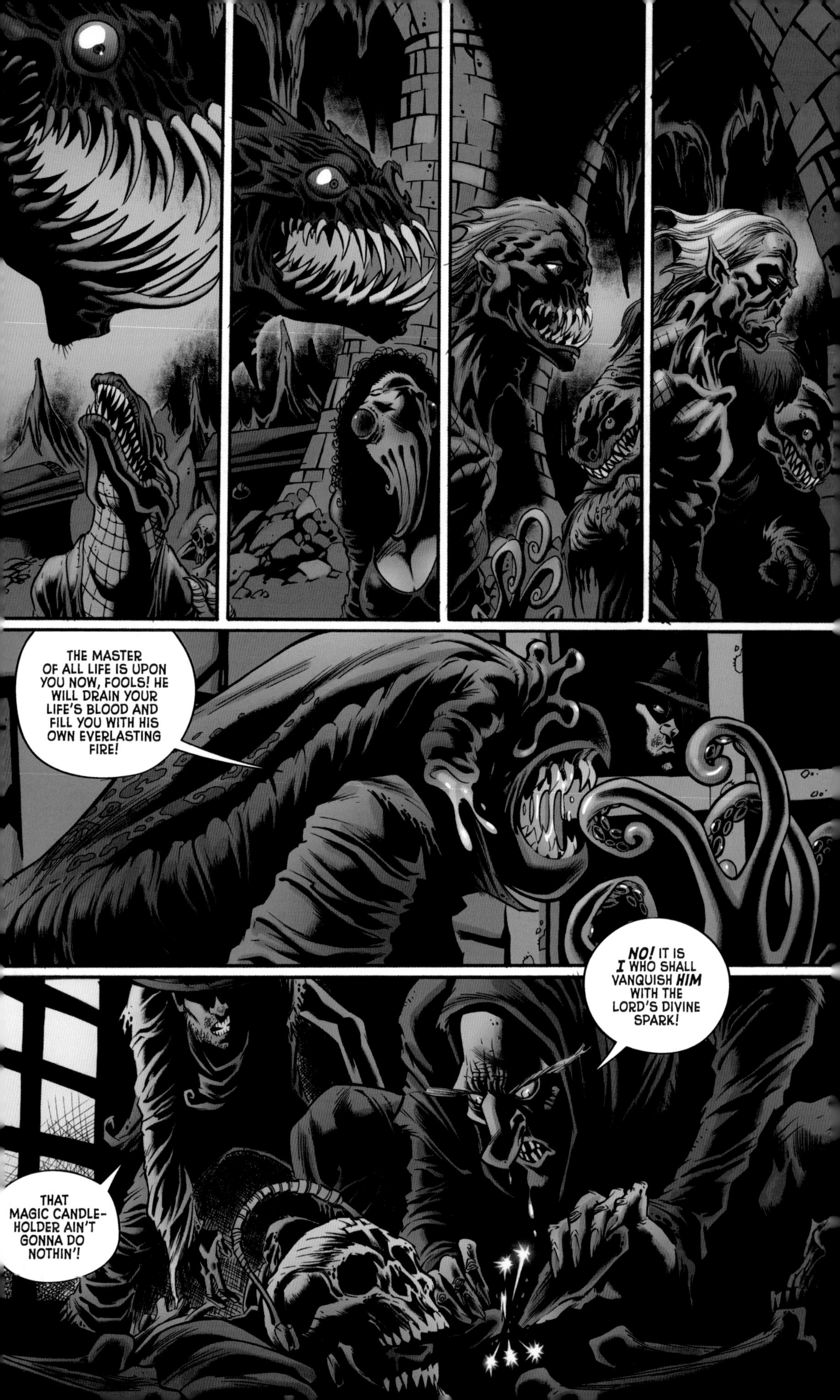
THE MASTER OF ALL LIFE IS UPON YOU NOW, FOOLS! HE WILL DRAIN YOUR LIFE'S BLOOD AND FILL YOU WITH HIS OWN EVERLASTING FIRE!
NO! IT IS I WHO SHALL VANQUISH HIM WITH THE LORD'S DIVINE SPARK!
THAT MAGIC CANDLE-HOLDER AIN'T GONNA DO NOTHIN'!

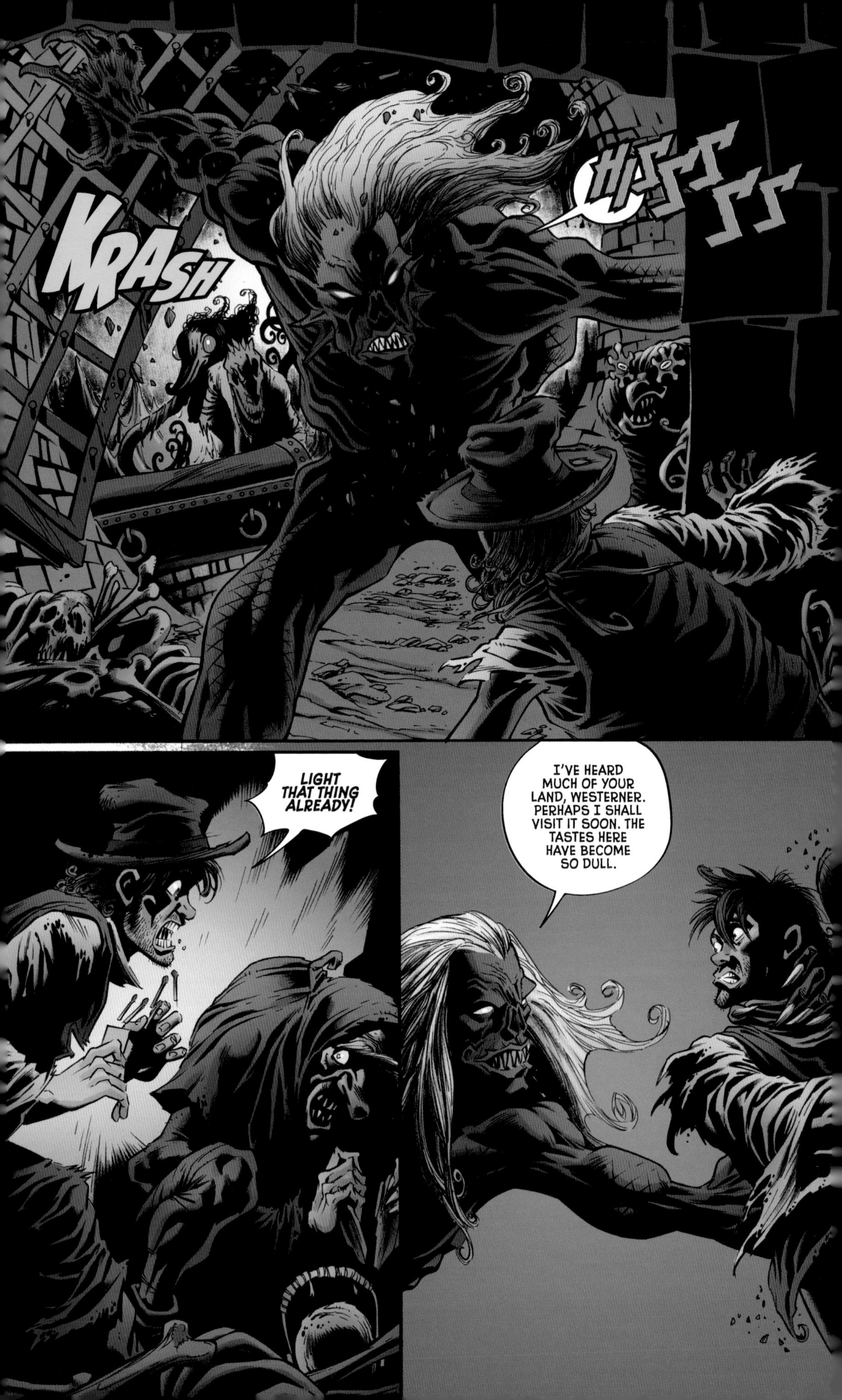
KRASH
HISSSSS
LIGHT THAT THING ALREADY!
I'VE HEARD MUCH OF YOUR LAND, WESTERNER. PERHAPS I SHALL VISIT IT SOON. THE TASTES HERE HAVE BECOME SO DULL.

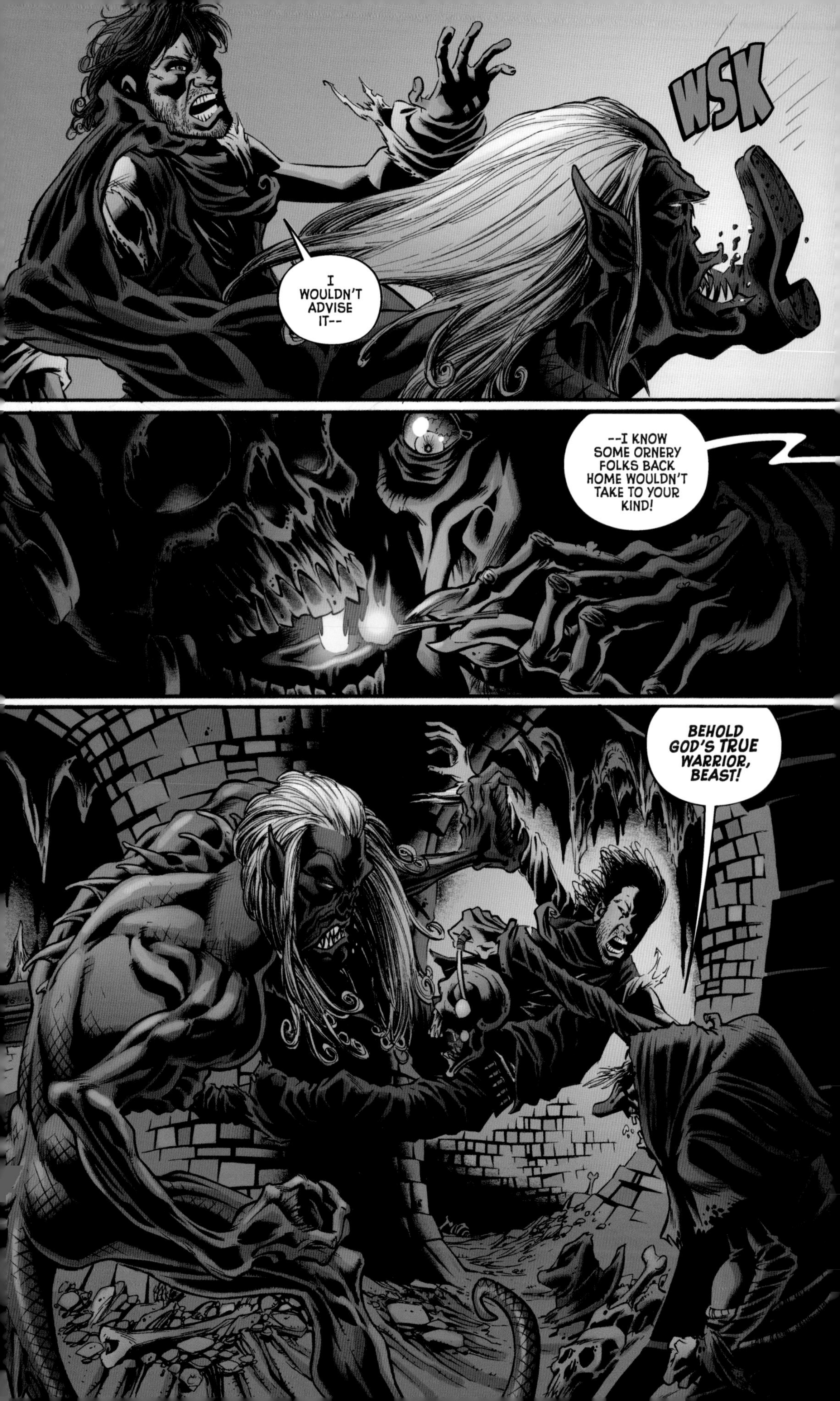
WSK
I WOULDN'T ADVISE IT--
--I KNOW SOME ORNERY FOLKS BACK HOME WOULDN'T TAKE TO YOUR KIND!
BEHOLD GOD'S TRUE WARRIOR, BEAST!

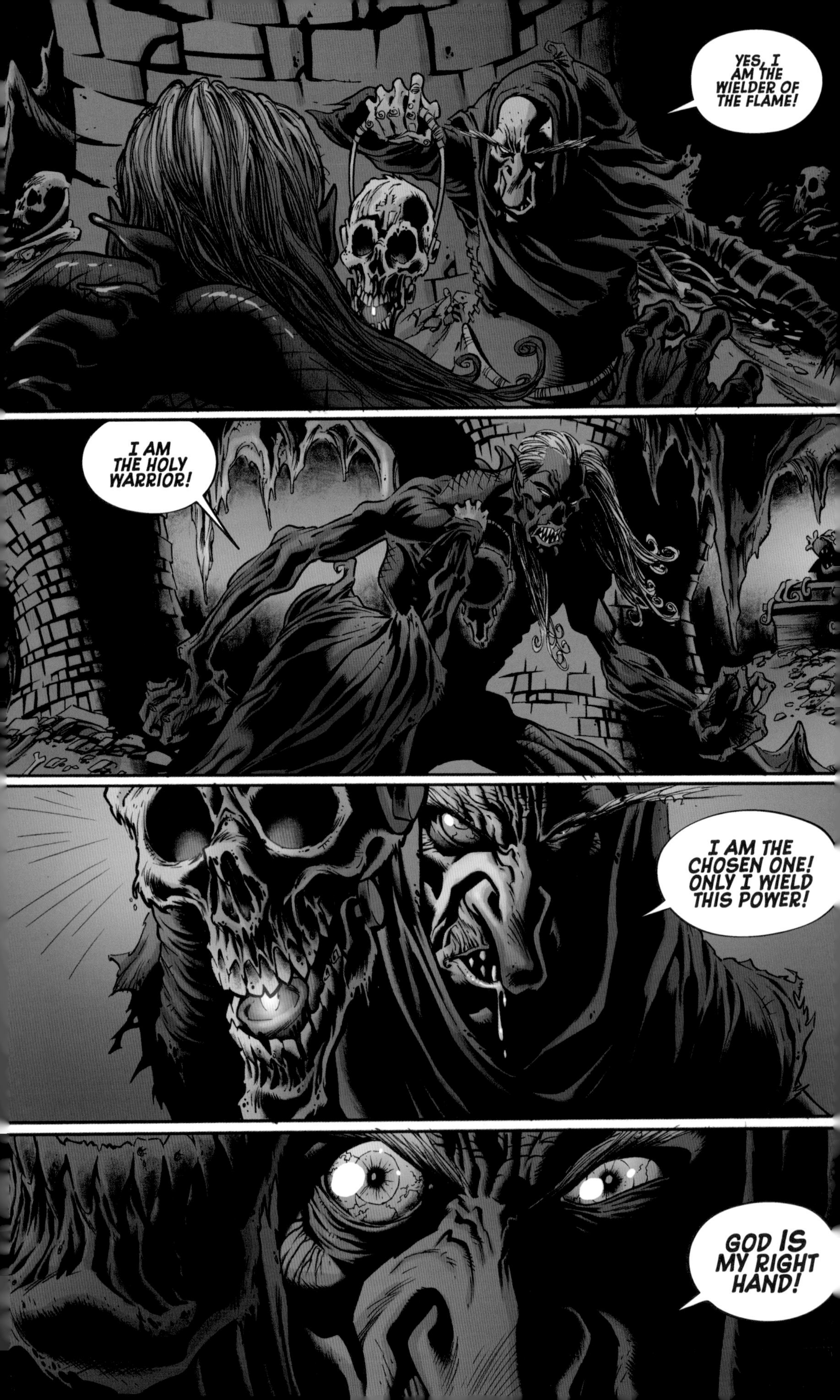
YES, I AM THE WIELDER OF THE FLAME!
I AM THE HOLY WARRIOR!
I AM THE CHOSEN ONE! ONLY I WIELD THIS POWER!
GOD IS MY RIGHT HAND!

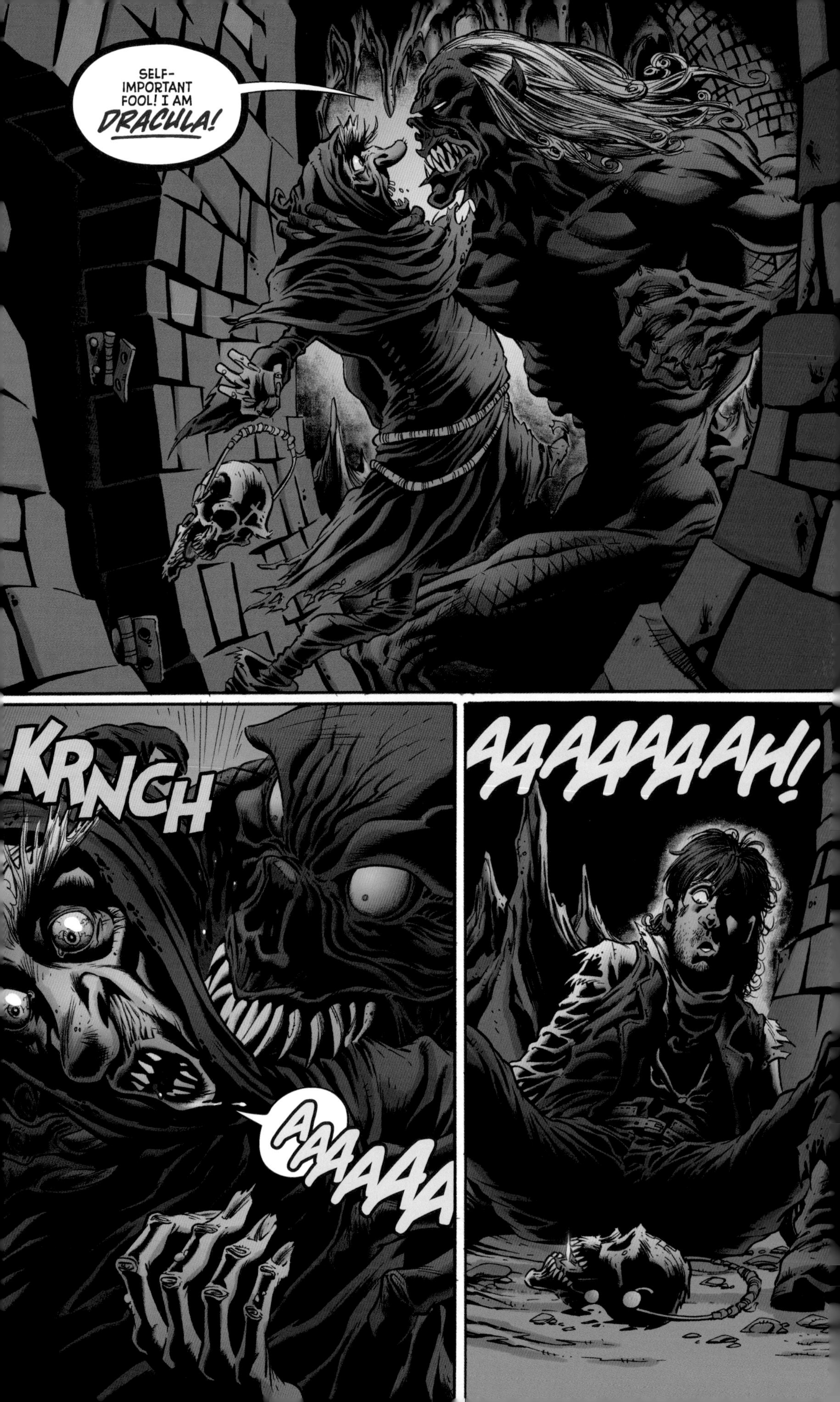
SELF-IMPORTANT FOOL! I AM DRACULA!
KRNCH
AAAAAA
AAAAAAAH!

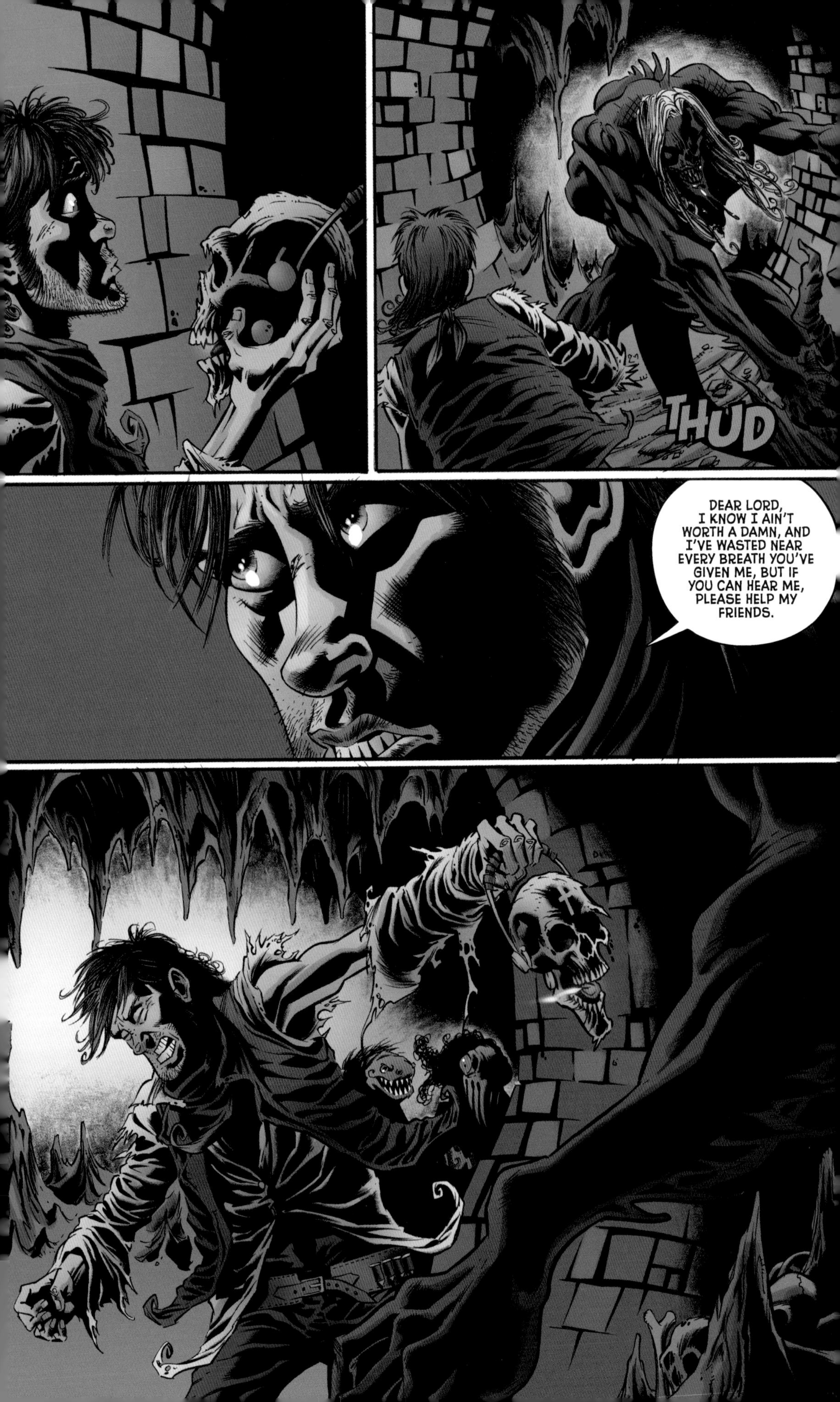
THUD
DEAR LORD, I KNOW I AIN'T WORTH A DAMN, AND I'VE WASTED NEAR EVERY BREATH YOU'VE GIVEN ME, BUT IF YOU CAN HEAR ME, PLEASE HELP MY FRIENDS.

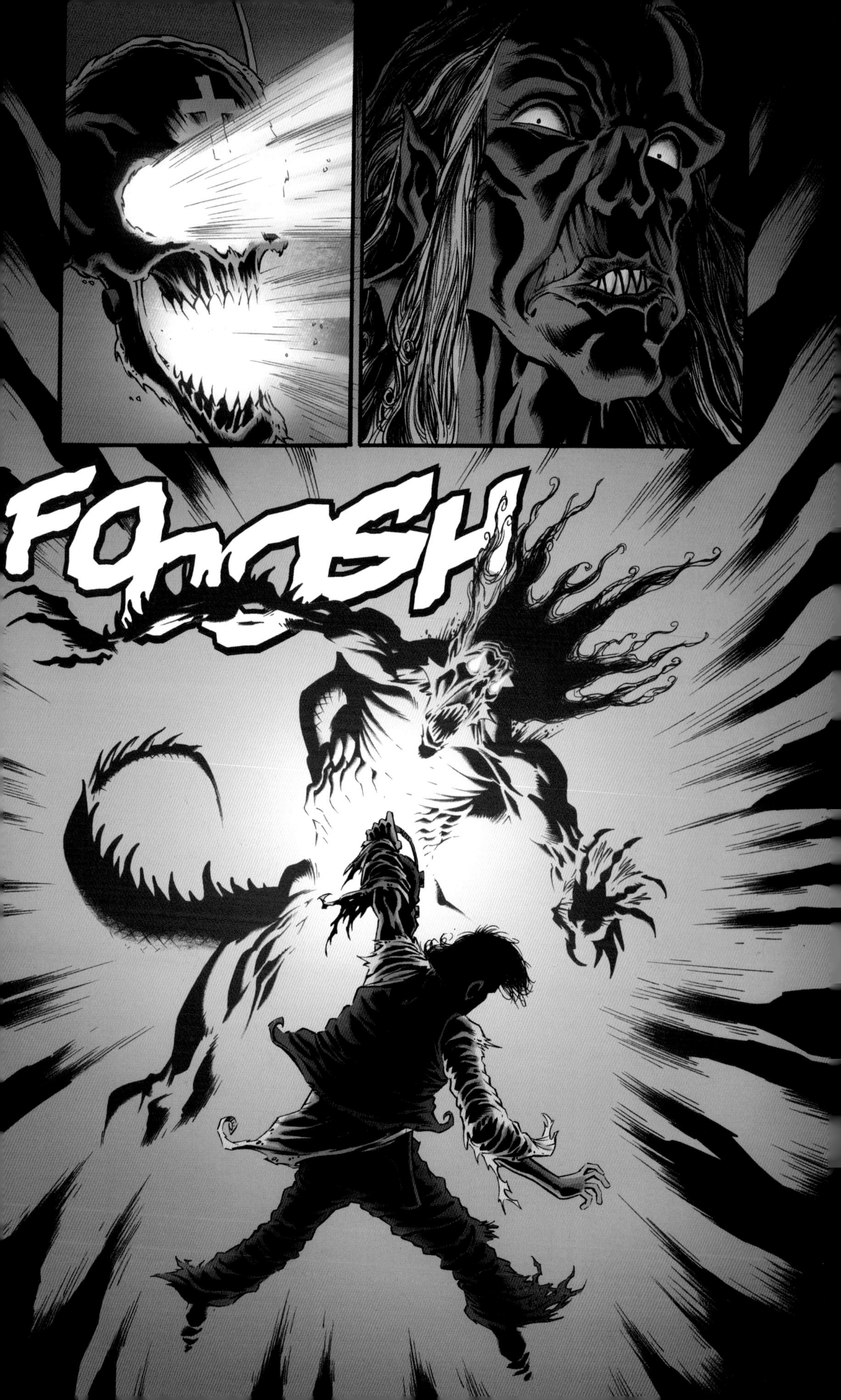
FOOSH

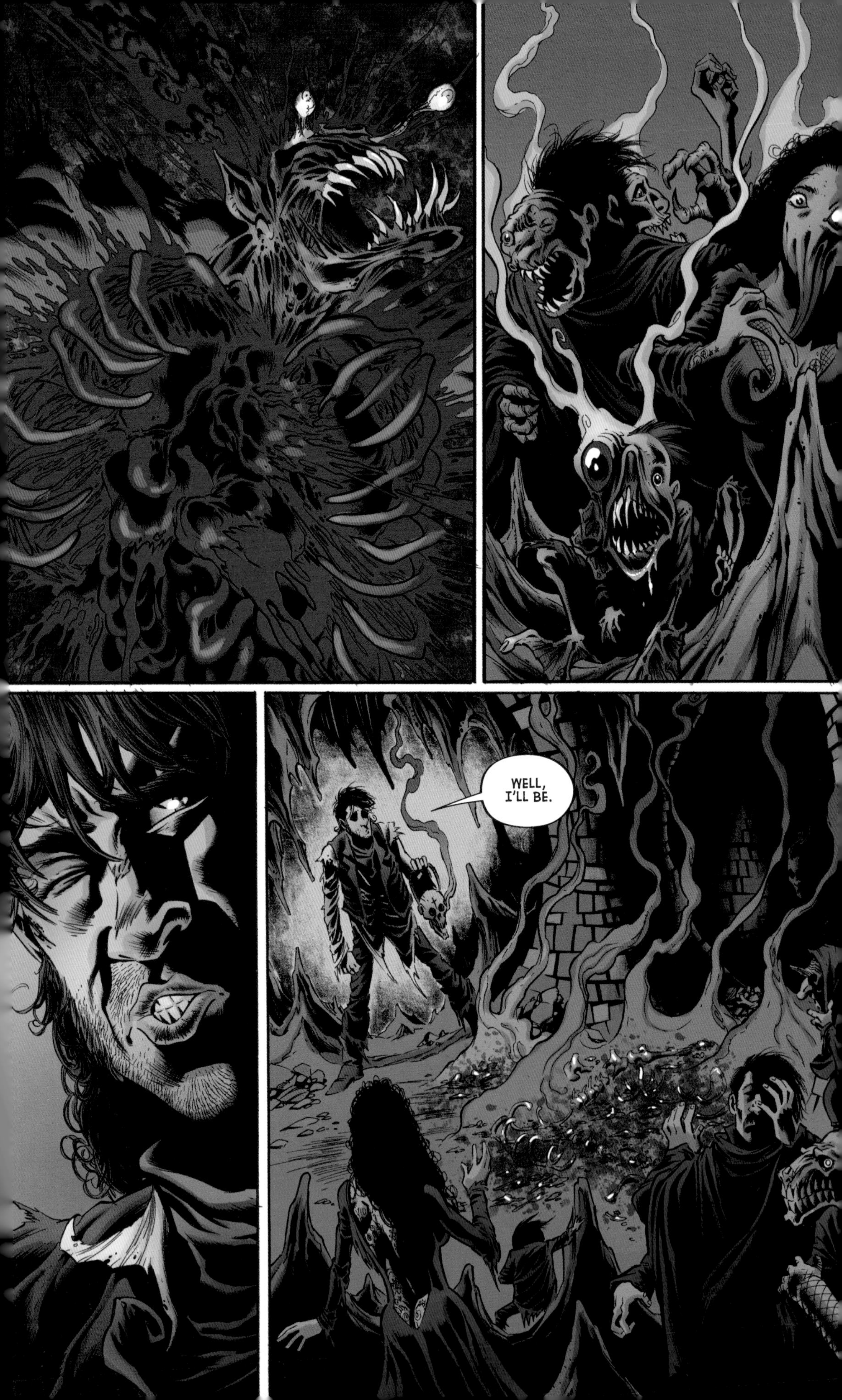
WELL,
I'LL BE.

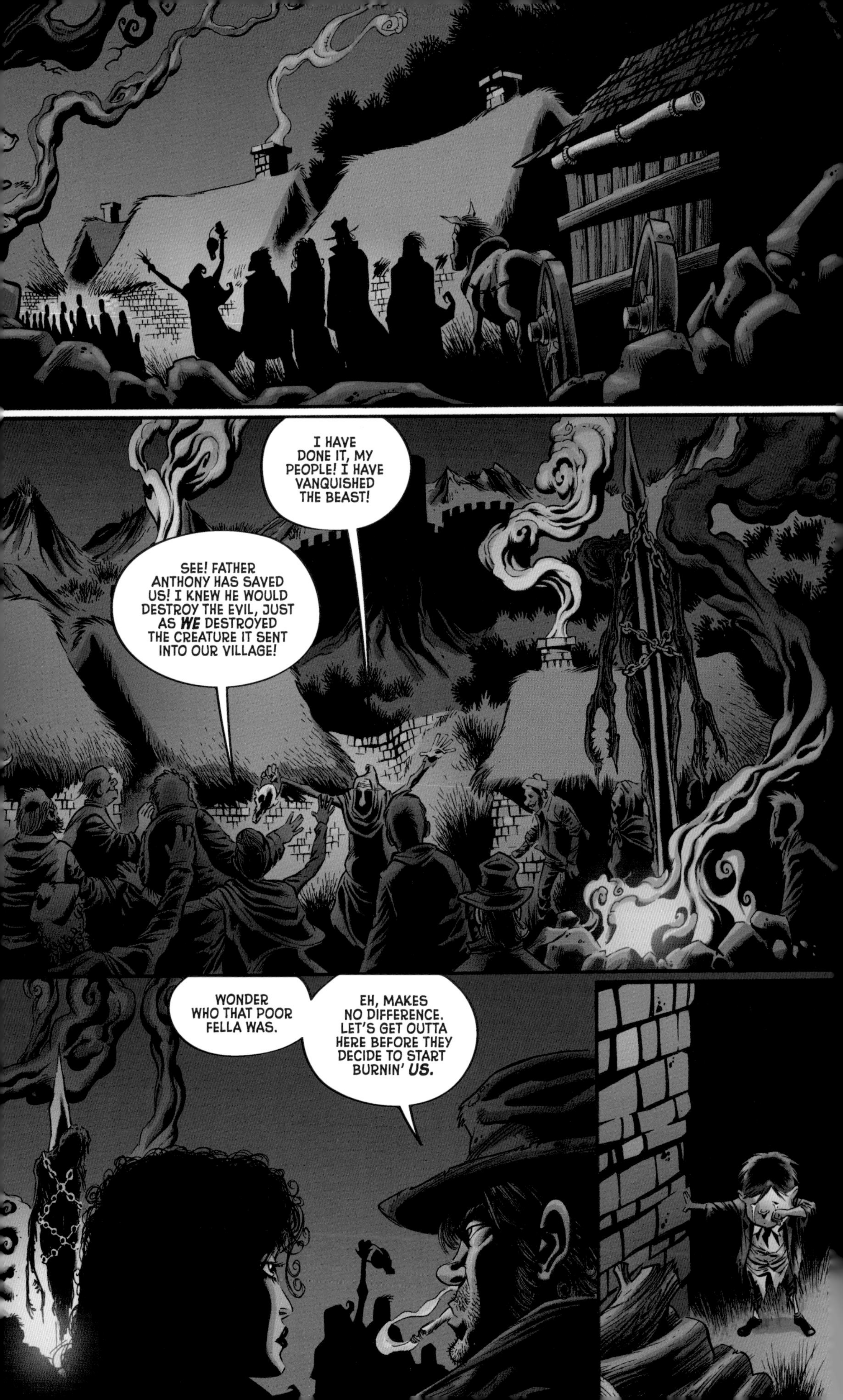
I HAVE DONE IT, MY PEOPLE! I HAVE VANQUISHED THE BEAST!
SEE! FATHER ANTHONY HAS SAVED US! I KNEW HE WOULD DESTROY THE EVIL, JUST AS WE DESTROYED THE CREATURE IT SENT INTO OUR VILLAGE!
WONDER WHO THAT POOR FELLA WAS.
EH, MAKES NO DIFFERENCE. LET'S GET OUTTA HERE BEFORE THEY DECIDE TO START BURNIN' US.

...KILLED THE MASTER, KILLED HIM...

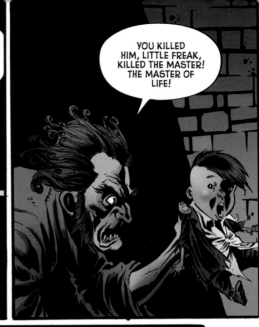

YOU KILLED HIM, LITTLE FREAK, KILLED THE MASTER! THE MASTER OF LIFE!

HE WAS TO MAKE ME GREAT! AND YOU TOOK HIM FROM ME!

NOW I KILL *YOU!* WORTHLESS FREAK! WORTHLESS F--

CLI

--ODDITY.

YOU--!

YOU KILLED HIM!

BLAM

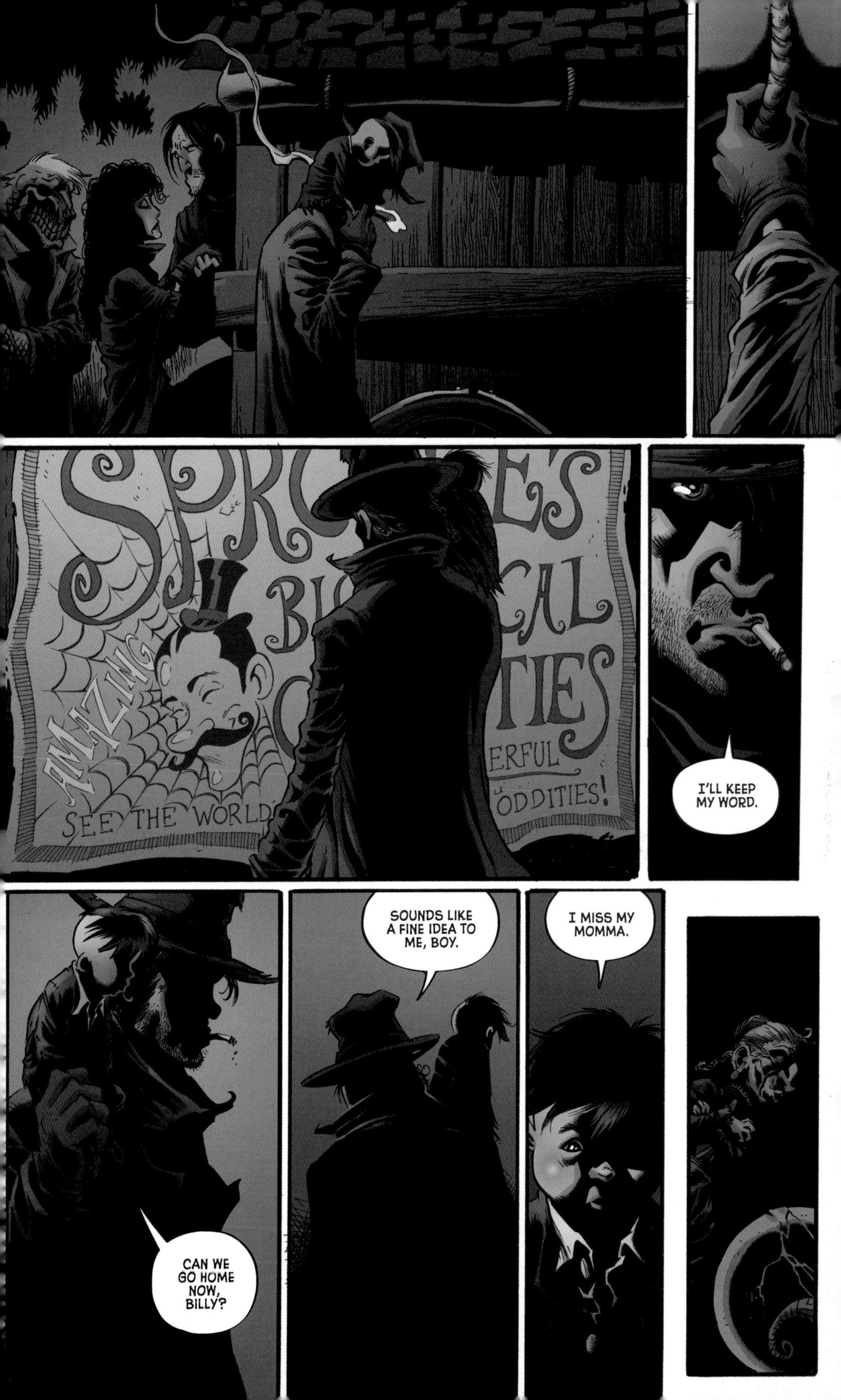
AMAZING
SEE THE WORLD
ERFUL
ODDITIES!
TIES
I'LL KEEP MY WORD.
CAN WE GO HOME NOW, BILLY?
SOUNDS LIKE A FINE IDEA TO ME, BOY.
I MISS MY MOMMA.

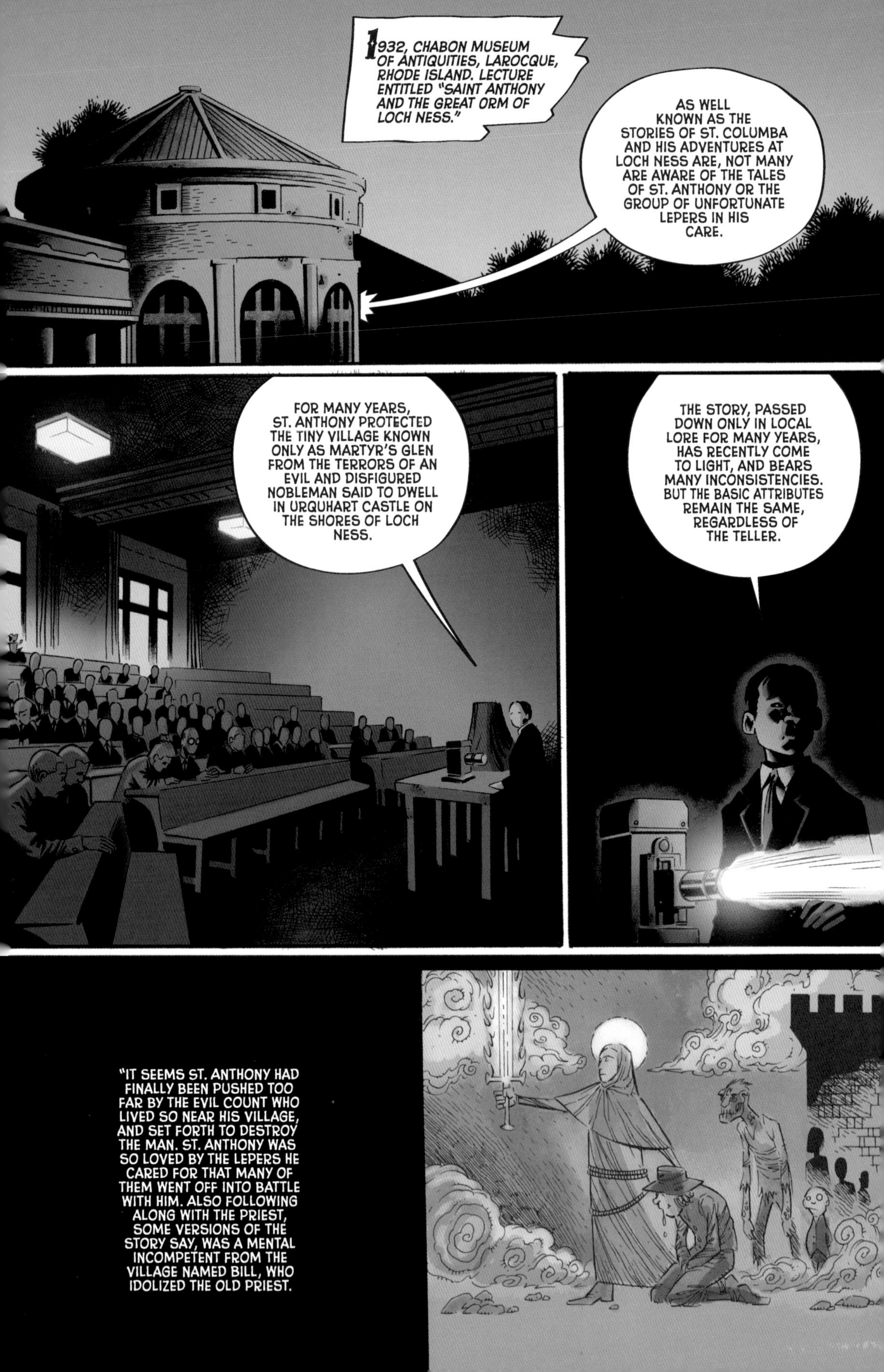
1932, CHABON MUSEUM OF ANTIQUITIES, LAROCQUE, RHODE ISLAND. LECTURE ENTITLED "SAINT ANTHONY AND THE GREAT ORM OF LOCH NESS."
AS WELL KNOWN AS THE STORIES OF ST. COLUMBA AND HIS ADVENTURES AT LOCH NESS ARE, NOT MANY ARE AWARE OF THE TALES OF ST. ANTHONY OR THE GROUP OF UNFORTUNATE LEPERS IN HIS CARE.
FOR MANY YEARS, ST. ANTHONY PROTECTED THE TINY VILLAGE KNOWN ONLY AS MARTYR'S GLEN FROM THE TERRORS OF AN EVIL AND DISFIGURED NOBLEMAN SAID TO DWELL IN URQUHART CASTLE ON THE SHORES OF LOCH NESS.
THE STORY, PASSED DOWN ONLY IN LOCAL LORE FOR MANY YEARS, HAS RECENTLY COME TO LIGHT, AND BEARS MANY INCONSISTENCIES. BUT THE BASIC ATTRIBUTES REMAIN THE SAME, REGARDLESS OF THE TELLER.
"IT SEEMS ST. ANTHONY HAD FINALLY BEEN PUSHED TOO FAR BY THE EVIL COUNT WHO LIVED SO NEAR HIS VILLAGE, AND SET FORTH TO DESTROY THE MAN. ST. ANTHONY WAS SO LOVED BY THE LEPERS HE CARED FOR THAT MANY OF THEM WENT OFF INTO BATTLE WITH HIM. ALSO FOLLOWING ALONG WITH THE PRIEST, SOME VERSIONS OF THE STORY SAY, WAS A MENTAL INCOMPETENT FROM THE VILLAGE NAMED BILL, WHO IDOLIZED THE OLD PRIEST.

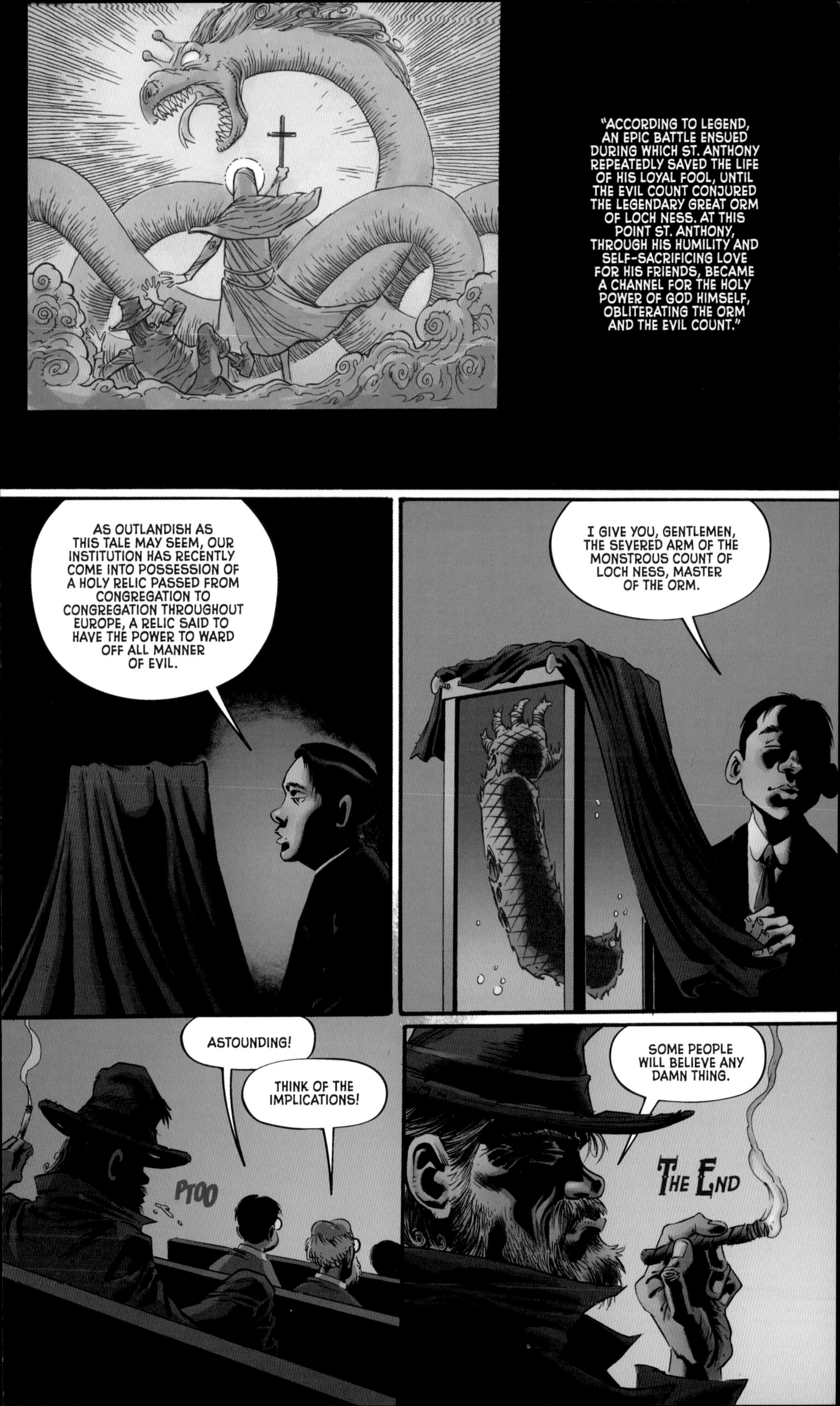
"ACCORDING TO LEGEND, AN EPIC BATTLE ENSUED DURING WHICH ST. ANTHONY REPEATEDLY SAVED THE LIFE OF HIS LOYAL FOOL, UNTIL THE EVIL COUNT CONJURED THE LEGENDARY GREAT ORM OF LOCH NESS. AT THIS POINT ST. ANTHONY, THROUGH HIS HUMILITY AND SELF-SACRIFICING LOVE FOR HIS FRIENDS, BECAME A CHANNEL FOR THE HOLY POWER OF GOD HIMSELF, OBLITERATING THE ORM AND THE EVIL COUNT."
AS OUTLANDISH AS THIS TALE MAY SEEM, OUR INSTITUTION HAS RECENTLY COME INTO POSSESSION OF A HOLY RELIC PASSED FROM CONGREGATION TO CONGREGATION THROUGHOUT EUROPE, A RELIC SAID TO HAVE THE POWER TO WARD OFF ALL MANNER OF EVIL.
I GIVE YOU, GENTLEMEN, THE SEVERED ARM OF THE MONSTROUS COUNT OF LOCH NESS, MASTER OF THE ORM.
ASTOUNDING!
THINK OF THE IMPLICATIONS!
PTOO
SOME PEOPLE WILL BELIEVE ANY DAMN THING.
THE END

SKETCHBOOK

Character sketches by
KYLE HOTZ

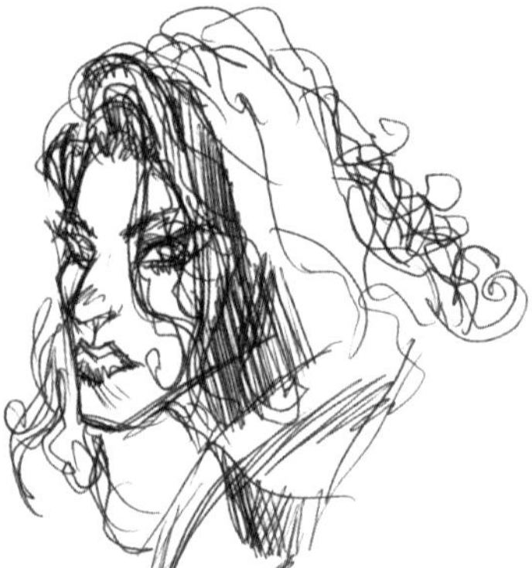

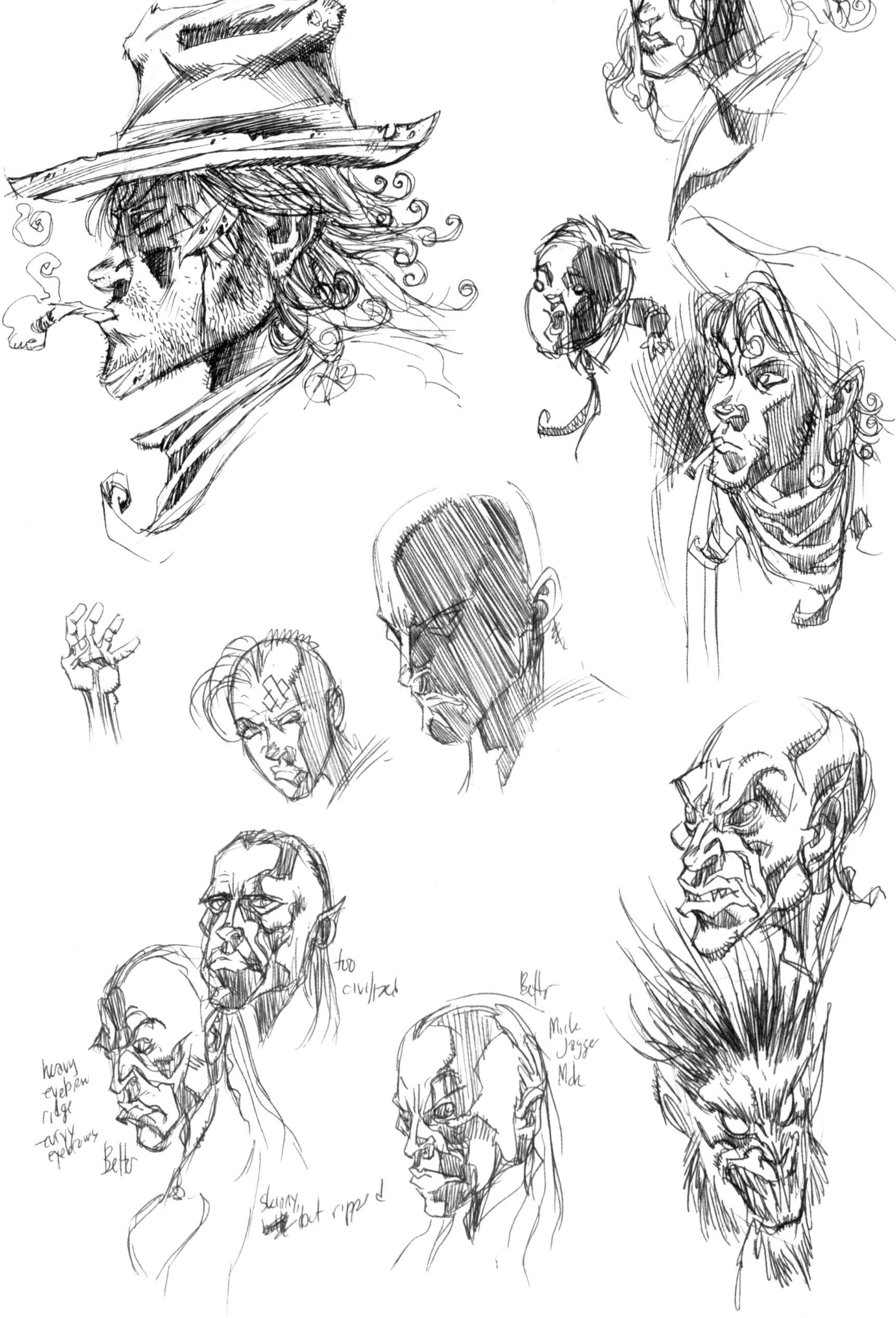
too civilized
Better
Mick Jagger
heavy eyebrow ridge
curvy eyebrows
Better
skinny, but ripped

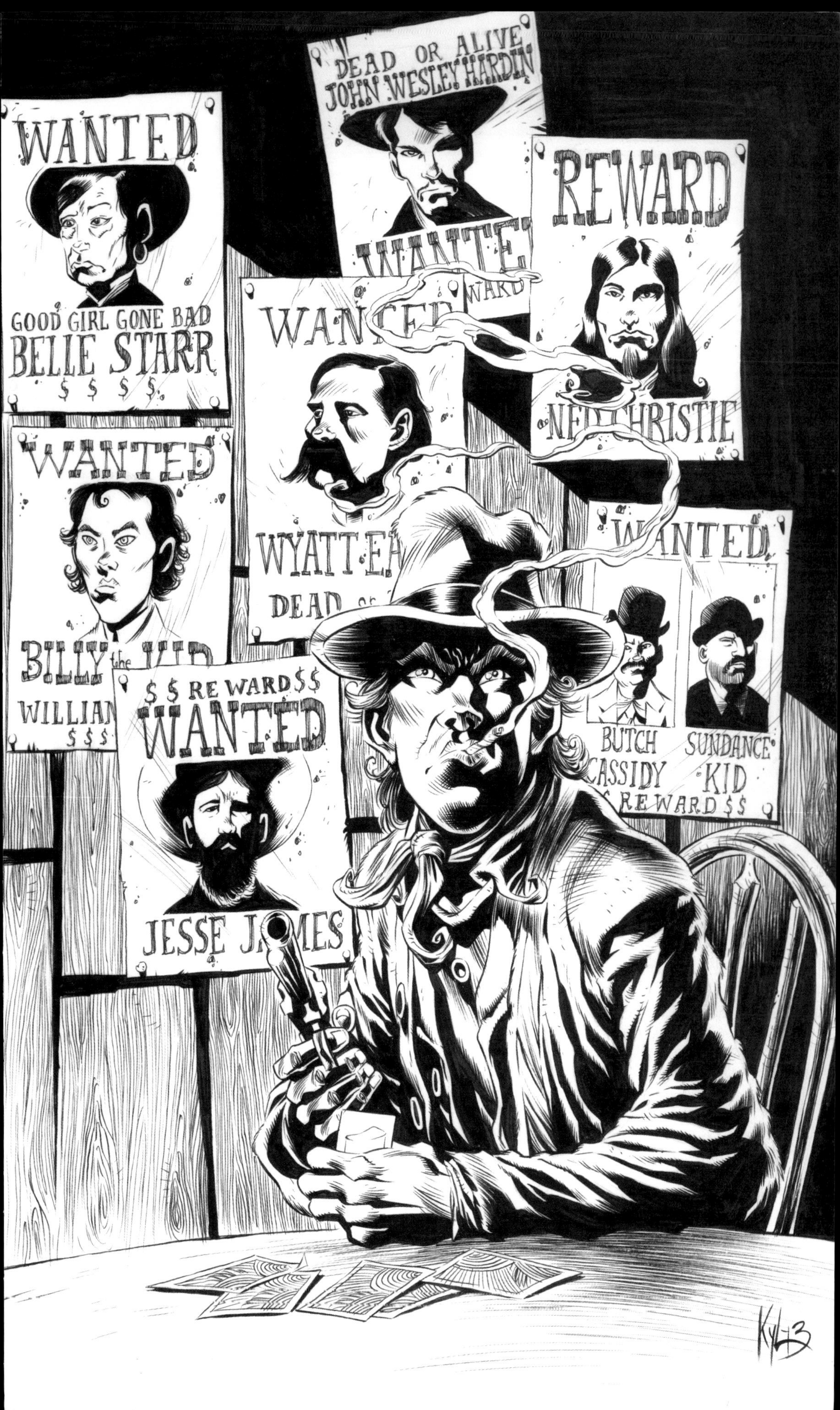
WANTED
GOOD GIRL GONE BAD
BELLE STARR
$ $ $ $
DEAD OR ALIVE
JOHN WESLEY HARDIN
REWARD
NED CHRISTIE
WANTED
WYATT EA
DEAD
WANTED
BILLY the KID
WILLIAM
$ $ $
$ $ REWARD $ $
WANTED
JESSE JAMES
WANTED
BUTCH CASSIDY
SUNDANCE KID
REWARD $ $

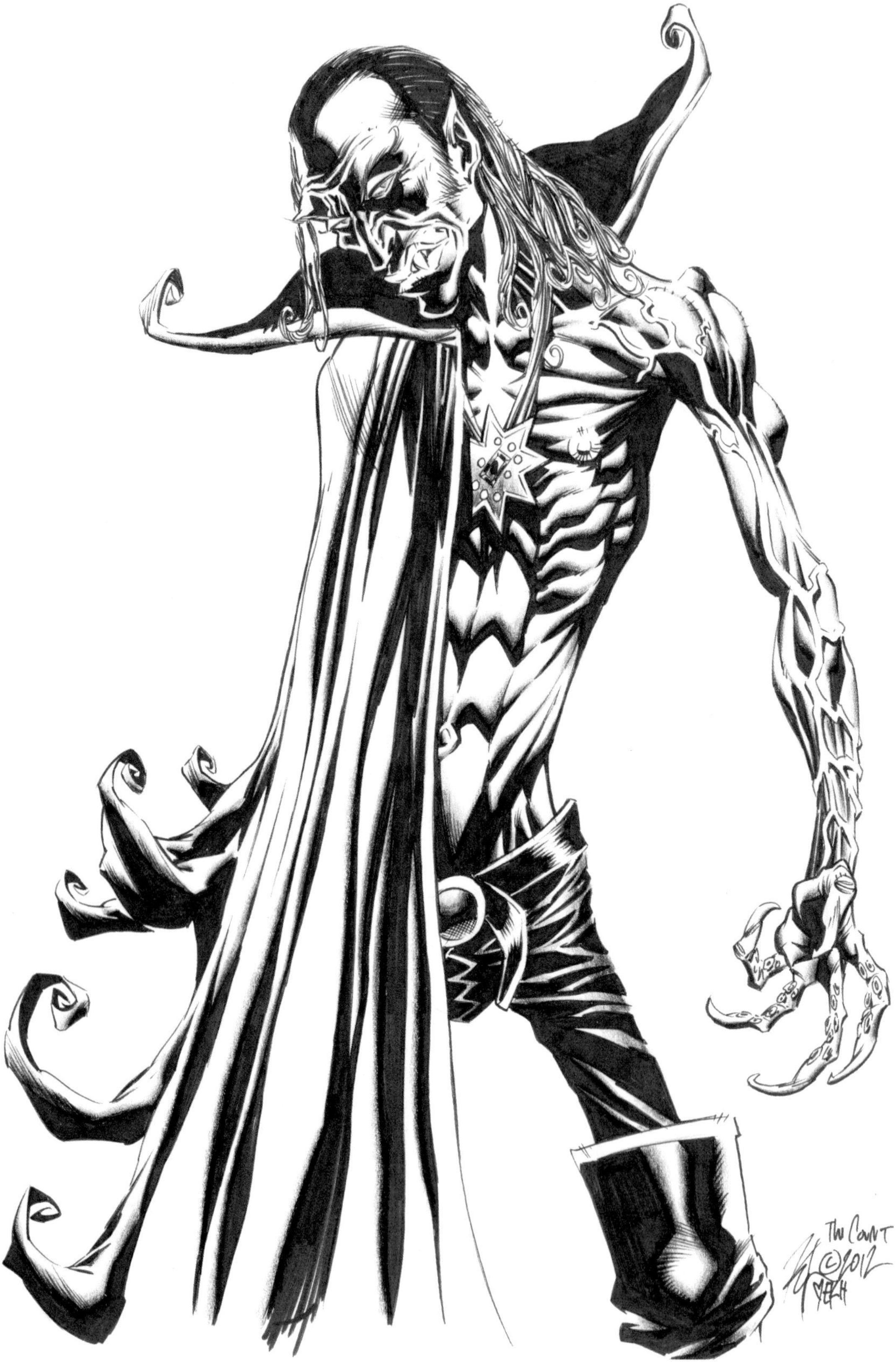
The Count
©2012

Issue #1 variant cover by Eric Powell.

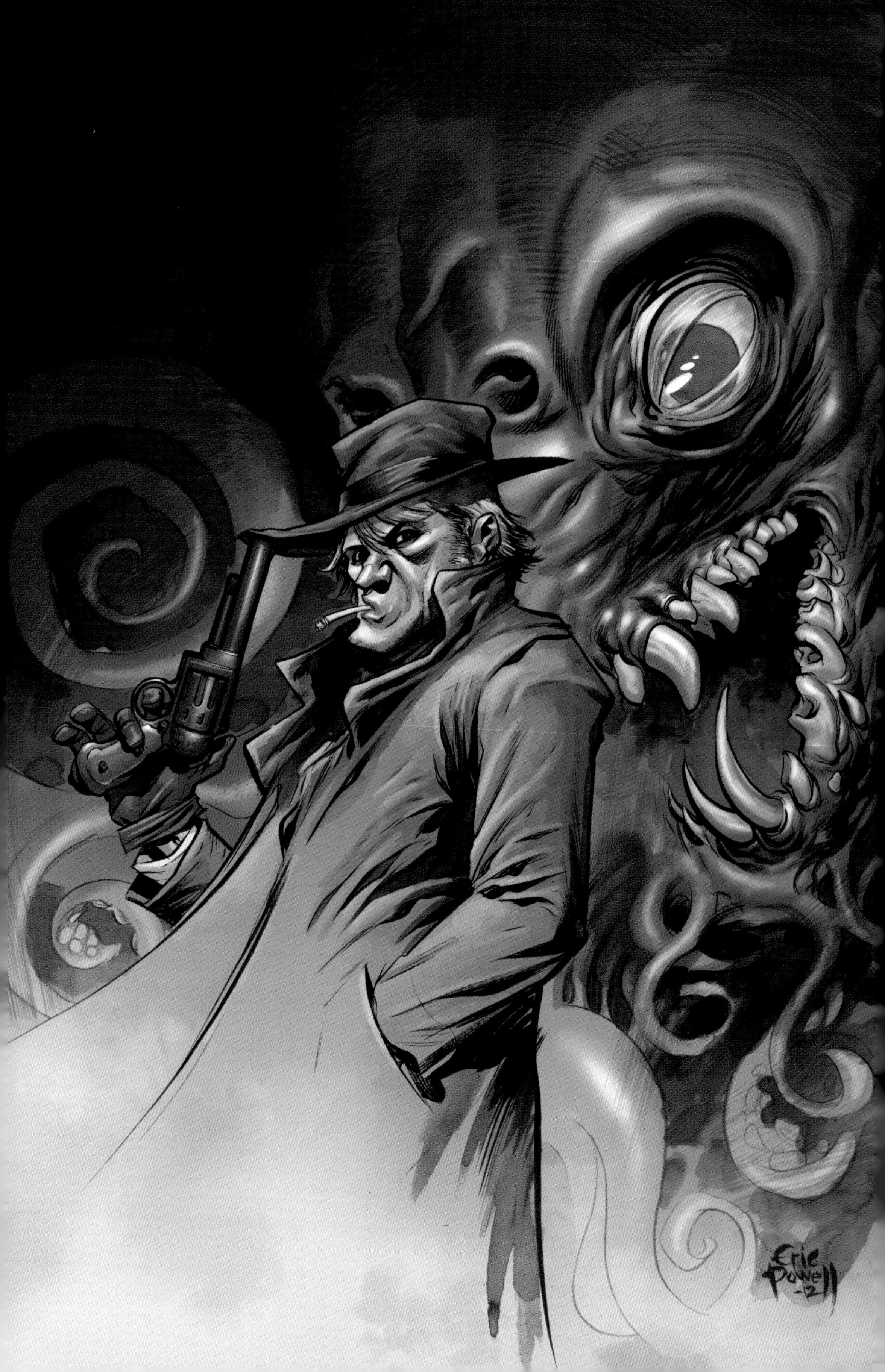
Eric
Powell
-12

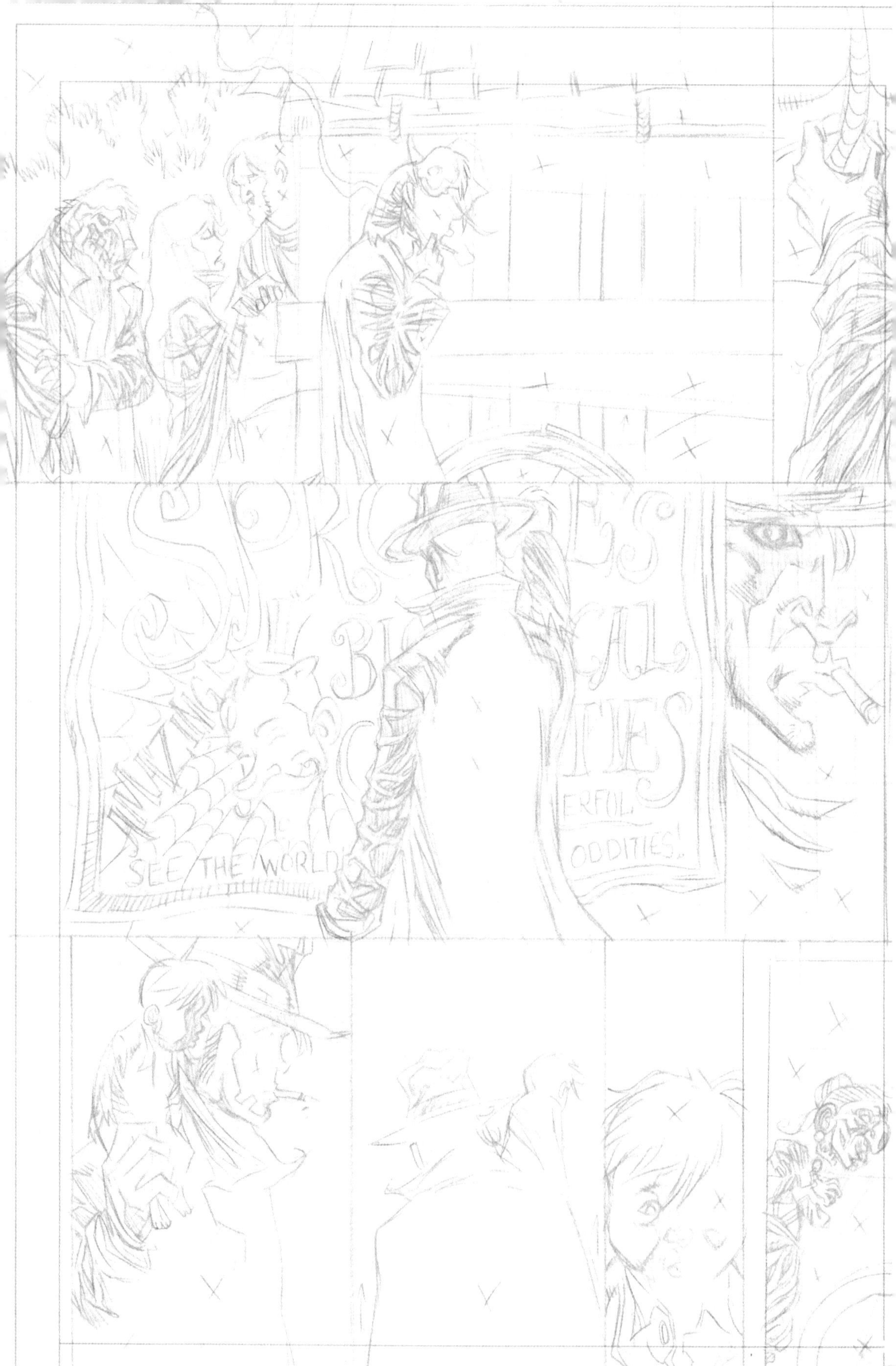
SEE THE WORLD
ODDITIES!

Pencils by Kyle Hotz.

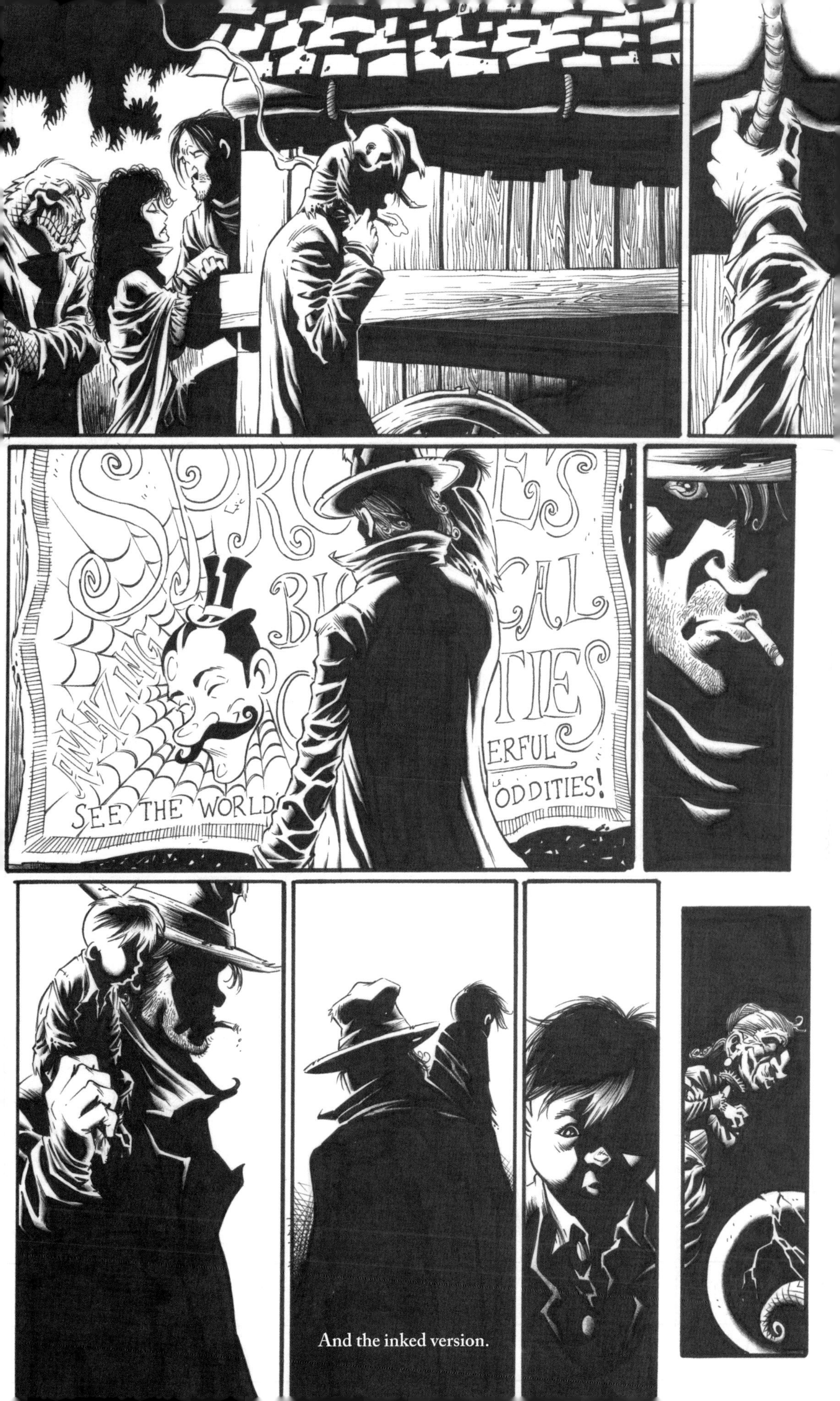
AMAZING
SEE THE WORLD
CAL
TIES
ERFUL
ODDITIES!
And the inked version.

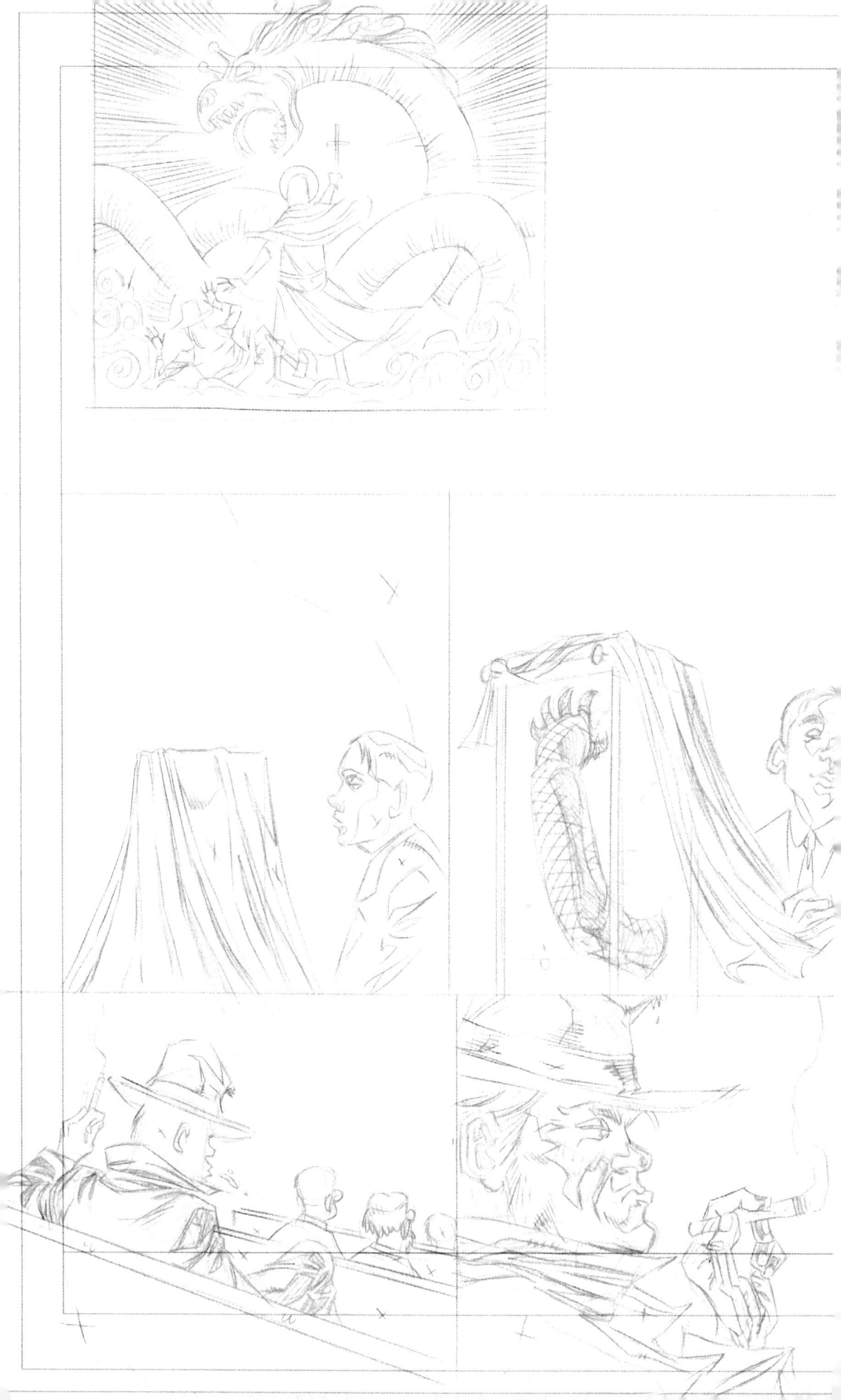

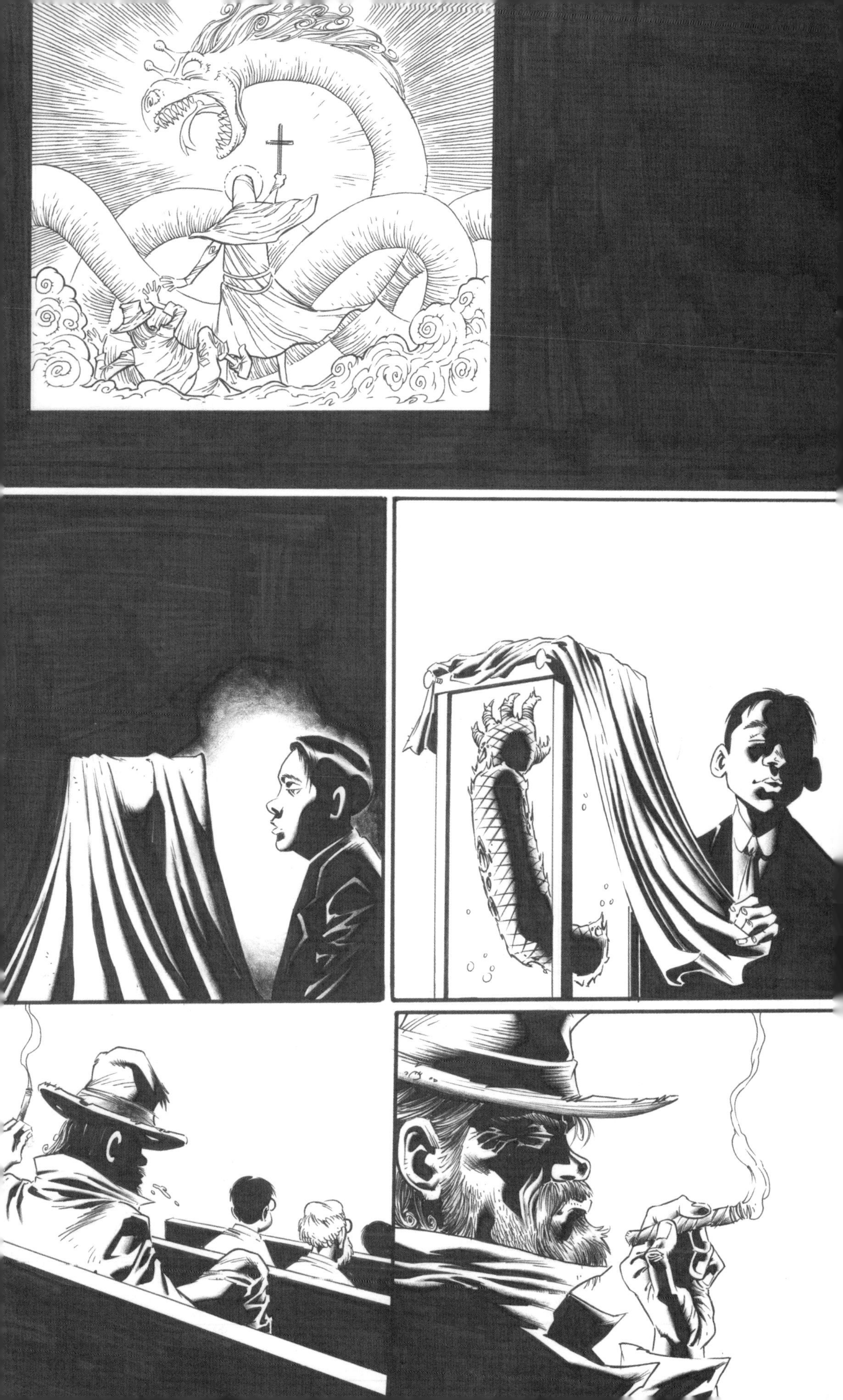

THE GOON™

by Eric Powell

Volume 0:
ROUGH STUFF
ISBN 978-1-59582-468-4 $13.99

Volume 1:
NOTHIN' BUT MISERY
ISBN 978-1-59582-624-4 $16.99

Volume 2:
MY MURDEROUS CHILDHOOD
(AND OTHER GRIEVOUS YARNS)
ISBN 978-1-59582-616-9 $16.99

Volume 3:
HEAPS OF RUINATION
ISBN 978-1-59582-625-1 $16.99

Volume 4:
VIRTUE AND THE GRIM
CONSEQUENCES THEREOF
ISBN 978-1-59582-617-6 $16.99

Volume 5:
WICKED INCLINATIONS
ISBN 978-1-59582-626-8 $16.99

Volume 6:
CHINATOWN hardcover
ISBN 978-1-59307-833-1 $19.99
CHINATOWN trade paperback
ISBN 978-1-59582-406-6 $15.99

Volume 7:
A PLACE OF HEARTACHE AND GRIEF
ISBN 978-1-59582-311-3 $15.99

Volume 8:
THOSE THAT IS DAMNED
ISBN 978-1-59582-324-3 $15.99

Volume 9:
CALAMITY OF CONSCIENCE
ISBN 978-1-59582-346-5 $15.99

Volume 10:
DEATH'S GREEDY COMEUPPANCE
ISBN 978-1-59582-643-5 $16.99

Volume 11:
THE DEFORMED OF BODY AND THE
DEVIOUS OF MIND
ISBN 978-1-59582-881-1 $16.99

Volume 12:
THEM THAT RAISED US LAMENT
ISBN 978-1-61655-006-6 $16.99

FANCY PANTS VOLUME 2: THE RISE
AND FALL OF THE DIABOLICAL DR. ALLOY
Limited-edition hardcover
ISBN 978-1-59307-918-5 $24.99

FANCY PANTS VOLUME 3: THE RETURN
OF LABRAZIO
ISBN 978-1-59582-503-2 $34.99

BILLY THE KID'S OLD TIMEY ODDITIES
ISBN 978-1-59307-448-7 $13.99

BILLY THE KID'S OLD TIMEY ODDITIES
AND THE GHASTLY FIEND OF LONDON
ISBN 978-1-59582-736-4 $15.99

CHIMICHANGA hardcover
ISBN 978-1-59582-755-5 $14.99

DARK HORSE BOOKS®
DarkHorse.com

To find a comics shop in your area, call 1-888-266-4226 For more information or to order direct: • On the web: DarkHorse.com • E-mail: mailorder@DarkHorse.com • Phone: 1-800-862-0052 Mon.–Fri. 9 AM to 5 PM Pacific Time